WALKING IN THE CANARY ISLANDS: VOLUME 1 WEST

TENERIFE, LA GOMERA, LA PALMA AND EL HIERRO

ABOUT THE AUTHOR

Paddy Dillon is a prolific outdoor writer with a score and more books to his name, as well as a dozen booklets and brochures. He writes for a number of outdoor magazines and other publications, as well as producing materials for tourism groups and other organisations. He lives on the fringe of the Lake District, and has walked, and written about walking, in every county in England, Scotland, Ireland and Wales. He generally leads at least one guided walking holiday overseas every year and has walked in many parts of Europe, as well as Nepal, Tibet and the Canadian Rockies.

While walking his routes, Paddy inputs his notes directly into a palmtop computer every few steps. His descriptions are therefore precise, having been written at the very point at which the reader uses them. He takes all his own photographs and often draws his own maps to illustrate his routes. He has appeared on television, and is a member of the Outdoor Writers' Guild.

Cicerone guides by Paddy Dillon:

Irish Coastal Walks
The Irish Coast to Coast
The Mountains of Ireland
Channel Island Walks
The Isles of Scilly
Walking in the Isle of Arran
Walking the Galloway Hills
Walking in County Durham
Walking the North Pennines
GR20 Corsica: High Level Route
Walking in Madeira
Walking in the Canaries: Vol 2 East

WALKING IN THE CANARY ISLANDS: VOLUME 1 WEST

TENERIFE, LA GOMERA, LA PALMA AND EL HIERRO

By
Paddy Dillon

CICERONE

2 POLICE SQUARE, MILNTHORPE, CUMBRIA LA7 7PY
www.cicerone.co.uk

ISBN 1 85284 365 9

A catalogue record for this book is available from the British Library.

Photographs by the author.

Advice to Readers

Readers are advised that while every effort is taken by the author to ensure the accuracy of this guidebook, changes can occur which may affect the contents. It is advisable to check locally on transport, accommodation, shops, etc, but even rights of way can be altered.

The publisher would welcome notes of any such changes.

Front cover: Climbing to Guajara with the peak of El Teide in the background

CONTENTS

INDEX OF MAPS

El Teide – the highest point in the islands – and in Spain

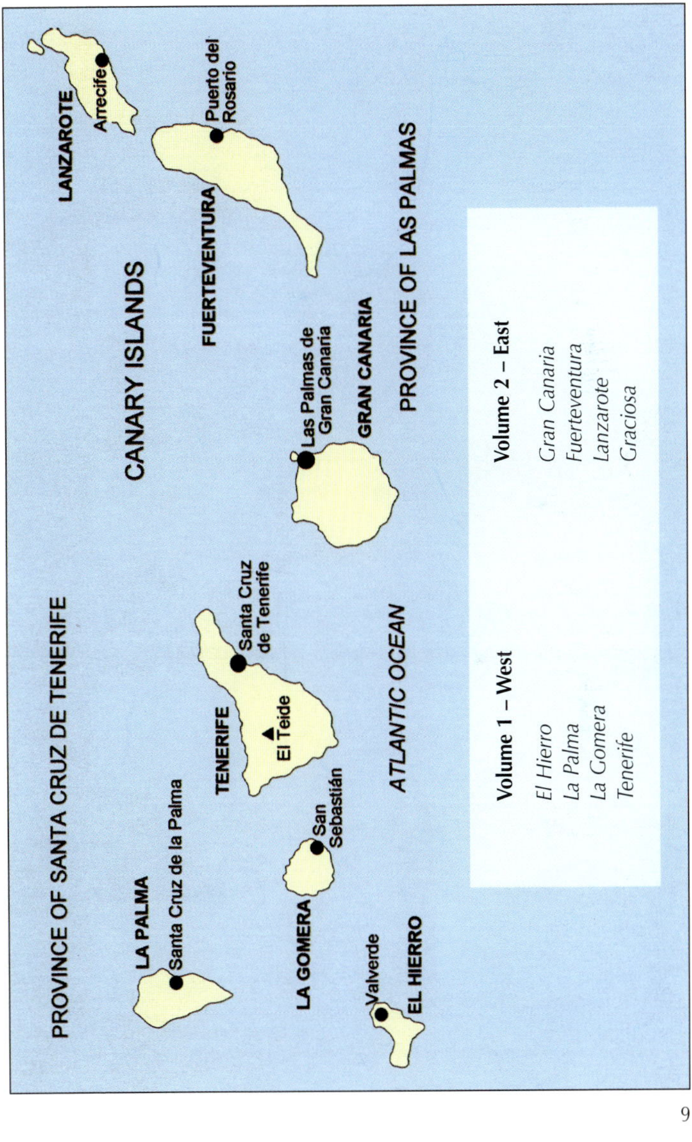
PROVINCE OF SANTA CRUZ DE TENERIFE
CANARY ISLANDS
LANZAROTE
Arrecife
Puerto del Rosario
FUERTEVENTURA
Las Palmas de Gran Canaria
GRAN CANARIA
PROVINCE OF LAS PALMAS
LA PALMA
Santa Cruz de la Palma
TENERIFE
Santa Cruz de Tenerife
El Teide
LA GOMERA
San Sebastián
EL HIERRO
Valverde
ATLANTIC OCEAN
Volume 1 – West
El Hierro
La Palma
La Gomera
Tenerife
Volume 2 – East
Gran Canaria
Fuerteventura
Lanzarote
Graciosa

Walkers on a rocky ridge near the top of the Roque de Los Muchachos

INTRODUCTION

The Canary Islands are a group of seven volcanic islands rising from the Atlantic Ocean off the coast of north Africa. They enjoy a sunny climate tempered by oceanic influences. Rainfall is rare and snowfall is confined to the highest peaks. Although the islands are often very rough and rocky, with impressive and often inaccessible cliffs, they are also criss-crossed with tracks and paths that offer a variety of interesting walking routes. Many areas are astoundingly beautiful and far removed from the major holiday resorts. There are mountain ridges and peaks to climb; deep and rocky *barrancos* to explore; extensive forests of pine and ancient 'laurisilva' woodlands; flowery hillsides, rugged cliff coastlines and cultivated terraces bearing all manner of fruit and vegetables. This guidebook includes a rich and varied selection of 50 walks on the islands of Tenerife, La Gomera, La Palma and El Hierro. A companion volume includes another 50 walks on the islands of Gran Canaria, Fuerteventura and Lanzarote.

LOCATION

The Canary Islands are more or less enclosed in a rectangular area from 13°30′W to 18°00′W and 27°30′N to 29°30′N. Interestingly, the small western island of El Hierro was long regarded as being at the very edge of the world; it was the original 0° meridian until supplanted by Greenwich! As a group, the islands stretch from east to west over a distance of 450km (280 miles). Although administered by Spain, the mother country is over 1100km (685 miles) away. The narrowest strait between the Canary Islands and north Africa is about 110km (70 miles) wide. There are seven main islands and a handful of much smaller ones. The total land area is nearly 7500km (2900 sq miles), but the islands occupy an area of the Atlantic Ocean nearly ten times that size. Apart from Morocco and the western Sahara, which are to the east, the nearest neighbours to the Canary Islands are Madeira, to the north, and the Azores, to the north-west.

GEOLOGY

The Canary Islands are essentially volcanic islands, and although much of the volcanic violence has long passed, there are still a handful of hot spots and there have been several recorded eruptions over the past 500 years. Magma from deep within the Earth spewed out onto the ocean floor over 100 million years ago. Gradually, enough material built up for land to rise above the water, so

Water is drawn away along channels from the valley head of Los Tilos on La Palma (Walk 6)

that the Canary Islands started appearing about 20 million years ago. The eastern islands of Lanzarote and Fuerteventura surfaced first, followed by Gran Canaria, Tenerife, La Gomera and La Palma. El Hierro, in the far west, probably surfaced only in the last three million years.

The volcanic rocks seen today range from ancient strata formed millions of years ago to lava flows that spilled out as recently as the 1970s. There is every reason to believe that there will be further eruptions; most likely at the southern end of La Palma. Perhaps the most spectacular result of volcanic activity is the conical peak of El Teide (the highest mountain in all Spanish territory at 3718m), itself surrounded by jagged lava flows and the awesome crater-like rim of Las Cañadas. However, it is easy to lose count of the number of smaller volcanic cones that can be spotted in their hundreds by a dedicated island-hopper. The deep-seated bedrock, volcanic dykes, later lava flows, cinder cones and almost everything else you see is essentially basaltic.

DISCOVERY AND HISTORY

Although the Spaniards are often credited with 'discovering' the Canary Islands, history has a lot more to say on the subject. The islands were convincingly described by Pliny the Elder in the first century AD, and it is thought he could have been drawing on information obtained by the Phoenicians or Carthaginians before the birth of Christ. Go back any earlier and the Canaries become lost in the mythology of Atlantis, but one thing is certain, the tribes known as the Guanches had already settled on the Canary Islands well before the birth of Christ, and Cro-Magnon Man was there as early as 3000BC. Where the Guanches came from, nobody can say for sure, though the simplest suggestion that they came from north Africa in fleets of canoes is probably the most plausable. Guanche civilisation has always been described as technologically primitive, even 'stone age', but was socially well ordered. The Guanches put up a fierce resistance when the Spaniards began their conquest of the islands from the 14th century, but one by one each island fell. Tenerife capitulated last of all, with the mighty volcano of El Teide grumbling throughout the conquest. Despite some of the Guanches entering into treaties with the Spaniards and converting to Christianity, they ultimately lost their land and freedom, and often their lives.

The Canary Islands have been viewed as stepping stones to the Americas. They were visited by Christopher Columbus on his voyages of discovery from 1492. Their position has, however, as with most exposed island colonies, left the islands subject to pirate raids, as well as disputes with the Portuguese, attacks by British fleets and wavering economic fortunes.

Buildings at San Sebastián dating from the conquest of the islands

There was constant rivalry between Tenerife and Gran Canaria, with the whole island group being governed from Las Palmas de Gran Canaria from 1808, but with Santa Cruz de Tenerife becoming the capital of the island group in 1822.

In 1927 the Canary Islands were divided into two provinces: Las Palmas and Santa Cruz de Tenerife.

In the early part of the 20th century the military governor of the Canary Islands, General Franco, launched a coup from Tenerife. This led to the creation of the Spanish Republic, the onset of the infamous Spanish Civil War and a long dictatorship. The islands were free from the worst of the strife, but were also left as a kind of backwater. It was largely as a result of Franco's later policies that the Canary Islands were developed from the 1960s as a major tourist destination for sun-starved holidaymakers from northern Europe.

Since 1982 the islands have been an autonomous region and there have been a few calls for complete independence from Spain. The islanders think of themselves as 'Canarios' first and Spanish second, though they can also be fiercely loyal to their own particular islands, towns and villages. It is a pity that so many visiting tourists remain largely confined to the resorts and holiday complexes, and understand little about the history of the islands or the character of the people.

Walking around the gravelly slopes of Montaña Blanca to reach El Tiede (Tenerife, Walk 26)

WEATHER

Most people have the impression that the Canary Islands bask in everlasting sunshine. While it is true that they have an enviable number of sunshine hours and the lower parts of the islands are warm and balmy even in the winter, the mountains can be covered in clouds, wreathed in damp mists or even subject to snowfall in winter. El Teide is high enough to catch snow every year and prominent enough to display it well. The high parts of La Palma and Gran Canaria may also see a little snow, but on the lower islands it is very rare and on the eastern islands it is unknown.

The prevailing trade winds blow from the north-west and tend to push a blanket of cloud against the higher western islands. The top of El Teide and the high parts of La Palma are often above the 'sea of clouds', while the uplands of El Hierro, La Gomera and Gran Canaria might be buried in it. There can be a vast difference in the weather at sea level and on the high mountains, as well as between the damp northern slopes of the islands and the arid southern slopes. Shift the wind direction around and you can get anything from showers of rain – of tropical intensity at times – or hazy dust blowing in from the Sahara, though these conditions are short-lived.

In practical terms, most days will be hot and dry, though potentially uncomfortably humid. You should protect yourself against the sun and carry plenty of water to drink. If there is any likelihood of rain, then a lightweight waterproof will suffice, and if venturing onto the mountains in winter, be prepared for cold winds and even snow. Do not expose yourself to the sun for too long, and try and rest in the shade at intervals if it feels uncomfortably hot. Keep reminding yourself that you are walking on a group of islands off the Sahara Desert!

LANDSCAPE

As a consequence of its volcanic origins, the Canarian landscape is often stark and severe. The islands are formed of layers of lava, some of which were weathered to a crumbly surface before being covered by more lava flows. The resulting beds of hard and soft layers weather most unevenly. Expect to find deep rocky valleys, or *barrancos*, and overhanging cliffs subject to rockfalls. Huge areas may be covered in soft pumice cinders that need to be emptied from your boots or shoes regularly. All the islands have rugged coastlines though sandy beaches are found on the eastern islands.

Vegetation cover varies from absolutely nothing – or a mere dusting of lichens – through rubbery 'taibaba' scrub, to dense 'laurisilva' and vast areas covered in pines. Where the volcanic soil is supplied with enough water, a bewildering variety of crops can be grown. In some areas banana plantations or vineyards are extensive, while on

Rocky peak on the side of Montaña Jala (Tenerife, Walk 42)

some terraced slopes every kind of fruit and vegetable is grown. The landscape contains plenty of variety, but how much of it you experience depends on your choice of walks. While some walks include several types of landscape, others may confine you to a pine forest, picking a way across barren rocky slopes, or to a day hidden deep in the 'laurisilva'.

LANGUAGE

Spanish is spoken throughout the Canary Islands, and if you have any proficiency in that tongue you will realise that Canarios have their own accent and colloquialisms. One of the most peculiar features is the way the letter 's' often vanishes from the middle and ends of words to be replaced by a gentle 'h' sound. Sometimes the origins of certain placenames is rooted in the pre-Spanish Guanche language. In the big resorts there are plenty of people who speak good English and German, but don't expect many people in remote locations to speak anything other than Spanish. It is useful to learn enough key phrases to negotiate a bus journey or ask for basic directions, and you'll find most Canarios very patient and helpful if you make the effort to communicate in Spanish.

While using a map, it is useful to know what some of the placenames refer to, so consult the topographical glossary in Appendix One for some commonly used terms. Don't be surprised if other walkers or Canarios assume you are German and speak to you in German, as there are plenty of German walkers around. Don't be afraid to practise a few words of Spanish. No matter how bad you think you sound, be assured that the Canarios have heard plenty of really bad pronunciation and yours is unlikely to be the worst!

ISLAND TREES AND FLOWERS

As each of the Canary Islands rose from the ocean, some attempt will have been made by terrestrial plants to gain a roothold. Maybe lichens and mosses managed to eke out an existence in tiny crevices, sometimes thriving, then being overwhelmed by lava flows. Later, a variety of plants, including flowers and trees, will have become established. The first seeds to reach these islands could have been deposited on the shore after floating on the ocean currents, or they could have been borne on the wind, or deposited in bird droppings.

The Canary Islands are remote from the African coast and have evolved a peculiar assemblage of plants that are not known elsewhere. While some plants may be related to others on nearby islands, or on the African or European mainland, others are unique to particular islands or even specific locations. Some striking and unusual plants are left over from the Miocene period, having become extinct elsewhere, such as the Dragon Trees. Some have adapted to particularly harsh conditions on the islands,

Two 'Tajinaste' or giant echiums, growing by the track on Las Cañadas (Tenerife, Walk 29)

Flowering candelabra spurge, or cardón, is a Canarian speciality

Prickly pears such as this one in bloom are common throughout the islands

such as the rubbery spurges, or *taibaba* and the thick candelabra spurges, or *cardón*. Canary pines flourish on many high mountainsides, defying the dryness of the ground and possessing an ability to regenerate even after severe forest fires. Some areas are densely covered in 'laurisilva' woodlands, containing various species of laurels and tree heather. These are the 'cloud forests' that sieve water droplets from the mist and keep the higher islands moist. Some of the lower arid slopes may be overwhelmed with Canarian palms, prickly pears and aloes. Flowers are abundant and form a specialist study. There are hundreds of flowers that are indigenous to the Canary Islands, and hundreds that are endemic. Even attempting to draw up a shortlist is futile, but anyone with a particular interest in flowers should obtain a good field guide to assist with identification of specimens. It is also a good idea to visit one or two botanic gardens, where most plants are name-tagged and information about them is close to hand. Keen botanists should visit the islands during May, when the flowers are at the blooming best. Good books inlcude: *Native Flora of the Canary Islands*, by Miguel Angel Cabrera Pérez, published by Everest; *Wild Flowers of the Canary Islands*, by David Bramwell and Zoë Bramwell, published by Editorial Rueda; and the more portable *Flora of the Canary Islands*, by David Bramwell, published by Editorial Rueda.

Dragon Trees survived the Ice Age in the Canaries and continue to flourish

When goats seek shade, should you be out walking in the sun?

ISLAND BIRDS

The Canary Islands attract plenty of passage migrant birds, but there are very few full-time residents and a mere handful of endemic species. The laurel pigeon and rock pigeon naturally prefer woodland and cliffs respectively, and the former is becoming rather scarce. Although buzzards and kestrels can be spotted hunting in barren areas, the real hunter is the shrike, which feeds off an abundance of insects. Many of the birds you see around the Canary Islands are varieties of pipits, chaffinches, warblers and chiffchaffs. One of the smallest birds is the kinglet. There are canaries, though these have no connection with the name of the island group. Parakeets may add a flash of colour, and some birds have no doubt escaped from the aviaries that exist around the islands. The littoral zones are very limited, but the Canarian oystercatcher can eke out an existence there along with other waders and divers. It is best to take a boat trip to be able to spot such things as shearwaters or storm petrels, though gulls are common.

ISLAND ANIMALS

It is not known what animal life existed on the islands before the Guanches settled there. Perhaps the most notable creature to have survived, and then only in small numbers on El Hierro and La Gomera, is the giant lagarte lizard. There are a few species of smaller lizards that can be seen in most sunny places. Rabbits were introduced to the islands and are hunted by man and dog most weekends, and end up on many Canarian restaurant menus. Feral cats make ruthless predators against all small animals, surviving in the outdoors throughout the year.

The Guanches started grazing goats on the islands. The Canarios have continued this tradition, making some areas look very close-cropped. There are some sheep and cattle, but these are only rarely seen; the usual array of farm and domestic animals are more common. Insect life is abundant in even the most desolate areas, such as Las Cañadas del Teide, where there are about 2000 species. In many places you see beehives, or signs warning of their existance. There are very few insects that bite or sting; it is safe to observe them, particularly the spectacular butterflies that sometimes flutter past.

You need to look to the sea to spot large wildlife. Whales and dolphins can be sometimes seen in great numbers. There are areas of the ocean near the islands that are sanctuaries for these animals. They can be visited on boat trips, which take you close enough to view them. Of course there are plenty of fish – more easily spotted on fish stalls than in the sea unless you include a diving trip in your exploration of the islands.

NATIONAL PARKS AND PROTECTED AREAS

Despite being of relatively small compass, the Canary Islands boast a higher concentration of protected landscapes than mother Spain. The most important of these is the strictly controlled Parque Nacional, or National Park. Conservation often takes priority over recreation in these places, so walking opportunities may sometimes be quite limited, though the scenery is often of the highest order. In this guidebook there are three national parks: the forested Garajonay on La Gomera, the rugged Caldeira de Taburiente on La Palma and the awesome Parque Nacional del Teide on Tenerife.

Other commonly observed land designations include Parque Rural (Rural Park), Parque Natural (Natural Park), Paisaje Protegido (Protected Land), Reserva Natural Especial (Special Nature Reserve), Especio Natural Protegido (Protected Natural Space), Monumento Natural (Natural Monument), Reserva de Biosfera (Biosphere Reserve) and so on. The military maps show many of these areas, though without always assigning them specific boundaries. While rampant building schemes are observed around the coast it is heartening to find so much of the rest of the islands under some form of protection. This guidebook makes a point of exploring many of these protected areas as they are often of great interest and usually display spectacular scenery. Usually there are signs telling you when you are entering and leaving these areas.

GETTING TO THE CANARY ISLANDS

Flights

Most visitors to the Canary Islands arrive on charter flights from all over Europe, but especially from northern Europe. Almost every travel agent in Europe offers competitive package tours to the Canaries, and most will be able to offer good flight-only deals on request. Charter flight destinations are usually to Tenerife, Gran Canaria and Lanzarote. Less often they are to Fuerteventura and rarely to La Palma. The small islands of La Gomera and El Hierro seem to be unknown to most travel agents! First-time visitors might be happy to fly to one of the popular islands, but those who want to visit the smaller and quieter islands will need to think about using onward flights or ferry services

Inter-Island Flights

All seven of the Canary Islands have airports and there are inter-island flights offering rapid (journeys are between 15 and 30 minutes) though expensive, routes from one to another. Canarias Binter, flies between the islands, with most flights operating out of Tenerife Norte or Gran Canaria. Flights from Tenerife serve all the other islands. Flights from Gran Canaria serve all islands except El Hierro.

Inter-Island Ferries

Ferries regularly ply between the islands. Heading west from Tenerife most ferries are operated by Lineas Fred Olsen. A large and slow ferry steers a triangular course around the western islands, while there are also fast and regular ferries between

The Ferries between the islands are fast and frequent

Tenerife and La Gomera. Ferries linking Tenerife to Gran Canaria are operated by Lineas Fred Olsen and Naviera Armas. Both companies offer onward links with Fuerteventura and Lanzarote, with a choice of long and short journeys, and fast and slow ferries. Local travel agents can supply current schedules and can handle bookings. Ferry journeys can take as little as 30 minutes or as long as 10 hours, and are fairly cheap.

GETTING AROUND THE CANARY ISLANDS

Car Hire

Car hire is usually offered at the time a package holiday is booked, but it can be arranged on arrival or later. Cars can be hired from the airports, sometimes the ferryports, or through travel agents and possibly your hotel or local tour representative. However, because of the nature of the terrain walks tend to be linear, rather than circular, so a car is not always useful, and is sometimes a liability. Many of the island roads are quite narrow and it can be alarming to meet large coaches on exposed bends. You need to balance the convenience of having a car with the inconvenience of having to retrieve it after a walk. There are plenty of useful bus services therefore they are often a better way of exploring the islands.

Bus Services

Canarios don't speak about the 'bus' or even the 'autobus', but use the term 'guagua'. The bus station is the 'estacion de guaguas' and the bus stop is the 'parada de guagua'. Oddly enough, most bus stops carry only a single word - 'bus' - but you never hear a local person say it. When using timetables, please be aware that there can be differences in the level of service on weekdays, Saturdays and Sundays, as well as during festivals. Each island in this guidebook has a single company providing bus services as follows.

El Hierro: The Sociedad Cooperativa de Transportes del Hierro (referred to as Cooperativa Bus in this guidebook) doesn't offer particularly helpful services. Timetables are seldom printed, so times have to be noted at the bus station in Valverde. Buses tend to leave the outlying villages early in the morning and converge on Valverde, then return to the villages some time in the afternoon. However, with careful planning it is possible to make use of them, but be sure to visit the bus station and find out what the latest timetables offer.

La Palma: The Transportes Insular La Palma buses offer plenty of useful services, mostly around the lower slopes of the island, running parallel to the coast, with a number of services crossing the crest in the middle of the island. Many, but not all, services run from very early until very late. Though some of their buses are used for tours along the highest mountain road they do not run scheduled services along here, which is unfortunate. Full details of services can be obtained on a single timetable sheet. A 'Bono Bus' card can be purchased to avoid fumbling with change, and offers a good discount on the usual cash fares.

La Gomera: The Servicio Regular Gomera buses run along only a handful of routes, but there are some early and late services, and as La Gomera is fairly small, the level of service is quite adequate. The earliest runs are from outlying towns and villages into San Sebastián. There are usually four runs out of San Sebastián during the day, along three main routes, with some cross-over routes from the airport to Valle Gran Rey or Vallehermoso. Full details of services can be obtained on a single timetable sheet.

Tenerife: The Transportes Interurbanos de Tenerife SA (referred to as TITSA Bus in this guidebook) offers plenty of excellent services around Tenerife. Some of the more popular routes have buses all through the night, though some outlying villages may have only one or two buses a day. Routes run all around the coast and a splendid network of services link most towns and villages. There are two bus routes that climb high into the mountains, almost to 2400m (7875ft). Full details of all services are contained on one large folding leaflet. Again a 'Bono Bus' card can be purchased.

It is important to be on the road in time to catch the bus – an up-to-date timetable is crucial

Tour Buses

Wherever you go in the Canary Islands, sooner or later you will find convoys of tour buses trundling along the roads. While these services are of limited use in reaching any destination, they can offer an easy insight into each island in turn. A good all-round tour will include many of the scenic highlights, a couple of places offering food and drink, and maybe an on-board commentary. If the tour passes through the countryside or climbs into the mountains, then there is a chance to preview some of the walking areas or even spot individual routes. After that, take to the public service buses and then start walking!

Taxis

There may come a time when a walk is both linear and awkward to reach, or the bus service isn't particularly helpful and a taxi may be required. Most towns in the Canary Islands have taxi services, and there are more in the big towns and resorts than in small towns. Taxis tend to be expensive, but prices for long runs are always negotiable, and if the cost is shared between three or four people it can be quite reasonable. If you find a good driver, be sure to take his phone number and favour him with either a pick-up at the end of the day or another journey on another day. On some walks, it can be useful to have a couple of phone numbers for taxis so that you can bail out easily if you miss an infrequent bus or find yourself running late.

ACCOMMODATION

The bulk of tourists reach the Canary Islands as part of an all-inclusive package deal. Accommodation is invariably provided in one of the major resorts, such as Playa de las Américas or Los Cristianos, or at least in a large hotel or apartment complex. It is a system that works well enough for most holiday makers, but it may not be ideal for walkers, especially those who do not want to be tied to a specific location. Ask detailed questions

Inside a well-stocked Canarian bar

The rugged mountains of the interior of the islands are far-removed from the resorts

about the precise location of your holiday accommodation before booking a package holiday, then check a detailed map to be sure that there is enough walking potential within easy reach, as well as good bus links.

Walkers who like to wander from place to place can easily book a flight and sort out accommodation 'on spec'. There are luxury Parador hotels, small hotels, apartments, *hostals* and *pensións* scattered throughout the Canary Islands. Tourist Information Offices can supply brochures or basic listings. Some farmhouses or country properties offer *casas rurales* (countryside apartments) for those who want to stay well away from the big resorts. Backpackers will have a hard time, as camping sites are very scarce. Wild camping is not permitted, and out-of-the-way mountain campgrounds require a special permit that has to be negotiated weeks in advance and may carry a limit of only a couple of nights in any one location. However, with such an equable climate there is nothing to stop you throwing down a sleeping bag in the wilderness for the night to bivvy out under the stars. It is hard to see how this could be policed!

Walkers who are not tied to packaged accommodation can travel from town to town, village to village, island to island, and generally please themselves with their choice of accomodation and what walking routes they wish to explore. Most walkers would be happy to stay in quiet mountain villages, far removed from the bustling resorts. Avoid the peak holiday seasons and there should be no problem finding a room for the night. During peak periods be sure to consult the available listings and phone ahead a day or so.

TOURIST INFORMATION

All the major towns on each of the Canary Islands has a Tourist Information Office. This may be ensconced in the Ayuntamiento, or Town Hall, or it may either be a small building or room in a central part of town, or just a street kiosk. Usually, but by no means always, English is spoken. Expect them to be able to offer some sort of accommodation listings, information on transport and tours, and sundry visitor attractions. Do not expect to be able to get any detailed information about walking opportunities. Some of them may have a small stock of basic maps and guides, but it is often better to head for the biggest bookshop in town for a decent choice.

MAPS OF THE CANARY ISLANDS

Maps of a quality similar to Ordnance Survey (OS) Landranger or Explorer maps of Britain are not available on the Canary Islands. The Spanish equivalent of the Ordnance Survey is the Servicio Geográfico del Ejército. They produce both 1:50,000 and 1:25,000 Cartografía Militar, or military maps of the islands. There are 29 maps in the 1:50,000 series covering the entire island group, and these are quoted at the beginning of each route description. Contouring on the military maps is good, and most landscape features are clear, but they tend to be out of date in terms of new roads and building developments. Many paths are shown rather vaguely or even erroneously. Some paths given great prominence on the maps may not exist on the ground. If you like OS style maps, then these are the best that are available. Private mapping offers a few alternatives. There is a good map of La Palma at a scale of 1:50,000, published by Juan José Santos. A good map of La Gomera at a scale of 1:30,000 is published by Compass. No-one has managed to make an adequate map of El Hierro, and maps of Tenerife tend to be large scale and are not really designed for walking. The Instituto Geográfico Nacional produces the 1:200,000 Mapa Provincial, which offers a complete overview of the islands. It gives a very honest impression of the relative size and position of each island, but leaves you feeling that you bought most of the Atlantic Ocean!

The maps quoted in this guidebook are the military maps of the Canary Islands. It is best to order them well in advance from map suppliers such as Stanfords (12-14 Long Acre, London WC2E 9BR, tel. 0207 836 1321), The Map Shop (15 High Street, Upton-upon-Severn WR8 0HJ, tel. 01684 593146), or Cordee (3a De Montford Street, Leicester LE1 7HD, tel. 0116 254 3579). More simple and free tourist maps of the Canary Islands can be obtained upon reaching the islands. The sketch maps in this book are simply for reference. Ensure you transfer details to your chosen maps and then use the route descriptions alongside them while actually walking.

Typical wooden signpost on the Camino de la Virgen on El Hierro (Walk 4)

THE PLAN OF THIS GUIDE

This guidebook covers walks in the Province of Santa Cruz de Tenerife, which includes the islands of Tenerife, La Gomera, La Palma and El Hierro. The first walking routes start in the far west, on the island of El Hierro; here five connecting routes are offered. The following walks are on La Palma. There is a five-day walk along the GR-131 that will enable those who wish to explore the high mountain crest of the island. There are a few other routes taking in some spectacular scenery. Another five-day walk explores half the island of La Gomera. There is also a coast-to-coast walk and routes around the high ground in the middle of the island. However, over half of the walks are on the biggest island of Tenerife. A four-day walk from sea-level to the summit of El

Los Roques on the main road from San Sebastián to Garajonay (Walk 22 on La Gomera)

Teide is offered, along with several walks that explore the amazing landscapes in and around Las Cañadas. There are also routes that can be linked end-to-end to allow an exploration of Teno, at the western end of Tenerife, and Anaga, at the eastern end of the island.

Cautious walkers should start with the shorter, easier walks. Read the route descriptions to decide if the walk is suitable, taking note of any difficulties mentioned. If using bus services, pace yourself carefully so that you are in time to catch the bus afterwards. More adventurous walkers will find plenty of longer and tougher routes, some of them involving scrambling on exposed rocks, or that are based in mountainous country. Those who desire to explore the countryside on long walks will find that many of the routes in this guidebook can be linked end-to-end, forming long treks across or around the islands. The GR131 over the mountains of La Palma is a classic mountain route, but you can enjoy similar long treks over the mountains on the other islands.

Each walk opens with a brief description, followed by details relating to the length of the walk, the start and finishing points, which maps to use, the nature of the terrain, plus information on bus services and refreshments along the way. The route descriptions lead step by step along each of the walks. If the places you pass are marked on the map, they are highlighted in the text.

As very few of the walks are circular, using a car is a handicap. In deference to the steepness of the slopes and the heat and humidity,

Looking across from La Gomera to Tenerife and El Tiede (Walk 20)

walks are sometimes downhill rather than uphill. However, there are many exceptions, and some routes are like roller-coasters with several ascents and descents.

Carry good maps, a compass and up-to-date bus timetables, then pace yourself to ensure that you reach the appropriate bus stop or pick-up point on time. The more remote or difficult the walk is, the more self-sufficient you need to be. Take enough food and water, and try not to walk too long in open sun without taking a break in the shade. Use sunscreen, a sunhat and long-sleeved clothing to prevent sunburn. A torch is essential if the chosen walk includes long tunnels.

EMERGENCY ASSISTANCE

Bear in mind that the Canary Islands have no organised mountain rescue service. If you need assistance it could be a combination of the ambulance, fire service or police involved in your rescue. All three services are contacted at the same emergency telephone number, which is 112.

Explorations of these islands can be continued with reference to the second volume *Walking in the Canary Islands - East* that covers walks on Gran Canaria, Fuerteventura and Lanzarote.

Picking a route along the northern cliffs of El Hierro (Walk 2)

EL HIERRO

El Hierro is the smallest and westernmost of the seven Canary Islands. There is a small airport near Valverde, the island capital, while ferries berth at La Estaca. Compared to the other Canary Islands, tourism is low-key and there are no big resorts or holiday developments. Walkers will find that the island is criss-crossed with tracks and paths, though very few of these are sign-posted. As maps are rather vague, you need to apply a lot of common sense to route-finding and navigation. Away from the small towns and villages there are extensive areas of scrub, bare slopes of cindery pumice, higher slopes of Canary pines and some damper areas of 'laurisilva'. As the highest point is only 1500m (4921ft), the 'sea of clouds' brought in by the trade winds often bury the high ground in mist, though sometimes the cloud just laps against the summits.

On a map it looks as though a huge bite has been taken out of El Hierro's northern side, a result of an enormous subsidence that literally tore the island in half. The bay of El Golfo is now overlooked by a splendid semi-circular cliff-line. The sheltered lower slopes are fertile and well watered, enabling an abundance of fruit and vegetables to grow here. Walkers who see the cliff-line will naturally want to follow it, and this is the subject of a two-day walk. Another two-day walk explores the course of the pilgrimage route called the Camino de la Virgen. A one-day walk from San Andrés leads to the southernmost point on the island at La Restinga.

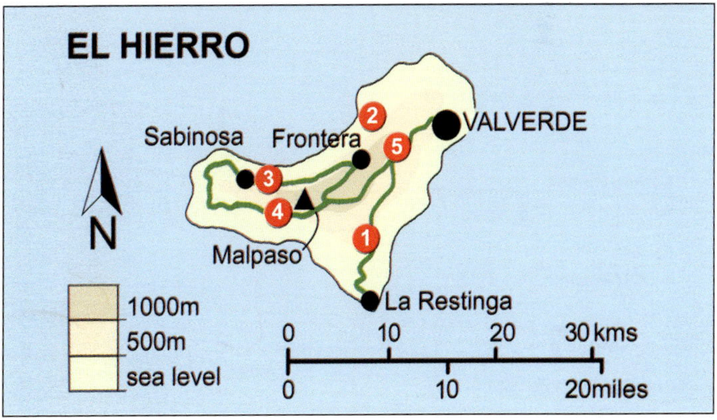

Mirador de la Peña
600m
Guarazoca
VALVERDE
600m
EL GOLFO
+ Ermita Virgen de la Peña
750m
Walk 5
785m
Jares
Reserva Natural
Especial Tibataje
900m
Tiñor
Puerto de la Estaca
1100m
Quatro Esquinas
1020m
Montaña Entremontañas
Izique
1232m
1100m
Camino de la Virgen
San Andrés
1040m
Walk 2
Frontera
Parque Rural
Frontera
Walk 1
La Torre
Fileba
1371m
Fuente de
Llania
Bermeja
1118m
1339m
1417m
Tenerife
EL HIERRO
Walks 1, 2 & 5
Mirador de las Playas
Las Playas
Las Casas
ATLANTIC OCEAN
820m
Taibique
Walk 1
N
500m
Lomito Pardo
Montaña del Jable
359m
El Miradero
SCALE
0 1 2 3 kms
0 1 2 miles
1000m
500m
sea level
Restinga
197m
La Restinga

WALK 1
San Andrés to La Restinga

Distance:	19km (12 miles)
Start:	Bar Restaurante Casa Goyo, San Andrés
Finish:	The harbour in La Restinga
Map:	1:50,000 Military Map Sheet 34/35-43-44
Terrain:	Mostly along good tracks and roads, with pathless scrub towards the end.

A series of tracks and paths can be linked southwards from San Andrés, to the southernmost point at La Restinga. The route includes flowery fields, pine forest and small villages that give way to barren slopes of scrub and cinders. La Restinga is a notable fishing harbour, where the little restaurants specialise in fish dishes. Please refer to the map on p. 34. This walk is best accomplished if you are staying at La Restinga, so that you can use the early bus to reach San Andrés and then walk back at your leisure during the day. This will allow time for a break in the middle and avoid the rush to make a connection at the end.

Take the time to wander around **San Andrés**, a cosy little village surrounded by small, walled fields. There is a little church tucked into a corner off the main road. The altitude is around 1040m (3410ft). Start the walk just beyond the Bar Restaurante Casa Goyo as if leaving the village along the main road for Frontera. Turn left down a minor road, until the road suddenly bends to the left. At that point, turn right along a clear track. Although the track is gently undulating, the trend is gradually uphill. Watch out for a water pipe running alongside, sometimes hidden in the undergrowth, as it marks the line of the route. The track suddenly turns left downhill, so turn uphill to the right to follow a water pipe and a more rough and rocky track. Cross a gentle gap around 1110m (3610ft) beside the rounded **Montaña de las Rosas**, passing small fields of grass and flowers enclosed by rugged drystone walls. You almost intersect with a broad dirt road, but turn left to continue down a narrower track. This track descends steeply at times, with rugged zigzags in places. You get a different perspective of the Montaña de las Rosas and realise that it is an old volcanic cone. There are a couple of pines and a lot of scrub on the way down through a shallow valley littered with boulders in places.

Transport: Cooperativa Bus Valverde-Restinga serves San Andrés, Las Casas, Taibique and La Restinga. Other Cooperativa Bus services pass San Andrés, such as those serving Frontera, Las Puntas, Tigaday and Sabinosa. There is also a bus service between Restinga and Pozo de la Salud.

Refreshments: bar restaurants and shops at San Andrés, Las Casas, Taibique and La Restinga.

When a minor road is reached, turn right to follow it over a rise, then head downhill to about 940m (3085ft). Keep right at a junction to climb uphill again. A sign on a building reads Calle la Ladera, the name of the road, while the cluster of houses is known as **La Torre**. The lower road in view, by the way, serves the village of Isora and has a bus service. Turn right up another road and keep climbing, ignoring a dip in the road and spurs to left and right. This road is the Calle Tajace, running above the buildings at Tajace de Abajo. The last prominent structure is for water storage. The road climbs across a scrubby slope and to the left at the top is the cindery bump of **Bermeja**, at 1118m (3668ft). It can be climbed in a matter of a few seconds for a view of the coast. Beware of the crumbly edge, where the trig point has already toppled over!

Beyond Bermeja the road turns right, but a narrow spur continues onwards and downhill a short way to a rocky streambed. A broad and gently undulating track continues with a water pipe running alongside. It runs very near a sheer drop where eroded gullies fall 1000m (3280ft) down to the coast at Las Playas. The Parador Nacional del Hierro can be seen at the end of the road, offering exclusive accommodation. Despite the steepness of the slope, there is a sparse covering of pines all the way round the vast hollow. The track narrows and is at times no more than a rough and stony path. It remains clear throughout and leads through pines to a road. It is worth making a left turn down the road for a couple of minutes to reach the **Mirador de las Playas**, where there is a car park and toilets in the shade of the pines, and another view of the rugged slope and coast.

Head back up the road and at a junction turn left down another road. The idea is to avoid a stretch of the main road, and you may hear traffic on the higher one. Note that the pines have scorched trunks and have obviously been burnt in the past. There are overgrown fields with very few plots under cultivation further down the slope. The area is known as El Pinar because of the abundance of pines. The settlements seen ahead are Las Casas

A dirt road leads down from Taibique in the direction of La Restinga

and Taibique, which are connected by the main road with its chequerboard patterned pavements alongside. When a road junction is reached, walk straight onwards to reach a bend on the main road, called La Curva, at **Las Casas**. Buses stop here. There is a supermarket and the Bar Restaurante La Sabina is just down the road. Follow the main road onwards to reach the middle of **Taibique**, where there is a small plaza with seating. The Bar El Mentidero and a supermarket are within easy reach. Buses stop at the little plaza. You are halfway through the walk so you have earned a break. Have a drink anyway as the next stretch is very dry and has very little shade.

As you leave Taibique along the main road there are a couple more shops and bars before the bendy road leads downhill and a sign announces that La Restinga is 15km (9 miles) distant. Don't worry, this is the distance by road; on foot it is 8km (5 miles). Follow the road towards a solitary building on the left. Just beforehand, also on the left, a narrow and rugged track drops steeply downhill. Cross the road and continue straight down another track. Don't turn right to a building, but continue straight onwards to cross another road. Walk straight down a narrow road that continues as a track. After passing a building, the surface deteriorates and becomes quite rugged. There is a narrow water pipe alongside. Turn right when a road is reached, then turn left down a much clearer track. There are spurs, but stick to the clearest track to pass a house, then avoid other tracks by roughly following the course of a pylon line further downhill. The track becomes steep, narrow and rather rocky. There are some beehives off to the left, so keep away from them. Stay on the clearest track, which now drifts well to the right of the pylon line. Turn right along a much clearer dirt road, then swing left near a building. When the dirt road suddenly bends right, head off down to the left along a narrower old walled track. It is very cindery underfoot and the track weaves through dense scrub. Looking ahead from **Lomito Pardo**, spot two pylons that apparently stand on two little knolls side by side. Watch for another narrow, rugged track on the left that approaches the pylon on the left. Follow this track, which keeps left of the pylon, and a cinder path leads down to a bend on the main road.

Cross the road and continue straight downhill along another crunchy cinder path. Swing to the right, then left, then right again as dictated by the lines of low stone walls. Continue downhill on a slope of cindery scrub by walking roughly parallel to the pylon lines. **Montaña del Jable** rises to the left and a small cluster of volcanoes are seen ahead. Although there is little trace of a path, the desert-like terrain is easy to cross. Don't follow any vehicle tracks across the slopes. Towards the bottom, drift to the right to reach the slopes of a small volcano called **Restinga**, crossing ropy lava to join a clear, walled, cindery track. This leads easily downhill on slopes that are too rough to walk, and a water pipe alongside reaches a large storage building. Continue along the track to join a road, and turn left to walk down into the village of **La Restinga**. The huddled white buildings are threaded by narrow streets, and a couple of these lead straight down to the harbour.

There are a few shops, bars and restaurants, as well as a little accommodation in this fishing village. The bus to and from Valverde stops at a small plaza opposite the Bar Zumeria. The bus service to Pozo de la Salud is worth bearing in mind to avoid all your bus transfers taking place in Valverde.

WALK 2

La Peña to Fuente de Llania

Distance:	10km (6 miles)
Start:	The Mirador de la Peña, near Guarazoca
Finish:	Fuente de Llania
Map:	1:50,000 Military Map Sheet 34/35-43-44
Terrain:	Upland, but often gently graded. Some short, steep ascents on cindery slopes.

This walk leads along the high crest of El Hierro, from the viewpoint Mirador de la Peña to the main road slicing across the crest at Fuente de Llania. Please refer to the map on p. 34. This is far enough for a day's walk and there is a chance to intercept bus services along the main road. Strong walkers who start early in the day could continue beyond Fuente de Llania and walk over the highest mountain on El Hierro, Malpaso, and descend to Sabinosa. With careful planning you could stretch it over a weekend by using bus services to break the route in the middle.This continuation is described in Walk 3.

The **Mirador de la Peña** is a fine viewpoint and one where you can study the whole of this walk from the altitude of 600m (1970ft) at a glance. The huge amphitheatre of near sheer cliffs falling to El Golfo are crowned by the gentle dome of Malpaso at 1500m (4921ft). Cowering beneath the cliffs are the settlements of Las Puntas, Frontera, Tigaday and Los Llanitos, with Sabinosa seen towards the farthest point.

The Restaurante Mirador de la Peña is rarely open early, so apart from the view there is little to detain the walker. Follow the nearby road uphill in a curve above a small graveyard. Rising to the right is the concrete lane called the Camino la Peña. The **Ermita Virgen de la Peña** is a tiny whitewashed structure tucked into a cliff, and a water tap is concealed nearby. This is another fine viewpoint. Follow a short tarmac road uphill from the ermita, and notice the steep, zigzag path called the Camino de

Transport: Cooperativa Bus Valverde-Guarazoca for La Peña. Cooperativa Bus services pass Fuente de Llania, including those to and from Valverde serving Frontera, Las Puntas and Tigaday.

Refreshments: Restaurante Mirador de la Peña at the start, though seldom open early. Water taps at Ermita Virgen de la Peña, Ermita Virgen de la Caridad and Fuente de Llania.

la Peña leading down to Las Puntas through the Reserva Natural Especial Tibataje. Don't follow it, but bear it in mind for another day. Continue up the road and turn left along a stony track. Almost immediately, swing right up a ramp once associated with a quarry, then pick up a rather vague and narrow path near the cliff edge. Although it looks unpromising at the start, it quickly becomes one of the best cliff paths on the island.

Follow the faint path faithfully. Generally, it runs between the walled fields and the cliff edge. There are small rocksteps and a couple of diversions into the fields, but for the most part the path is true to the cliff edge. There are clumps of tree heather, but only seldom do these obstruct the views that simply get better and better as height is gained. At a couple of points where the tree heather blocks the cliff edge, you will have to walk just inside the small fields. Take care not to damage walls, but cross at the makeshift stone stiles positioned at low places. There may be cattle in the fields of grass and flowers. Goats may be hobbled to prevent them climbing walls and grazing along the cliffs. A trig point is reached where an overgrown, walled track reaches the cliff edge around 1100m (3610ft).

Continue along the cliff edge and turn a prominent corner to reach a higher trig point at **Izique**, at 1232m (4042ft). There are good views around much of El Hierro from this point. The cliff path gives way to a wide, stony track that in turn leads to a road. Turn right up the road to reach parking spaces at the Mirador de Jinama. The Ermita Virgen de la Caridad is alongside. Enjoy the views over the cliff edge, and also note the steep zigzag path called the Camino de Jinama leading down to Frontera through the Parque Rural Frontera. A water tap is located near the start of the path, but don't follow the path itself.

It isn't easy to continue along the main crest of El Hierro, but it is possible. If things get too difficult, then note that the main road is only a short distance away, and in fact it will have to be followed for at least a short stretch in due course. If you go behind the *ermita* a rather faint path can be traced uphill beside a line of pine trees. Unfortunately, there are abandoned terraces on the higher parts of this steep-sided little hill, and the pine branches tend to push you onto these rather than let you use the path. Walking along the top of the hill is easier, and leaving it is even better, crunching along a cindery crest towards La Mareta. Awkward patches of scrub sometimes cover the crest, but the road is close to hand and there are a couple of dusty tracks leading towards it. If you get as far as a small observatory on the crest, then head left to join the main road anyway, then turn right to follow it into a shady pine forest, which is part of the **Parque Natural Frontera**.

A stone by the roadside is marked '23km' and at this point a track drifts off to the right. It leads out of the pine forest for a sudden view of a huge volcanic crater at Fileba. Keep to the left side of the crater, as the ridge on the other side is too steep, rocky and crumbly to be followed safely. The crater walls are mostly cindery slopes, studded with heather trees along with a few pines and laurels, while a rug of grass sits at the very bottom.

A notable feature of this walk is the immense cliff-line overlooking the broad bay of El Golfo. In a cataclysm that is hard to imagine, half the island collapsed into the ocean, leaving this huge amphitheatre.

The Restaurante Mirador La Peña and a distant view of Malpaso above clouds

The deep cinder crater of a volcano is passed near the main road at Fileba

Come down to the main road at a sign reading 'Fileba 1330' and walk alongside the road for the space of two telegraph poles. Turn right uphill on a gritty path between laurels and heather trees. Cut across an open slope, then continue along a narrower path through denser laurel and heather, more typical of the original 'cloud forest' of El Hierro. Emerge on another broad, cindery path and swing right at a signpost to reach the Mirador El Golfo at 1369m (4491ft). Enjoy the views once more, which are as striking as ever, though you are still only halfway round the enormous cliff amphitheatre. The cinder path signposted for La Llania leads down into tall, dense 'laurisilva' to reach a road junction. There are a series of water taps off to the left. If you are running short of time, then hopefully there will be useful bus services along the main road. If you wish to continue with the second half of the walk, be sure that you will be able to finish it in daylight. The walk is less than half completed at this point; the second half is longer and more difficult.

WALK 3

Fuente de Llania to Sabinosa

Distance:	13km (8 miles)
Start:	Fuente de Llania
Finish:	Sabinosa
Map:	1:50,000 Military Map Sheet 34/35-43-44
Terrain:	Upland, but often gently graded. Some short, steep ascents on cindery slopes. There is a long and difficult forested descent to Sabinosa. The high parts are prone to cloud cover and care is needed with navigation.

The walk along the high crest of El Hierro continues from the main road at Fuente de Llania, over the highest mountains on the island. For much of the time you walk across grey cinder slopes, sometimes among pines and sometimes in the open. Cloud cover is common and where paths are vague, careful navigation is required. Please refer to the map on p. 44. From time to time the route along the high crest coincides with the route of the Camino de la Virgen, and this route across the island is described in Walks 4 and 5. There is a long, forested descent to Sabinosa beyond the summit of Malpaso

Walk 3 continues the second half of the walk that began in Walk 2. It starts on top of the main road at **Fuente de Llania** and continues along the high crest of El Hierro. There are a series of water taps available and water is virtually absent from the high crest. Follow the road signposted for the Santuario Virgen de los Reyes. There are open, cindery slopes close to the road that can be used instead of the tarmac, so look out for opportunities to leave the road to left and right. Keep an eye on the bald dome of a mountain called **Tenerife** ahead, and leave the road at a sign for the Camino de la Virgen to reach its slopes. Although the *camino* cuts across the cindery slopes of Tenerife, it is possible to climb straight up the steep, crunchy crest to reach the summit trig point at 1417m (4649ft). There are only a few clumps of heather on these otherwise barren slopes. Cloud is common and views might be completely obscured.

Walk down a short, steep, cindery slope then follow the undulating, crunchy crest, which has only sparse vegetation cover. In mist, take great care with route finding,

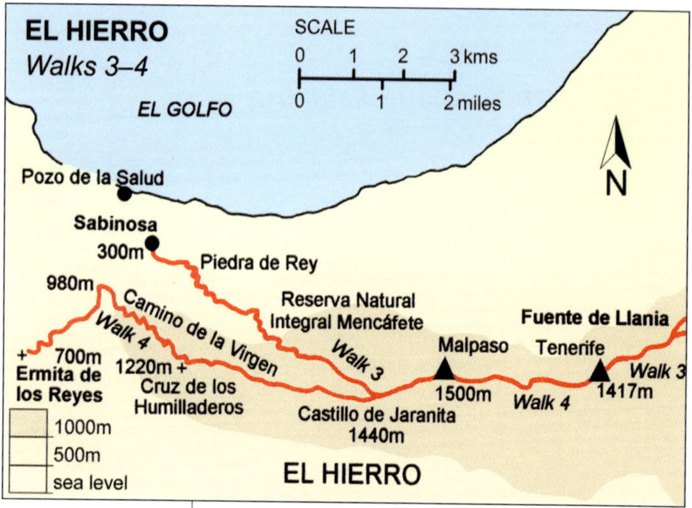

Transport: Cooperativa Bus services pass Fuente de Llania, including those to and from Valverde serving Frontera, Las Puntas and Tigaday. Cooperativa Bus Valverde-Sabinosa or Restinga-Pozo de la Salud reach Sabinosa.

Refreshments: Water taps at Fuente de Llania. Bar restaurants at the end in Sabinosa.

keeping away from the northern slopes, and bearing in mind that there is a good road a short way down the southern slopes. Clumps of heather appear later, then a gap is crossed at Raya del Cepon. Walk uphill to reach the summit cairn and heather clumps on Tábano at 1387m (4550ft). Pick the best line you can along the cindery crest, as there is no real path and the cinders are arranged in awkward ripples. Descend towards a prominent wooden cross at Cruz de los Reyes, which is at the end of a tarmac road, where a broad dirt road continues onwards.

Follow the dirt road a short way down through a cutting, then head off into a dip on the right and start climbing a broad, cindery path on the slopes of **Malpaso**. Pines and heather keep their distance and there are good views when the clouds permit. This path is part of the **Camino de la Virgen**, and although it hits a couple of bends on a vehicle track serving the summit, simply keep climbing straight uphill. The track is used for a short stretch on the final approach to the summit, crossing a dip where there is a twisted juniper (sabinosa) trunk. A direct line can be taken up the last cindery slope. There is a tall mast, a few smaller masts, and a trig point at 1500m (4921ft). This is the highest point on El Hierro and views naturally take in the whole island, so try to be there in clear weather. Looking out to sea, the islands of La Palma, La Gomera and Tenerife are often in view.

Descend from Malpaso along a gentle cindery slope, following the line of the Camino de la Virgen, which is marked by parallel lines of stones. There are some stony patches, areas of heather and pines, and a few undulating stretches, but generally the trend is downhill and the route is easy. The true crest is up to the right and is often too rugged to be followed safely or easily. A sign is reached at Castillo de Jaranita, where the Camino Sabinosa branches off down to the right. The altitude is about 1440m (4725ft).

The path slices down across the forested slope, among pines, tree heather and laurels. After crossing a cindery slope it heads back among the trees. It descends gently, then becomes steeper and rougher before levelling out to cross a gap at Tanganasoga. Rougher zigzags lead onwards and downwards and a sign announces entry into the **Reserva Natural Integral Mencáfete**. The path sometimes runs down a narrow groove and is usually clear to follow. The 'laurisilva' woodland may be rich with bird song, unlike the high mountains. A series of sweeping zigzags give way to tighter zigzags as the path drops more steeply on the forested slope, eventually landing on a track.

Turn left along the level track as signposted for the Camino Sabinosa. At a junction another signpost points left uphill for the Camino Sabinosa and Fuente Mencáfete. Walk uphill and another signpost shows the course of the Camino Sabinosa off to the right down a narrow path. This can be a bit overgrown in places, maybe including plants that have escaped from old cultivation terraces. At a sign for Piedra de Rey the path starts zigzagging down a steep and cindery slope. There is at last a view down to Sabinosa, and although it looks

The 'sea of clouds' laps against the high mountain crest of El Hierro

fairly close, the path needs care and should not be hurried. The zigzags pass spikes of rock and eroded buttresses, then the descent becomes more gradual, slicing across the slope and joining a fine track to approach **Sabinosa**. Turn right steeply downhill into the village at the first opportunity. Turning left or right at the bottom leads quickly to bars. The village stands at an altitude of around 300m (1000ft).

There is limited accommodation in Sabinosa and occasional bus services. If accommodation cannot be secured, then follow the winding road down to the coast at **Pozo de la Salud**, where there is a health resort type hotel.

WALK 4

Ermita de los Reyes to Fuente de Llania

Distance:	15km (9½ miles)
Start:	Ermita de los Reyes
Finish:	Fuente de Llania
Map:	1:50,000 Military Map Sheet 34/35-43-44
Terrain:	Good tracks and paths for the most part, sparsely waymarked as the Camino de la Virgen. Open mountainside with some forested patches.

Every four years, in the month of July, a statue of the Virgin is carried in procession all the way across El Hierro. The Bajada, as it is known, is a procession of people that starts at the Ermita de los Reyes in the far west of the Island, moves over the highest mountain, Malpaso, arriving at Valverde the same day. Ordinary walkers might well be amazed at the spectacle and awed at the endurance of those who walk the whole way. Thus for a less purgatorial walk this walk covers the distance over two days. This first stretch of the Camino de la Virgen runs from the Ermita de los Reyes to Fuente de Llania, where handy bus services allow the journey to be broken. Please see the map on p. 44.

The **Ermita de los Reyes** is not served by buses and the only reliable way of reaching it is to hire a taxi to travel the whole length of El Hierro. Be sure to carry all your provisions for the day as there are no places offering food and drink, though there are water taps at intervals. Have a look around the Ermita, which is situated at 700m (2300ft). If the building is open you can have a look at the doll-like image of the Virgin and the wooden carriage used to carry it over the mountains on the Bajada. The full distance has been measured very precisely as 28,686 metres (17¾ miles).

Start by following the road round the back of the Ermita. A broad dirt road continues through a little gap between two little hills. A junction is reached at Piedra del Regida, where there is a water tap. Turn right up the dirt road signposted as the Camino de la Virgen and Camino de Sabinosa. Follow the dirt road uphill and through a gate, where there is another water tap, and there are a couple more taps further uphill. At a point where tracks cross, take note of a distance marker, stating

Transport: Taxi to the Ermita de los Reyes. Cooperativa Bus services pass Fuente de Llania, including those to and from Valverde serving Frontera, Las Puntas, Tigaday and Sabinosa.

Refreshments: Water taps at the Ermita de los Reyes, Cruz de los Humilladeros and Fuente de Llania.

that 835m (½ mile) has been walked. There are more of these markers at uneven intervals.

Prickly pears and twisted junipers (sabinas) grow alongside the walled track. Keep climbing uphill through all other track junctions, then the track swings left as it rises. At a fork, head right and the track climbs between fences. Walk straight on past a junction where a marker states that 2000m (1¼ miles) has been covered. Zigzag up past a sign reading 'Descansadero La Gorona', at 980m (3215ft), and keep right to continue climbing.

The **Camino de la Virgen** is very roughly aligned to a high crest as it climbs further. Always keep to the left at junctions with other tracks, rising past a house and passing flowery fields. The track gradually pulls away from the crest, but continues its gradual ascent, winding up past fields and patches of tree heather. A reservoir is reached, where there is a water tap and a set of gates. Rising to the left is the cindery, pathless dome of Montaña de los Humilladeros. The track cuts across the bare slopes and is lined with heather, laurel and a variety of trees. A broad stretch of the track passes a cross at the **Cruz de los Humilladeros**, where there are water taps. The altitude is 1220m (4000ft).

Further along the track there is a Camino de la Virgen sign, and a less obvious track rises to the left. Follow it and note the little pits that have been dug for individual trees on the slope. These little pits encourage mist to condense and so supply a tiny amount of moisture to each young tree. The track becomes grassy and slices across another track. The slope, covered in clumps of heather, then becomes rough and stoney. Cross a cindery slope, then rise through a pine forest on a good track. Leaving the trees, a sign points out that 6000m (3¾ miles) have been covered. Cross another slope of cinders and scrub, then curve round and uphill to reach Fuente de Binto. This is a possible source of water as heather trees collect moisture from the mist and the drips collect in a small cistern and a hollowed-out log. The altitude is 1380m (4525ft) and this may be the last offer of water for the day.

Continue steeply up the cindery slope, which levels out as you pass a sign reading 'Raya de Binto'. There is a small, stone windbreak shelter up to the left. The high-level track boasts retaining walls for a while, then the cinder path crosses a cinder slope, followed by a dip and gentle ascent to the 8000m (5 miles) marker. Pines, heather and scrub are passed as the path climbs more steeply up a little rocky valley, passing a signpost for the Camino Sabinosa at **Castillo de Jaranita**. Walk uphill, then down through a rocky cutting. Leave the sparse pines and climb up another cindery slope, where the Camino de la Virgen is marked by parallel lines of stones. A sign marks the route as it crosses a dirt road on top of **Malpaso**. There is a tall mast, a few smaller masts, and a trig point at 1500m (4921ft). This is the highest point on El Hierro and views naturally take in the whole island, so try to be there in clear weather. Looking out to sea, the islands of La Palma, La Gomera and Tenerife are often in view.

Leave the summit of **Malpaso** and walk down to the dirt road, crossing a dip where there is a twisted juniper (sabina) trunk. Pass a marker giving the distance walked as 10,000m (6¼ miles) and climb uphill a little, then branch left from the dirt road to follow a path. This runs downhill and clips a bend on the dirt road at a lower level. Keep left, as signposted for the Camino de la Virgen, passing heather trees and pines and enjoying open views, provided there is no mist. The path runs down a cindery slope to reach a broad dirt road. Follow this up through a little cutting to reach a tarmac road and a prominent wooden cross at Cruz de los Reyes.

Go behind the cross to continue along the Camino de la Virgen. Although not easy to spot on the slope, steer a course between a line of telegraph poles and the crest of the ridge. A line of stones later marks the route, and these lead almost to the summit of Tábano at 1387m (4550ft). Swing to the right and walk down below a cliff studded with houseleeks, to reach a sign at Raya del Cepon. A distance marker for 12,000m (7½ miles) is passed. Walk up another cindery slope, and although

The Ermita de los Reyes as at the start of the Camino de la Virgen

the way is vague, aim for a line between the telegraph poles and the crest. Eventually the path becomes broad and clear, crossing a loose, steep slope of cinders on the slopes of the domed mountain, Tenerife. Enjoy views stretching south to La Restinga. The track enters a pleasant patch of laurel and heather and swings right to reach a Camino de la Virgen sign by the roadside.

Cross over the road to continue, walking over a low, cindery dome, veering left to head back down to the road. There is a sign across the road indicating the Camino San Salvador, but walk a short way along the road to another Camino de la Virgen sign. Veer off to the left of the road and follow the route into a forested area. When the way becomes overgrown, it is easier to cross back over the road and use a bare strip on the other side. Follow the road onwards to reach a junction with the main road and turn right as signposted for Valverde. There are several water taps off to the left at a parking space. Tall heather trees and laurel grow alongside the road. There are bus services to and from Valverde, so this is a good place to break the journey.

WALK 5
Fuente de Llania to Valverde

Distance:	13km (8 miles)
Start:	Fuente de Llania
Finish:	In the middle of Valverde
Map:	1:50,000 Military Map Sheet 34/35-43-44
Terrain:	Good tracks and paths for the most part, sparsely waymarked as the Camino de la Virgen. Mostly open country with some forested patches.

Start from the road junction at **Fuente de Llania** and follow the main road in the direction of Valverde. Tall heather trees and laurel grow alongside the road. Useful water taps are positioned near a parking space. Walk gently down the road and pass the turning for Hoya del Morcillo. The main road has a slight dip, then it rises gently to a sign at Fileba, at 1300m (4265ft). There is a Camino de la Virgen sign on the left. Climb away from the road and roughly follow a line of telegraph poles across a cindery slope. Only a few paces away to the left it is possible to walk along a shrubby crest and look down into an awesome volcanic crater. There is a rug of grass down at the bottom.

The route passes a distance marker for 16,000m (10 miles) as a track leads into a forest and back to the main road. Follow the main road onwards through the forest, then leave the trees and climb gently uphill at Raya la Mareta. To the right of the main road there is another Camino de la Virgen sign and a broad track crosses a rise, roughly parallel to the main road. Follow the track over the rise and down through a fairly level area. There are old quarries and fields as the track pulls away from

The middle parts of the Camino de la Virgen run roughly parallel with the walk describing a high-level trek along the crest of El Hierro. Not far beyond Fuente de Llania, however, the Camino de la Virgen commences its long descent towards Valverde. Please refer to the map on p. 34. The route uses a series of old, walled tracks and skirts close enough to San Andrés for a brief visit to be made. After continuing onwards through undulating country, the little village of Tiñor is passed. New road construction has sliced through some of the old tracks and roads in this area, and it is easier to head straight for Valverde to finish the walk.

Transport: Cooperativa Bus services pass Fuente de Llania, including those to and from Valverde serving Frontera, Las Puntas, Tigaday and Sabinosa. Cooperativa Bus services also run between San Andrés and Valverde.

Refreshments: Water taps at Fuente de Llania and Raya Cuatro Esquinas. Bars off-route at San Andrés. Plenty of shops, bars and restaurants around Valverde.

the main road. Follow the clearest track at all times, generally running straight onwards at any junctions. At a set of gates, turn left down a grassier track, though it is rocky underfoot in places. Pass a marker for 18,000m (11 miles). A walled track leads down to the main road again at Raya Cruz del Niño.

Cross over and continue straight along the next walled, grassy track through fields. A winding stretch is followed by a steep and rocky descent to cross the main road again. There is a sign for the Camino, then a stretch of the track is shaded by tall pines. Cross the main road again at a building, where another sign indicates a walled track running level between fields. Pass a marker for 20,000m (12½ miles), then follow the track gently downhill and keep walking straight onwards. A track junction is reached where there is a sign for the Camino de la Virgen at Las Cuatro Esquinas. Go straight through, but note that a right turn could be useful if you want to visit **San Andrés** for food and drink. Walk down through another junction and continue down to the road at Raya Cuatro Esquinas, where there are water taps at a car park.

Just across the road are signs for the Camino de la Virgen and Arbol Santo. Walk down a dirt road into a forestry plantation, then up and over a rise to pass a distance marker for 22,000m (13½ miles). When a fork is reached, Arbol Santo is signposted up to the left, so keep to the right to continue along the Camino. The track runs along the level, then climbs at Raya Tejeguete. Once over a rise, turn left at a junction, passing another sign for the Camino de la Virgen. Follow a grassy track to a rock cutting, then head off to the right, down an overgrown, boulder-paved track, keeping below a forest. An overgrown, bouldery track leads down to the main road at **Tiñor**.

On the day of the Bajada, pilgrims take a long break at the little village of Tiñor, but anyone following the Camino de la Virgen as a walk will wish to keep moving. The main road has been cut straight through old tracks and roads in the area, so use it to make progress straight downhill through a deep cutting. When the road

The final descent to valverde, the largest town and capital of El Hierro

bends to the right, look out for a turning to the left. A steep, rough, stone-paved road leads more directly to Valverde. Follow it down towards the town as it turns to tarmac at the first few houses. Walk down a steep one-way street and under an arch, then down Calle Licenciado Bueno to reach the centre of **Valverde**. There are lots of shops, bars and distractions, but leave them all for a few minutes. Turn left, then right, and walk down the Calle Pérez Galdós. The pleasant Plaza de Quintero Nuñez is passed and a flight of steps lead down to the church.

Entering the savage, rocky and steep sided Caldeira de Taburiente on Walk 8

LA PALMA

Though La Palma is one of the smaller Canary Islands, it is the second highest after Tenerife. It is claimed that for its size and height, La Palma is one of the steepest islands in the world, and the slopes certainly rise relentlessly from the sea to the top of the Roque de los Muchachos at 2426m (7959ft). The high crest is often above the 'sea of clouds'. There is an airport near Santa Cruz de la Palma, while ferry services berth almost in the heart of town. Tourism is evident around La Palma, but there is no particular resort or huge holiday development. In fact, Santa Cruz de la Palma exhibits some of the most attractive old Canarian architecture.

On a map it looks as though a vast crater occupies the centre of the island. This is the Caldeira de Taburiente, protected as a national park. Although nothing more than a deeply excavated valley, it is awe-inspiring to look into. One of the finest long-distance walks in these islands is the GR131, a five-day walk along the crest of La Palma combining the Ruta de la Crestería and Ruta de los Volcánes. There are three other one-day walks offered, taking in some of the most interesting and scenic places. The southernmost parts of La Palma have seen a lot of volcanic activity over the past few centuries, and as the most recent eruption was in 1971, there is every likelihood it will flare up again. In the meantime, walkers will find signposting of routes around La Palma is excellent, and compares favourable to many other parts of the world.

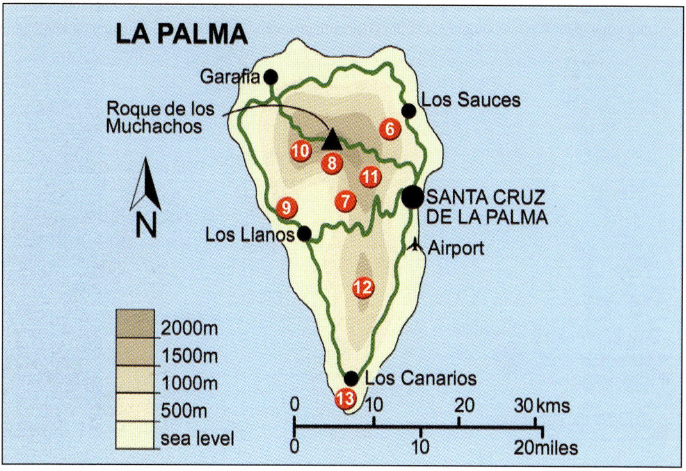

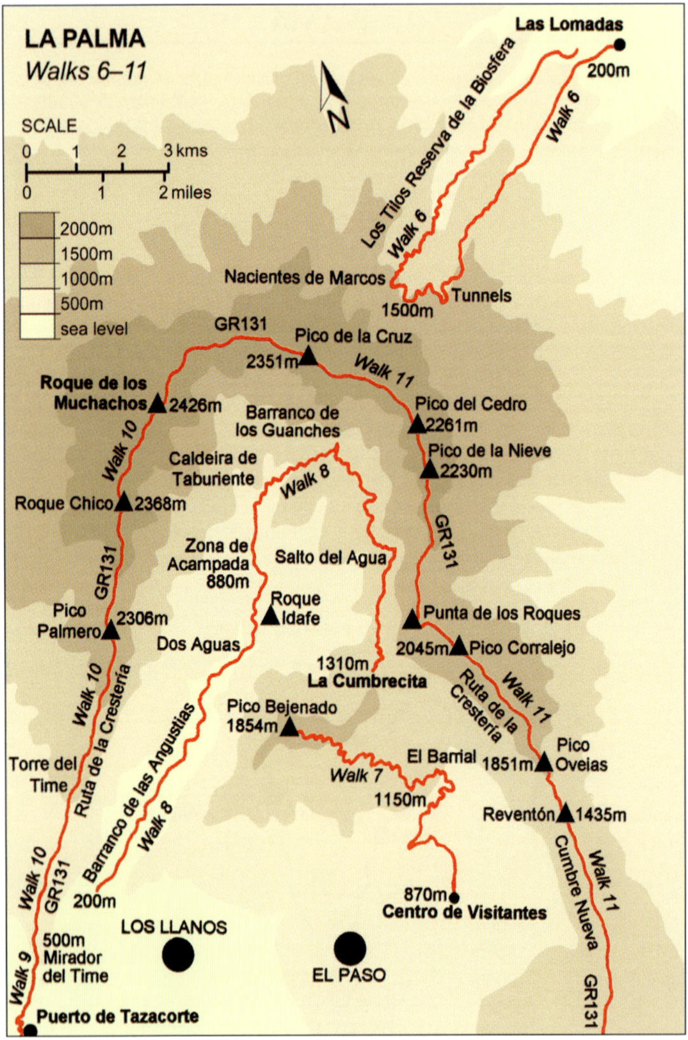
LA PALMA
Walks 6–11
SCALE
0 1 2 3 kms
0 1 2 miles
2000m
1500m
1000m
500m
sea level
N
Las Lomadas
200m
Los Tilos Reserva de la Biosfera
Walk 6
Walk 6
Nacientes de Marcos
Tunnels
1500m
GR131
Pico de la Cruz
2351m
Walk 11
Roque de los Muchachos
2426m
Barranco de los Guanches
Pico del Cedro
2261m
Walk 10
Caldeira de Taburiente
Pico de la Nieve
2230m
Walk 8
Roque Chico
2368m
GR131
Zona de Acampada
880m
Salto del Agua
GR131
Roque Idafe
Pico Palmero
2306m
Punta de los Roques
Dos Aguas
2045m
Pico Corralejo
1310m
La Cumbrecita
Walk 10
Ruta de la Crestería
Ruta de la Crestería
Walk 11
Barranco de las Angustias
Pico Bejenado
1854m
Torre del Time
El Barrial
1851m
Pico Oveias
Walk 7
1150m
Walk 8
Reventón
1435m
Walk 10
GR131
Cumbre Nueva
Walk 11
200m
870m
Centro de Visitantes
LOS LLANOS
500m
Mirador del Time
EL PASO
Walk 9
GR131
Puerto de Tazacorte

WALK 6

Los Tilos Reserva de la Biosfera

Distance:	19km (12 miles)
Start:	On the bridge between Las Lomadas and Los Sauces
Finish:	Las Lomadas
Map:	1:50,000 Military Map Sheet 35-37
Terrain:	Easy tracks give way to steep and rugged paths on the ascent. The walk along the watercourse is narrow and exposed at times, with a dozen tunnels, some of which require a torch. The descent links a series of paths and tracks and forested slopes give way to cultivated slopes.

The Camino de la Reserva de la Biosfera is a waymarked path encircling the Biosphere Reserve at Los Tilos. The area is essentially a forested valley that has precipitous slopes. At first sight, it doesn't look as though it would support a walking route, but the trees hide tracks and paths that climb ever upwards. Please refer to the map on p. 56. Springs gush from the base of a cliff and are immediately channelled away through a series of tunnels. Walkers who know the *levadas* of Madeira will find the walk along this watercourse remarkably similar. Paths can be very narrow and a little exposed, but only for a short while. Afterwards comes a long descent to Las Lomadas.

The bus running between Las Lomadas and Los Sauces turns round a bend where there is a bridge, at 200m (655ft), at a junction sugnposted for Los Tilos. Follow the road up into the valley. You will pass banana plantations and cross the *barranco* before a 1km marker. Keep climbing gradually and cross the *barranco* again before a 2km marker. Climb further among chestnuts to reach a rise where there is a parking space, a mapboard and a track heading off to the left. The altitude is 500m (1640ft). Further along the road, for those who are interested, is the Bar Restaurante Casa Demetrio and the Centro de Visitantes Los Tilos. If you go in search of food, drink and information, then retrace steps to the parking space afterwards.

The track climbing up from the road is waymarked as the 'PR LP 6' or Camino de la Reserva de la Biosfera. Trees offer shade and some of them are labelled with

Transport: Transportes Insular La Palma Bus 11 serves Las Lomadas.

Refreshments: Plenty of cold water gushes into the watercourse on the highest part of the walk. There is a small bar at Las Lomadas at the end of the walk.

their names. There is a tunnel big enough for a truck to drive through and at a higher level there is an old building. The track zigzags uphill between stout retaining walls and is later hewn from the rock. A marker post is reached where a path climbs to the left, but stay on the main track as marked for the Nacientes de Marcos y Cordero. Walk downhill for a while, noticing walls of rock covered in ferns. The track reaches a junction with another path where there is a warning sign for the Sendero de Marcos y Cordero. It basically says that you continue at your own risk.

Follow the path down steps into the *barranco* to reach a clutch of big boulders. Carefully cross a wobbly wooden bridge, then turn left and climb up log steps. There is a level stretch of path before a small side *barranco,* then you climb steeply again. Another level path crosses another side *barranco,* then climbs up more and more log steps. Yet another level stretch crosses another small *barranco,* then there is a more sustained ascent. The path is mostly good, though some of the log steps may be broken. A thick pine tree might be noticed just to the left of the path, then there are other big pines that can be seen on the slopes. The path climbs further and sometimes runs on the level, crossing another three little ravines. Descend a little to a viewpoint with a railing and enjoy the steep-sided forested valley. It's mostly 'laurisilva', which is a mixture of tree heather and laurels, though there are other species too.

Descend a little further then follow a level stretch of path round into the *barranco*. Climb uphill and cross another wobbly wooden bridge. A short path leads into the bouldery *barranco,* where you pick a way along the bed. Obviously, this is not a good route if there is any amount of water flowing. There are markers on the boulders, and a marker post on the right indicates a path rising from the *barranco*. The path later crosses back over the *barranco* and continues upstream. Zigzags and stone steps climb steeply at times, then the bouldery *barranco* is followed still further. Watch carefully for markers and especially for a path rising to the left, towards the sound of cascading water. Sheer cliffs rise above the forested slope and the path reaches a series of springs where water gushes from the base of the cliff. These springs are the Nacientes de Marcos, at 1500m (4920ft).

Water is captured by a channel and runs downstream to the left. Follow the path alongside the watercourse in the direction of Casa del Monte. The path is level and easy at first, looping across the slope, passing pines and tree heather. Enter a tunnel where a torch is useful. There is low headroom at first but more room further inside, though the path is narrow throughout. Leave the tunnel and follow the bendy path until it turns a pronounced corner. Drop down flights of steps below the watercourse, noting that the wooden handrail has been smashed in places by rockfalls. More springs, called the Nacientes de Cordero, pour water into the canal. Enter a low and dripping tunnel using a torch. The tunnel is bendy, with 'windows' feeding more water from a waterfall outside into the watercourse inside. There is a viscious side-spout of water that will leave you drenched, and most other parts of the tunnel drip continually. There is water on the path as well as in the channel, so expect wet feet on top of everything else, and low headroom! After leaving the tunnel there is a good view back to the steps.

Enter the next tunnel, which is also bendy and has low headroom, but is quite short. The next tunnel after that features a bend and has a section of low headroom. A spell in the open leads to a fine viewpoint, taking in sheer bouldery walls and looking back to the Nacientes de Cordero. The path drops below the watercourse to pass a small storage tank, then meanders easily for a while. There is a short tunnel with good headroom, but a narrow path. After a short walk in the open there is another short tunnel. After a longer walk comes a short tunnel cut through a ridge, with a bendy channel. The next tunnel is bendy too, with low headroom at the start and finish thus requiring a torch to negotiate it. The watercourse proceeds round a short curve to reach the next tunnel, which slopes downwards at the entrance.

Spring water gushing from a cliff at the head of the valley of Los Tilos

The path is wet, but is separated from the watercourse by a tall wall, and there is good headroom most of the time. Leave the tunnel and cross a side *barranco,* where the channel is part of a concrete bridge.

Leave the *barranco* and go through a short tunnel with low headroom, immediately followed by another tunnel, which is long and bendy, requiring a torch. The wet path has a tall wall between it and the watercourse. Emerge for a brief view across the valley to the little lake at Barlovento. A longer stretch runs in the open, high above the valley, then comes another short tunnel with good headroom. After another view across to the lake at Barlovento, the final tunnel is reached. This is a peculiar structure; after little headroom at the start, you are given more room, before slabs laid accross the channel cause it to become rather constricted again. There is plenty of headroom and the exit is through an old gateway. The channel is covered as you continue across a slope, following what appears to be simply a path. The water emerges and leads into 'laurisilva' woods.

A small parking space and mapboard are located near the Casa del Monte, where the watercourse begins to run faster as it slopes more steeply downhill. Follow a good track past the Casa del Monte, then walk down a grassy path waymarked for Las Lomadas. When this suddenly turns right, continue straight onwards down a grooved path. The path is actually on a well-defined ridge, but the tree cover tends to obscure this fact. Keep following either the ridge or the grooved path downhill, which are steep at times. The path intersects with a track several times, and three times the way along the path is signposted, while at other times there are smaller markers. It is a steep, rough, grooved path at times, and one stretch is covered in ribbed concrete.

The descent leads along a narrow, overgrown, but passable path, with a water pipe alongside. A track continues, again with the water pipe next to it. A junction is reached where Las Lomadas is signposted to the right for vehicles and to the left for walkers. There is only a view of the neighbouring village of Los Sauces at first, but as the track drops more steeply, **Las Lomadas** also comes into view. The track is covered in concrete as it passes the topmost houses in the village, and is too steep for comfort. This is the Calle Verada de Lomadas, which continues straight downhill as a tarmac road, joining the main road at the point where buses stop.

WALK 7
Pico Bejenado

Most of the mountains on La Palma shoulder each other up, so very few peaks manage to stand out on in isolation. Pico Bejenado rises proudly on the rim of the Caldeira de Taburiente and its shape is easily recognised whenever it crops up in view. Its steep, forested flanks are traversed by a single path, so this route is a there-and-back walk. Please refer to the map on p. 56. If you have a car, then you can drive onto the forested slopes before walking. If you are relying on buses, then the walk starts at the Centro de Visitantes near El Paso. The national park visitor centre has plenty of information and should be included at the outset if there is time.

Distance:	11 or 21km (6½ or 13 miles)
Start/Finish:	El Barrial or the Centro de Visitantes
Map:	1:50,000 Military Map Sheet 35-38
Terrain:	A lengthy road-walk is necessary if arriving by bus. Good tracks and paths lead up steep, rugged, pine-covered slopes to the summit.

Anyone arriving by car can use these initial route directions to reach a parking space, then refer to the next paragraph to start walking. If bus services are being used, then start at the national park visitor centre near El Paso. The altitude is 870m (2055ft). The visitor centre is a curious, blocky, concrete structure that is well worth exploring, preferably before attempting any walks in the national park. They have plenty of literature available and some of it is in English. There is a road signposted Parque Nacional alongside the visitor centre, and this road runs straight to a crossroads. Most people turn right as signposted for the Virgen del Pino, but continue straight on for Pico Bejenado. At the next junction, keep straight on as signposted for Valencia, where most people would turn right for La Cumbrecita. The road is called the Calle Valencia and it rises in a series of bends, offering wide-ranging views as height is gained. There are a number of houses along the way, and at one point the road overlooks the lower road to La Cumbrecita.

Drivers may wish to park after reaching the end of the tarmac at **El Barrial**, though it is possible to continue along a dirt road and park at a higher level. The dirt road is quite rough and stony, climbing and bending even further, then rather surprisingly there is tarmac again. Keep walking gently uphill to reach a small car park and mapboard at 1150m (3775ft). Follow the track rising left from the road, bending further uphill on a sparsely forested slope with an understorey of guelder rose. Pass a large sign for the Parque Nacional de la Caldeira de Taburiente, then turn left as signposted for Pico Bejenado. There is almost immediately a fork, so keep left on the clearest track and climb gently further uphill. A series of little *barrancos* are crossed, and rock cuttings beside the track feature interesting lava tube cross sections. A track junction is reached where Pico Bejenado is signposted to the right.

The track climbs only a short way from the junction and there is a good carpet of guelder rose. A zigzag path continues uphill, reaching a path junction where a signpost points right to draw your attention to a petroglyph. This short detour leads to a fenced enclosure where a single boulder has a vague, wavy line carved on it by the original Guanche inhabitants of La Palma. Retrace steps to continue up the path, climbing in long, lazy zigzags at a fairly gentle gradient, with sparse shade from the pines. As height is gained, the views stretch further afield, taking in the populated seaward slopes. Turn round a rocky corner and climb to a rocky gap on the ridge. A little further up the ridge is a sign for El Rodeo, where there are splendid views down into the Caldeira de Taburiente and around its rocky rim.

Keep zigzagging up the steep and rocky slopes and finally reach the summit ridge on **Pico Bejenado**. There is a cairn at 1854m (6083ft), while a little further along the ridge is a trig point overlooking the Caldeira de Taburiente at 1844m (6050ft). Pines almost reach the summit, but the view is clear in all directions. Spend a while observing the deepest recesses of the Caldeira de Taburiente and trace the skyline ridge round to the Cumbre Nueva and Cumbre Vieja, where volcanic cones can be distinguished. Further afield, on a clear day, it is possible to see the islands of El Hierro and La Gomera, as well as the peak of El Teide on Tenerife.

Transport:
Transportes Insular La Palma Bus 1 serves the Centro de Visitantes from Los Llanos and Santa Cruz.

Refreshments:
The Restaurante Parilla Las Piedras is opposite the Centro de Visitantes at the start.

Pico Bejenado as seen from the far side of the Caldeira de Taburiente

The descent is simply a case of retracing your steps all the way to **El Barrial**, if you arrived by car, or the **Centro de Visitantes**, if you arrived by bus. The Restaurante Parilla Las Piedras is opposite the visitor centre if food and drink are required.

WALK 8
Caldeira de Taburiente

Distance:	21km (13 miles)
Start:	At the car park at La Cumbrecita
Finish:	At the car park at Barranco de la Angustias
Map:	1:50,000 Military Map Sheet 35-38
Terrain:	Very steep and exposed rocky slopes, crossed by narrow paths that are subject to frequent rockfalls and landslides. Not to be attempted in unsettled conditions.

This is one of the most spectacular walks anyone could attempt in the Canary Islands, but it is also one that needs great care. Narrow paths pick their way along exposed ledges and are subject to frequent rockfalls and landslides. The idea is to traverse around the head of the Caldeira de Taburiente on steep slopes, below sheer cliffs, crossing deep-cut *barrancos* and airy ridges. Please refer to the map on p. 56. Access to the route is from a high gap at La Cumbrecita, and the exit is from a remote campsite in the valley, basically following the riverbed to reach a car park. This is a long and difficult day's walk.

The drive to **La Cumbrecita** is impressive, as the road runs through forest, is hemmed in by rock walls, then finally zigzags up to a viewpoint car park. There are mapboards and a national park information kiosk. Most people who walk around here either head for the Mirador de los Roques, and walk back again, or complete a loop by walking downhill, then climb back up to the car park. Many who set out with the intention of following this particular walk quickly turn back when they realise how narrow and exposed the path is. It is better to turn back while there is still a chance, rather than risk getting stuck further along.

Enjoy the views from the car park, at 1310m (4298ft), then follow the path down from the information kiosk. A short ridge walk leads to a mapboard under the rocky prow of the **Punta de los Roques**, which towers high above. Follow a path zigzagging downhill to a junction and signposts. To the left is the easy loop to the Mirador de los Roques, while the path uphill to the right is signposted for the Zona de Acampada. The campsite is actually straight downhill in the bottom of the valley,

Transport: Buses do not run close to this route, so arrange a drop-off and pick-up at the car parks at either end. Taxis can be hired at Los Llanos.

Refreshments: None on route, though water may be available from a couple of the *galerias* along the way.

but it will take most of the day to traverse round the rugged slopes before you can find a path leading down to it.

The path climbs uphill on a steep slope of pines, with a few guelder roses on the ground. Pass through a little notch and walk downhill along tight little zigzags. A buried water channel contours across the slopes and there are magnificent views as you follow it. The path is narrow, stony, gritty, exposed and not for sufferers of vertigo. Pass beneath a prominent fang of rock, which pierces the sky above, and weave in and out of gullies. The path becomes even narrower and crosses bare buttresses where every step must be placed with great care. Pass a sign for the Galeria Aridane, then the path becomes so narrow that it is necessary to go down and up rough steps below the line of the water channel. Pass a building and pause to enjoy the view back to La Cumbrecita and Pico Bejenado.

There is a bit more forest cover on the slopes, and every corner turned reveals another splendid view. The path remains narrow and exposed, crossing more bare buttresses. A water pipe spans a ravine, where you need to edge round the slope with the aid of a chain bolted to the rock. A tunnel mouth and old metal bogie truck are passed at the Galeria la Faya, where there are a few laurels and a ruined building. The path becomes quite awkward, turning round crumbling buttresses and gullies. Head gradually up the slope, then down with the aid of a chain. Turn into a bouldery *barranco* surmounted by towers of rock. This is Hoyo de los Pinos, also known as **Salto del Agua**.

The Zona de Acampada is, unbelievably, signposted up the ravine. Follow a path weaving up between the boulders, following little cairns. There are sheer cliffs rising above, but the path cuts off to the left, and the base of the cliff dictates the line of onward progress. The path crosses stony slopes that look like heaps of rubble. Scramble on bare rock towards the top, using a chain if required, to reach the Lomo del Escuchadero. Looking round from a rocky little gap, leaning towers of rock

Steep and crumbling rocky slopes deep in the Caldeira de Taburiente

The Roque Idafe may have had some ritual significance to the Guanches

loom menacingly above. The path zigzags down through pines, guelder rose and broom to cross the Barranco Limonero. After rising and falling on the slope beyond, the path zigzags down to another *barranco,* where there may be a waterfall. A couple of lengths of chain assist on the climb from the waterfall and the path remains in pine forest with a ground cover of guelder rose. When you reach the ridge at Lomo de las Goteras, take a break to enjoy the rock scenery.

Take care on the descent as the path is vague in places and there are some steep scrapes where it is easy to slip. Three lengths of chain assist on the drop down into the bouldery Barranco de Altaguna. Scramble across to continue along the path until you reach a signposted junction. There is a turning to the Galeria de Altaguna, but keep straight on as signposted for the Zona de Acampada. A hut stands just below the path. Zigzag up the steep, forested slope, then continue up along the base of a cliff-line to reach another rocky ridge at Lomo Cumplido. A short descent features another chain, then carefully pick a way across slopes of rubble beneath a cliff. After passing a point of rock, things get a little easier and there is a path across a forested slope. Turn into the awesome, sheer-sided **Barranco de los Guanches** and take great care on the loose and broken slopes. There is a chain part-way down into the *barranco.* Although the Guanches took refuge from the Spaniards in the Caldeira de Taburiente, it is unlikely that they were pressed this far into its recesses.

Care is needed leaving the *barranco,* and again there are crumbly paths and lengths of chain. Looking down into the *barranco,* water can be seen pouring from a galeria below a hut. An easy walk across a forested slope leads to the Lomo Lajuraga, then the path zigzags downhill for a while. Another crumbling, awkward, chained path leads across steep, unstable slopes, then reaches a junction. Up to the right is a dead-end path to the Nacientes y Galeria Verduras de Alfonso, and the short detour is worth it just for the view. Return to the junction and continue downhill as signposted for the Zona de Acampada.

Zigzag down the forested slope, crossing streams further downhill. Waterfalls can be seen at times, but more often you just hear the water in the gorge alongside. The path finally reaches a mapboard beside the main river, the Río Taburiente, on a wide, bouldery area called the Playa de Taburiente. Follow the bouldery riverbed downstream. There may or may not be water in the river, but either way simply pick what seems to be the best way through the boulders and cobbles. Take the time to examine the skyline of buttresses and peaks all around the Caldeira de Taburiente. Looking ahead, woody scrub seems to fill the riverbed, and before this point a ramp and track on the left lead up into a pine-shaded area with picnic tables. This is the **Zona de Acampada**, and a path leads onwards through the trees to a national park visitor centre and toilets. The altitude is 880m (2890ft). There is no road access and there is still a long walk down through the valley.

A path leaves the visitor centre and undulates as it crosses a gap near the Roque Salvaje. There are splendid views from either side of the gap, at Somada de El Palo.

There's a narrow path, then rough zigzags leading downhill, with views across the Río Almendro to the **Roque Idafe**. It is said that the pinnacle was venerated by the Guanches, but there is no hard evidence to prove this. Pass a sign for the Cuesta del Reventón and reach a path junction. Walking down to the left is quite rugged, while the path rising to the right, signposted for the Barranco de las Angustias, is labelled 'Salida Normal', meaning it is the way most people should walk. The paths join again at Las Lajitas del Viento. Continue down through the gorge, passing a sign for Cruce de Barrancos, as well as an altar where Mass was once said in this remote area. Walk down the pebbly riverbed almost to a water intake building at **Dos Aguas**, where two rivers converge.

The path continues on the bank opposite the water intake building, and is signposted for the Barranco de las Angustias. Exactly how you proceed depends on your inclination. The path drops back into the riverbed and passes under what looks like a footbridge but is actually a water pipe. After the water pipe there is a path heading up to the left, though it is also possible to continue along the riverbed; this sort of choice occurs many times along the way. The path leads back down to the riverbed, then where the word 'Salida' is painted on the rock walls, take another path rising to the left. After turning round a big bend, the path descends to cross the riverbed and rises on the other side. After turning another bend, rising and falling, a little stone building is passed at Morro de la Era. Cross a water channel and descend to the riverbed again for a while. Watch for a signposted path up to the left again, which later zigzags back down to the riverbed, crosses over and climbs up the other side. The path crosses the Barranco de El Fraile and drops down to the main riverbed one last time. Simply walk down the broad, cobbly bed until a prominent dirt road crosses from one side to another. There is a mapboard to the left, and a little further along the dirt road is a small car park at 200m (655ft). If you can arrange to be collected here, then it saves having to climb out of the valley and walk all the way over the top to reach Los Llanos.

WALK 9
Puerto de Tazacorte to Mirador del Time

Distance:	3km (2 miles)
Start:	Puerto de Tazacorte
Finish:	Mirador del Time
Map:	1:50,000 Military Map Sheet 35-38
Terrain:	Good paths and tracks, rugged at the beginning and steep for most of the way.

The GR131 is a challenging waymarked trail that climbs from the coast to the highest mountains on La Palma, then descends to the southernmost point. A tough walker travelling lightweight could cover it in three days, but most prefer to take five days. This first stretch is short, but steep, and involves climbing from the coast at Puerto de Tazacorte to reach a bar restaurant at the Mirador del Time. Please see the map on p. 56.

There is a main road and bus service, so the route can be broken at that point.

This short walk is a mere sample, allowing walkers to experience something of the steepness, ruggedness, heat and humidity associated with the trail.

Stronger walkers could simply continue onwards and upwards to reach the Roque de los Muchachos.

There are banana plantations all around **Puerto de Tazacorte**, but the village itself has the air of a little seaside resort. The bus turns around in front of the Restaurante Casa del Mar and there are plenty of other colourful bars and restaurants. Start by walking along the coast in the direction of a steep and prominent rocky headland, admiring buildings along the way. Look out for the Kiosco Teneguía, and walk behind it to find a mapboard outlining the GR131, or at least the Ruta de la Crestería that comes first. A paved zigzag path leads up to a rugged cliff, passing a series of caves, some of which are used for storage. The zigzags seem interminable on a hot and humid day, and looking up, an occasional glimpse of a small wooden cross marks the top of the cliff. Take as many breaks as are necessary and enjoy the bird's-eye view over Puerto de Tazacorte, as well as the unfolding view further along the coast and up towards the mountains.

A path leads along the cliff top to a junction at a road-end by an old Unipalma banana store. The waymarked GR130 heads off to the left here, but the **GR131** continues straight on up a narrow, overgrown

Transport: Transportes Insular La Palma Bus 2 to Puerto de Tazacorte and Bus 5 from the Mirador del Time. Both operate to and from Los Llanos.
Refreshments: Bars and restaurants at Puerto de Tazacorte, and a bar restaurant at the Mirador del Time.

path that was formerly a stone-paved track. A concrete ramp at the top leads onto a road. Turn right up the road and left around a bend. When the gradient eases, turn right as signposted up another steeper road between huge tents covering banana plantations. At the top of the road, swing right and left up dirt roads, then climb up another steep tarmac road to reach a bar restaurant at the Mirador del Time. The altitude is 500m (1640m). A sign by the roadside says it is 594m (1949ft), though this refers to a point further uphill. If this is as far as you are going today, then take a break and enjoy the view from the terrace. Bear in mind that there are no facilities on this walk for the next couple of days.

Banana plantations seen from the cliffs above Puerto de Tazacorte

WALK 10
Mirador del Time to Roque de los Muchachos

Distance:	14km (8¾ miles)
Start:	Mirador del Time
Finish:	Roque de los Muchachos
Maps:	1:50,000 Military Map Sheets 35-37 and 35-38
Terrain:	Good tracks and paths, gradually rising from cultivated slopes onto steeper forested slopes. The final stages are on open mountain slopes.

The GR131 climbs relentlessly from the Mirador del Time to the Roque de los Muchachos. Along the way there are transitions from cultivated terraces to dry pine forest, then beyond the forest is mountain scrub and a series of bare rocky peaks. Walkers engaged on this ascent will usually climb into a band of cloud, then rise above it and enjoy clear skies on the mountain tops. There is nothing technically difficult about the ascent, which is along clear tracks and paths, signposted and waymarked as necessary. Please refer to the map on p. 56. However, it is a steep ascent at times and the heat and humidity can be uncomfortable. Take plenty of water and take breaks in the shade. Decide whether to spend the night on the open mountain, or arrange to be collected on the summit.

Start on the main road at the **Mirador del Time**. If food or drink are required at the outset, then visit the bar restaurant and stock up on supplies. There are no other refreshment points on this walk, and indeed no water either. There is a GR131 signpost pointing up a very steep concrete road, indicating the way to Torre del Time and the Roque de los Muchachos.

Keep to the right of a house at the top of the concrete road, then follow a path up and along an arid ridge, with water pipes running alongside. The **Torre del Time** is just up to the right, at 594m (1949ft). There is a view of Los Llanos from a gap on the ridge, looking like a Lego-brick construction. Above and beyond the town is the Caldeira de Taburiente and the volcanic peaks of the Cumbre Vieja. A battered concrete track leads uphill to the right for a short way, then as you reach a gateway marked as private, keep left to follow a terrace path. The path contours across the slope, passing both cultivated and overgrown terraces, with stacks of water pipes in places. Cross over a tarmac road and continue straight

Transport: Transportes Insular La Palma Bus 5 serves the Mirador del Time. There are no buses along the high mountain road.

Refreshments: There is a bar restaurant at the Mirador del Time.

along, always following the waymarked, trodden path onwards and up. A few houses are passed, then a broad dirt-road is reached. Turn left along it to pass a wayside shrine, then head up a ramp to the right as signposted for Torre del Time and the Roque de los Muchachos.

Walk along a terrace, then up to another terrace, and swing left at the end to climb up past a derelict house among prickly pears. Continue along a walled path, then turn right up a rough track for a short way. A left turn leads along another terrace path, then there is a steep and rocky climb up old terraces covered in cistus and charred pines. The ridge is called the Lomo del Pico and there is a gap offering a view down into the Barranco de las Angustias. Climb steeply again to a signposted path junction, where a route known as La Travesia heads left to Briestas and La Mata. The **GR131** is to the right, climbing up a broad and rocky path. It is steep at first, crossing terraces at a higher level. There is also a view from a rocky ridge, overlooking the lower parts of the Caldeira de Taburiente and Los Llanos. The path rises to join a track, and the track is followed up to the right, signposted for Torre del Time. Cistus, shrubs and flowers grow alongside as the track wriggles up the slope to reach a prominent fire lookout tower at **Torre del Time**. A viewpoint overlooks the Caldeira de Taburiente, though this part of the ascent might be covered in a band of cloud. The altitude is 1160m (3805ft).

Vines and scrubby slopes flank the track, which swings around a small valley. There is a signpost at a bend, where you follow the GR131 up a steep and rocky path off to the right. Cross the track again at a higher level, then continue up the rocky path. When you meet the track yet again, turn left and follow it uphill. It rises in a curve, then ends rather suddenly. Continue straight along a path, crossing terraces covered in vines. The path leads back onto a slope of charred pines and keeps climbing, later contouring across the mountainside. A gap is reached at Hoya Grande, at 1387m (4550ft), where there is another view of the lower part of the Caldeira de Taburiente. Follow the path as it twists and

Looking over the Caldeira de Taburiente from the mountain at its head

turns up the forested slope and reaches a well signposted junction with another path. There is a line of descent here to El Jesús and Tijarafe, but the GR131, signposted for the Roque de los Muchachos, keeps climbing. The ridge is clothed in pines, but there are views from time to time of the Caldeira de Taburiente. Pass a sign at the Risco de las Pareditas and keep climbing. At a higher gap there is a good view across the Caldeira to Pico Bejenado on the far side. Make the most of this, as there is a steep pull up the forested slope before the path rises more gently to the next viewpoint. This higher gap is bare and gritty, then the path climbs again in zigzags up a steep and rocky slope covered in charred pines. There is a slight descent to cross a gap at Hoya del Estrabito, at 1920m (6300ft).

Follow a rough and stony ridge path. Notice how the gabbritic rock has disintegrated in places, leaving gritty slopes scattered with beautiful little black polygonal crystals. Keep climbing to pass a sign at Pinos Gachos, another viewpoint, then climb up a bouldery crest. The path begins to run at a gentler gradient, away from the top end of the forested ridge, across slopes of scrub, passing the last of the pine trees. On a bouldery shoulder there is a sign for the Barranco de Tajodeque, one of the steep rocky gullies falling into the Caldeira de Taburiente. However, the path rises and crosses the slopes of **Pico Palmero**, whose summit rises on the right to 2306m (7566ft). A stony path runs downhill with a fence alongside. Look into the enclosure and notice the giant 'tajinaste' or echiums that are protected within.

The path crosses a gap called the Degolladas de las Palomas, and observant walkers will already have spotted the Roque de los Muchachos ahead. Climb uphill and cross an easy, rounded crest where the path is flanked by sticky broom. Follow the path up and across a slope, then cross a little gap where the rock is grey, though the rock either side of the gap is pink. A zigzag path leads almost to the spiky rocks on top of **Roque Chico**, at 2368m (7769ft). Walk down to a gap where there is a sign for the Barranco de Marangano, or Barranco Bombas de Agua. This is another of the steep rocky gullies falling into the head of the Caldeira de Taburiente. The path rises round to another gap, the Degollada de Hoyo Verde, again flanked by sticky broom. There are good views of the volcanic peaks of the Cumbre Vieja, seen across the Caldeira. The path cuts up and down across the slope, passing below a booster station, then rising to a road. A signpost points up the road for the Roque de los Muchachos with a signboard alongside. Walk up the road and pass an observatory building. After passing a Parque Nacional sign, a path leads away from the road, climbing more directly to the summit of the Roque de los Muchachos.

The topmost spiky rocks on the summit of the **Roque de Los Muchachos** rise to 2426m (7959ft) and are actually out of bounds for conservation reasons. There are paved paths leading to a handful of fine viewpoints, where you can peer down into the Caldeira de Taburiente. If cloud is filling the Caldeira, it looks even more attractive, and there is a feeling of being on top of the world. At any rate, this is the highest point on La Palma and you have to look towards El Teide on Tenerife to spot anything higher. The islands of La Gomera and El Hierro may also be visible above the 'sea of clouds'. Looking ahead along the GR131, it is possible to pick out the line of the route around the Caldeira, across the Cumbre Nueva to the volcanic peaks of the Cumbre Vieja. The problem with reaching the top of the Roque de los Muchachos is that there is no food, no water and nowhere to stay. If you can arrange for back-up, however, then someone can drive to the car park on the summit and supply your needs, or simply give you a lift down the mountain. If this is being considered, please note that the road to the summit is closed during the hours of star-gazing, between 8pm and 9am. There is a national park information kiosk in the car park, as well as a noticeboard giving information about the observatories.

WALK 11

Roque de los Muchachos to Refugio del Pilar

Distance:	25km (15½ miles)
Start:	Roque de los Muchachos
Finish:	Refugio del Pilar
Maps:	1:50,000 Military Map Sheets 35-37 and 35-38
Terrain:	Good mountain paths, though steep and stony in places. Tracks are used later in the day, along a lower forested ridge.

Transport:
Taxis or backup vehicles would need to be arranged at both ends of the route.

Refreshments:
Water is available at the Refugio del Pilar.

An early morning start on top of the **Roque de los Muchachos** offers the chance to look across the 'sea of clouds' to El Teide on Tenerife, Garajonay and La

After all the effort involved in climbing the Roque de los Muchachos from sea-level, walkers on the GR131 can enjoy walking along the mountain tops before making a long descent. The route offers splendid views down into the Caldeira de Taburiente, but beyond the Punta de los Roques there are ferocious cliffs, so a change of direction to the forested Cumbre Nueva is necessary. This keeps the GR131 on the central crest of La Palma, and although the Cumbre has the appearance of a low gap in the middle of La Palma, it is actually quite high. This day's walk ends at the Refugio del Pilar, where a campsite in a forested setting with basic facilities is available. Please refer to the maps on p.56 and 84.

Fortaleza on La Gomera, and Malpaso on El Hierro. It is also a good viewpoint from which to study the layout of day's walk. You will see the high crest above the Caldeira de Taburiente, then the forested crest of the Cumbre Nueva. Cloud often spills over the Cumbre Nueva, but the volcanic ridge beyond is usually clear. From the top of the Roque de los Muchachos, the GR131 is signposted as the Ruta de la Crestería to the Refugio del Pilar and Cumbre Nueva. If you plan to get a lift to the summit in the morning, please remember that the road is closed between the hours of 8pm and 9am.

The path zigzags downhill, clipping the road serving the observatories, but avoiding following the tarmac. As usual, there are fine views from the rugged edge looking deep into the Caldeira de Taburiente. Pass some weather measuring devices and again note how the path appears to run down to the road. Watch for a marker and fork right, then pick a way down past a blade-like dyke. Cut across and up the steep slope overlooking the caldeira, still avoiding the road, and descend through a gap in a wall-like dyke at Pared de Roberto. The path briefly touches the road at a fine viewpoint at Degollada de Franceses. Staying close to the road, the path is easy and undulates across a broad gap, then climbs up across a little heap of boulders to reach a signposted junction. A path to the left is signposted downhill for Los Sauces and Barlovento, but keep walking ahead and uphill to continue along he GR131. A gritty path passing between boulders is littered with lovely little black crystals. Climb to the top of **Pico de la Cruz**, at 2351m (7713ft), where there is a blocky little hut as well as a trig point. The hut isn't a refuge, so don't plan on staying there. It is locked and contains monitoring equipment.

Zigzag down a gritty slope covered in more black crystals, then continue walking along the crest, gently downhill. The path rises and falls, avoiding little summits, crossing slopes of scrub, and gradually pulling further and further away from the road. A sign points ahead for Pico de la Nieve and the path zigzags down a slope covered in colourful scrub in early summer. There are

fine views down into the Caldeira. Cross a bare, rounded gap and follow the path as it rises up the next slope. Once you have cut across the flanks of a couple of little peaks, a path on a stony slope reaches a signposted junction. There is an exit down to the left to the Pista Pico de la Nieve, as well as a short climb uphill to the right for the summit of **Pico de la Nieve**. The detour to the summit takes only a couple of minutes, reaching an altitude of 2230m (7316ft). There is a cross on a cairn, some aerials and great views.

A peak passed on the Caldeira rim deserves the name Half Dome

The GR131 actually leaves the mountain as if heading for the Pista, but turns right at a junction further downhill, signposted for the Refugio del Pilar. Walking down the stony path leads to a number of pines with charred trunks. Drop down from the crest and zigzag down onto the pine-covered slope. A sign points ahead for the Ermita de la Virgen del Pino, and the path slices across the slope to reach a gap called the Degollada del Barranco de la Madera. Follow the path as it heads to the left of the ridge, then to the right, overlooking the

Caldeira, then left again to descend. Overgrown sticky broom and guelder rose flanks the path, which is still on a slope covered in pines. At one point there is a view of a little peak that deserves the name Half Dome.

Continue zigzagging downhill, then run out onto a gap and enjoy the views. There is another shrubby stretch, again to the left of the ridge, leading back among pines. A pleasant stretch of path contours to the next gap, which is the Degollado del Rio. A fanged peak rises dramatically ahead, and the path zigzags uphill, then slices across a steep cliff face. A steep slope of pines follows, leading to a gap where things look very dry and stony. The path descends a short way to reach the Refugio Punta de los Roques. Here, a building is tucked into the mountainside, and while it offers accommodation, it lacks water and is usually locked. There is a tap alongside, but the tank may well be empty, as it relies entirely on rainfall to fill it. Enjoy the views towards the Cumbre Nueva and Cumbre Vieja.

Follow the path as it zigzags down another steep slope of pines to reach a gap. Climb up a rough and stony path, apparently aiming for a rocky stump. However, on reaching a gap below the stump, follow the path as it swings to the right and follows a kind of rock wall onwards. When you reach another gap at a sign for Pico Corralejo, there is the option of swinging sharply left to climb to a trig point at 2045m (6709ft); a matter of a few minutes walk.

The GR131 continues along the crest, then zigzags down through more pines. For the most part, the path stays on the crest, where it is flanked by guelder rose and pines. A fine, easy walk leads gently downhill. A sign indicates the nearby summit of **Pico Oveias**, requiring only a few seconds of a detour at a height of 1851m (6073ft). Zigzag down a steeper, rockier part of the crest, still among pines and guelder rose, but also with clumps of heather alongside. There may be good views, though sometimes cloud wells up and spills across the Cumbre Nueva. More zigzags lead down onto a clear track signposted as the Pista de Cumbre Nueva.

Path slicing up the cliff face on the approach to Refugio Punta de los Roques

The track falls, then rises, then swings sharply left downhill. Tree heather rises high on both sides, along with a few laurels and pines. Swing sharply right, still heading downhill, before the track becomes bendy and features a particularly sharp corner before reaching a signposted junction. A waymarked coast-to-coast route called the PR LP 1 is signposted left, down to Santa Cruz, and right down to El Paso and Puerto de Tazacorte. The

GR131, however, continues straight onwards, signposted for the Refugio del Pilar. It is a level, easy walk for a while. There are views left to Santa Cruz, though to the right of the wooded crest, there are few openings for sightings. A clutch of communication masts stand on top of Reventón at 1435m (4708ft). The track rises and falls across the flanks of **Reventón**, then undulates, generally climbing uphill in stages. Views now mostly extend over El Paso, rather than Santa Cruz. The track crosses a rise, runs level among pines, then reaches a signboard at a road junction. Turn right to walk downhill a short way through a cutting, to find the **Refugio del Pilar** in the forest on the left. Although there are stone buildings, the area is essentially a campsite with a water supply and cooking areas.

WALK 12

Refugio del Pilar to Fuencaliente

Distance:	16km (10 miles)
Start:	Refugio del Pilar
Finish:	Fuencaliente (Los Canarios)
Maps:	1:50,000 Military Map Sheets 35-38 and 35-39
Terrain:	Good tracks and paths lead over old, arid and cindery volcanoes. The long descent is on a slope through a sparse pine forest.

Transport: Taxi to Refugio del Pilar. Transportes Insular La Palma Bus 3 serves Fuencaliente (Los Canarios), linking with Santa Cruz and Los Llanos.

Refreshments: Water is available at the Refugio del Pilar. Fuencaliente (Los Canarios) has a number of shops, bars and restaurants.

Leave the **Refugio del Pilar** and follow the GR131 up from the buildings as signposted for the Ruta de los Volcánes and Los Canarios. There is also a large mapboard covering the Parque Natural Cumbre Vieja, as well as a map of the trail. Follow a path zigzagging uphill among tall, shady pines, reaching a fine viewpoint looking out towards the Caldeira de Taburiente. Keep climbing and slice across steep cindery slopes on a good path.

A signposted junction is reached, where there is an option to climb **Birigoyo**. The GR131 continues across the slope and around a corner, where the trees thin out and the path descends across a slope of stones and cinders to reach a track.

Turn left up the broad, stony track, as signposted for Los Canarios (also known as Fuencaliente). There are more pines on the slope, becoming quite dense before another signpost is reached. There is another opportunity to climb Birigoyo here, though the GR131 heads off to the right, again signposted for Los Canarios. The path undulates and is forested in places, with clearings full of sticky broom and guelder rose. Later, there is a more sustained climb on smooth, gritty slopes, crossing a footbridge over a small ravine, then zigzagging uphill. On reaching a stony crest, turn right and climb further uphill, and enjoy the views stretching back to the Caldeira de Taburiente, as well as across the sea to El Teide on Tenerife. Continue straight up past a signpost, climbing along a crest using a gritty path, while the slope either side is covered in stones and boulders. After walking over a rise, and a short way downhill, detour a few paces to the right to study a huge, deep, crater. This is the **Volcán de Hoyo Negro**, which erupted in 1949. Don't stray too close to the crumbling crater rim.

Continue up and along the path, through a stand of pines, then downhill with a view of the next steep-sided volcano ahead. A dark, thick lava flow can be seen off to the left, and the path actually runs across a gap where the lava has solidified, leaving big blocks and fissures. At this point the GR131 actually heads down to the right, then later climbs to Volcán Deseada. However, it is well worth leaving the waymarked trail and making a direct ascent of Volcán Deseada, as the volcanic scenery along the way is quite remarkable. So, climb straight uphill from the gap to reach a prominent crater, then walk round one side or the other to reach the far side. Either way, be careful on the crumbling crater rim. Cross another gap and climb uphill, and again there is a view into a crater. The path traces the crater rim and reaches

The Ruta de la Crestería on the GR131, traversing the high mountains of La Palma, gives way to the Ruta de los Volcánes beyond the Refugio del Pilar. This is a classic walk in its own right, crossing a range of ash-grey volcanoes full of interest and strange scenery. The route weaves between summits and the path is often crunchy with cinders. Please refer to the map on p. 84. The highest of the old volcanoes is Volcán Deseada, and there are other craters that can be studied closely. Eruptions along or beside the range have taken place as follows: Volcán Martin in 1646, Volcán San Antonio in 1677, Volcán Montaña del Charco in 1712, Volcán de Hoyo Negro in 1949, and Volcán Teneguía in 1971. Experts say the area is unstable and will one day collapse into the Atlantic!

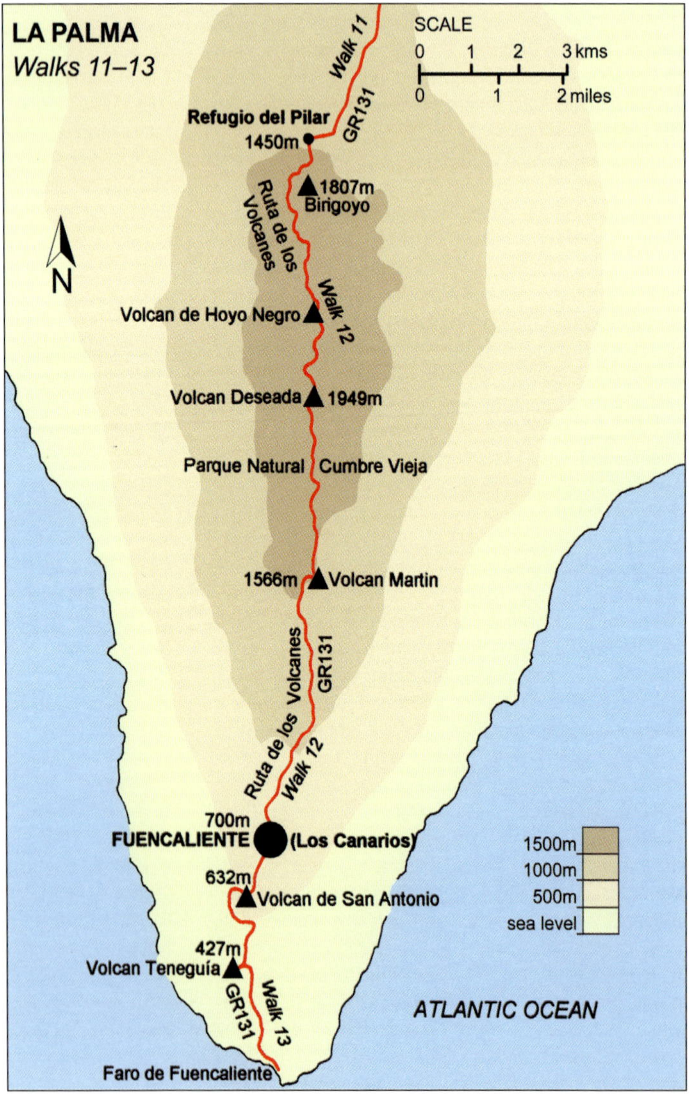
LA PALMA
Walks 11–13
SCALE
0 1 2 3 kms
0 1 2 miles
N
Walk 11
GR131
Refugio del Pilar
1450m
1807m
Birigoyo
Ruta de los Volcanes
Walk 12
Volcan de Hoyo Negro
Volcan Deseada
1949m
Parque Natural
Cumbre Vieja
1566m
Volcan Martin
Ruta de los Volcanes
GR131
Walk 12
700m
FUENCALIENTE
(Los Canarios)
632m
Volcan de San Antonio
427m
Volcan Teneguía
GR131
Walk 13
Faro de Fuencaliente
ATLANTIC OCEAN
1500m
1000m
500m
sea level

a trig point on **Volcán Deseada** at 1931m (6335ft). It should be noted that the other side of the crater rim rises to 1949m (6394ft), if anyone is inclined to make a detour for the extra height. Splendid views stretch all the way back along the GR131, as well as across the sea to El Teide on Tenerife, Garajonay and La Fortaleza on La Gomera, and Malpaso on El Hierro.

Markers for the GR131 are encountered again on the descent from Volcán Deseada. Follow a loose and stony path that leads down the ridge to the bottom where pines offer shelter on a hot and sunny day. The path continues along the crest to a gap with a signposted junction. Walk straight onwards, gently uphill, then down through a long, shallow valley. The path is loose and cindery. The slopes alongside are bare and grey but towards the end there are more tall pines offering shade. The path rises gently from a signpost on a stonier slope, then the pines thin out as another gentle gap is crossed. Looking ahead, the colourful cone of **Volcán Martin** is seen, the path descends and follows a short ridge to reach its slopes. If time can be spared, it is worth making short detours around the volcano. A path off to the left leads to a reddish gap, from where a steep and very loose path drops down into the crater. This path can be followed up to a prominent cave where water drips from the roof into hollowed-out log troughs. The volcano last erupted in 1646.

The GR131 slices across the stony slopes of the volcano, then crosses a gentle gap, continuing down a gritty slope to reach a signpost. If water is needed desperately, take the path off to the right leads to the Fuente del Tion. Continuing along the main path to another signpost, however, the slope is loose and gritty and any turnings should be avoided . There is a good view back to Volcán Martin, taking in a long, blocky lava flow on its slopes. Walk down among pines to reach a signposted junction. The Fuente del Tion is straight onwards, while the GR131 heads down to the left, signposted for Los Canarios. The path is steep and gritty, then swings right alongside the lava flow, then left and more gently

Skirting a crumbling crater on the way to the Volcán Deseada

downhill. Cross over a track called the Vereda de las Cabras as signposted. The path continues on an undulating course over forested cinder mounds, then drifts alongside the lava flow again. Slice down a forested slope to reach a signpost and walk straight onwards. A path contours across a steep slope, then at another signpost, descend gently on slopes of cinders and pines. The path is quite broad and is marked with parallel lines of stones. Look ahead to spot a prominent mast.

Before reaching the mast, the path crosses a track. Here there are signposts for the GR131. Swing round the hill bearing the mast, keeping to the right side, and cross the access track as signposted. A rough and rocky path makes its way down through the forest, crossing another track as signposted. The forest path remains rough and stony, and is enclosed by stone walls for a while. Pass a small area planted with vines, then go straight down through a signposted intersection with the GR130, which completely encircles La Palma. Cross a track, then follow a walled track and water pipe down the forested slope. Turn left, as signposted, down a forest road. This rises gently past cultivated plots. A signpost points left along a rugged, gritty path. Where the path forks, take the left fork that leads steeply down to a dirt road. Another signpost points down towards the church in the village of **Fuencaliente**. Walk in front of the church, then follow a road straight down to the main road, landing by the Bar Parada.

There are plenty of places offering food and drink in Fuencaliente, also known as Los Canarios, and anyone who has been roughing it on the route so far will welcome the facilities. There is a little accommodation, as well as bus services.

WALK 13

Fuencaliente to Faro de Fuencaliente

The final part of the GR131 is fairly simple and straightforward. The route leaves the village of Fuencaliente and takes in the Volcán de San Antonio and Volcán Teneguía on its way to the southernmost point of La Palma at the lighthouse, Faro de Fuencaliente. Even casual strollers find it easy, but there is a catch. There is no transport between the lighthouse and the village. Astute walkers will make an arrangement with a taxi driver before leaving Fuencaliente, while tougher walkers may prefer to walk all the way downhill, then turn around and walk all the way uphill afterwards. Either way, be sure to allow plenty of time as the old volcanoes are well worth studying. The Volcán Teneguía last erupted in 1971 and there are still hot spots in the crater. Please see the map on p. 84.

Distance:	9 or 18 km (5½ or 11 miles)
Start:	Fuencaliente (Los Canarios)
Finish:	Faro de Fuencaliente
Map:	1:50,000 Military Map Sheet 35-39
Terrain:	A fairly steady descent on cinder paths and tracks, with a short, rugged ascent in the middle. If no transport can be arranged at the end, then it is necessary to climb all the way back to Fuencaliente.

Start at the Bar Parada in **Fuencaliente** and cross the main road. Go straight down the Calle Emilio Quintana Sanchez, then continue downhill, passing a turning for the Restaurante Llanovid Bodega. The Volcán de San Antonio is signposted further downhill, down the Calle los Volcánes. Go straight through the crossroads at the bottom, which is signposted for the Volcán de San Antonio. A dirt road leads to a car park and an interesting visitor centre devoted to the volcanoes of La Palma. Just beyond the centre, an easy and well-trodden path wanders round the crater rim to reach a trig point at 632m (2073ft). Pines and scrub fill the crater, which last erupted in 1677. You cannot make the full circuit around the rim, so retrace steps to the visitor centre after enjoying the view southwards. There are also camel rides available for those who don't like getting cinders in their boots!

The Faro de Fuencaliente is signposted near the visitor centre, and a loose and cindery path winds down a slope sparsely planted with pines and vines. Turn left along a firm cinder road and walk gently downhill. The road cuts across the steep, cinder slopes of the Volcán de San Antonio and occasional vehicles send up clouds of choking dust. If you wanted to leave the waymarked GR131, there are interesting little paths allowing an exploration of the colourful prominance of the Roque Teneguía. Otherwise follow the dirt road running down to a junction, where a sharp right turn leads further downhill to reach a point where motorists are obliged to park.

Turn left, and although the GR131 is marked as heading off to the left at a path junction, it is worth keeping to the right to visit the shattered **Volcán Teneguía** first. A rough and rocky path leads up to the crater rim, and if you scramble a short way into the crater and look very carefully, you can find hot-air vents. If there are other people scrambling around, just watch for a few minutes and you will soon realise who finds them! The volcano last erupted in 1971 and there is still a sulphury whiff in the air. A rocky ridge path can be followed around the crater, leading to the summit cairn and trig

Transport: Transportes Insular La Palma, Bus 3 serves Fuencaliente (Los Canarios), linking with Santa Cruz and Los Llanos. Either make an arrangement with a taxi to be met at the Faro de Fuencaliente, or be prepared to walk back up to Fuencaliente.

The Faro de Fuencaliente at the southernmost tip of La Palma

The Volcán Teneguia last erupted in 1971 and is still hot in places

point at 427m (1401ft). Views southwards take in the Faro de Fuencaliente, while out to sea it is often possible to spot El Teide on Tenerife and the islands of La Gomera and El Hierro. Double back to the path junction to continue along the GR131, which is marked with red and white paint.

The path passes close to a small crater, and a few seconds detour to the left is all that is needed to inspect it. Continue downhill alongside a blocky lava flow. The path runs close to a slope of vines, then slices straight across the lava flow. Fortunately, the path has been well engineered, or this would be a difficult crossing. Drop steeply down a slope of barren, grey cinders. There are a few patches of scrub and occasional reddish hues further downhill. Having walked through a shrubby defile and reached a road, turn right and follow it a short way. Watch for a signpost and markers that indicate that the path drops down to the left, away from the road. Follow this as it cuts out a road bend, crossing the road again at a lower level. Keep following the path downhill to reach the final GR131 signboard on the road near the **Faro de Fuencaliente**.

The red and white lighthouse stands alongside an older structure which has been restored. Strangely coloured pools nearby are old salt-pans, or *salinas*. Walk down to the cobbly beach to find the Bar Faro tucked in among a few boat sheds at the southermost point of La Palma. Drinks and snacks are offered here. If arrangements have been made to be collected here, then the walk is over. If it is necessary to walk back up to Fuencaliente, then allow plenty of time as it is tougher than the descent, especially in the heat of the afternoon.

Refreshments: Fuencaliente (Los Canarios) has a number of shops, bars and restaurants. There is also the Bar Faro at the Faro de Fuencaliente.

A fine rocky ridge seen from the zigzag path descending from the forest on Walk 15

LA GOMERA

La Gomera is the second smallest of the Canary Islands and is notable for having an extensive area of 'laurisilva' forest covering its higher parts. As the highest point on the island, at Garajonay, is only 1485m (4872ft), the uplands are often brushed by the sea of clouds and the forest can be a damp and dripping place. The cloud forest keeps the island topped-up with water, and as you explore the arid lower slopes and deeply-eroded *barrancos*, you realise how dry the island would be without it. The forested central area is protected as a national park. La Gomera's airport is near Playa de Santiago, while ferries berth at San Sebastián. Many walkers choose to stay at the scenic Valle Gran Rey, but accommodation is spread all round the island. Amazingly, for such a popular island, there is little in the way of big holiday complexes and the place has a nice relaxed air about it.

Driving around La Gomera generally means following roads over the higher parts, as there is rarely a coastal road. Paths and tracks for walkers are abundant, criss-crossing the whole island, but they are only vaguely signposted outside the national park. The deep *barrancos* that radiate from the centre of the island are truly awesome by the time they reach the sea. The rocky *barrancos* need care and many of the high ridges end abruptly. A five-day half-circuit round the island is offered, from San Sebastián to Valle Gran Rey, as well as a two-day coast-to-coast route from Valle Gran Rey to Hermigua, and a couple of one-day walks explore other scenic and interesting places.

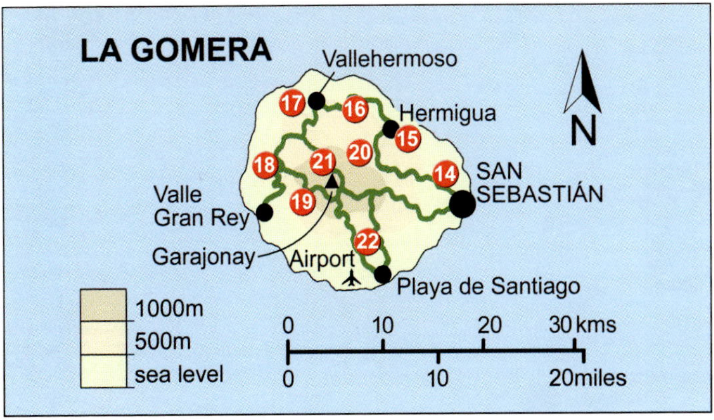

LA GOMERA
Walks 14–16, 20 & 22
Agulo
200m
Embalse
600m
700m
Walk 16
Centro de
Visitantes
Playa de Hermigua
1000m
500m
sea level
Hormiga
HERMIGUA
700m
Walk 15
Casas El Moralito
Walk 20
700m
Degollada
de Hayeton
Walk 15
Arroyo
de El
Cedro
960m
Parque Natural Majona
Casas El Helechal
Walk 20
Encherada
600m
676m
Jaragán
Las Casetas
500m
Walk 14
500m
Parque Nacional Garajonay
Lomo de
las Nieves
Walk 14
Roque de Agando
1070m
Reserva Natural Integral
Benchijigua
600m
SAN SEBASTIÁN
833m
Walk 22
N
Targa
200m
El Rumbazo
ATLANTIC OCEAN
500m
Walk 22
SCALE
0
1
2
3 kms
0
1
2 miles
PLAYA DE
SANTIAGO

WALK 14

San Sebastián to Las Casetas

Distance:	10km (6 miles)
Start:	Nuestra Señora church in San Sebastián
Finish:	Las Casetas
Map:	1:50,000 Military Map Sheet 37-41/42
Terrain:	Roads, tracks and paths climb gradually uphill. The higher parts are rocky and need care. The descent is along a good, clear dirt road.

A five-day route from San Sebastián leads through an assortment of lovely villages and varied countryside to reach Valle Gran Rey. Any one of the five stretches can be completed as a fine day's walk. This first stretch climbs from San Sebastián, taking in desert-like slopes and an exciting terrace route across the face of Jaragán. Although you could continue all the way to Hermigua, it is rather a long way and passes through arid countryside. Please refer to the map on p. 94. Better to take things easy and descend to Las Casetas to catch the bus back to San Sebastián, then continue the next day.

Face the front of Nuestra Señora church in San Sebastián, then head round the back on the left-hand side. Take a moment to look directly uphill as the higher parts of the town can be reached using flights of steps, some of which can be spotted from below. Make your way up the first flights of steps until you reach a higher road. Turn right and continue up more flights of steps, enjoying widening views over the town. You should exit onto the Calle de la Orilla del Llano. Turn left to follow this road straight up to the top edge of San Sebastián. The road continues out onto dry, scrubby slopes. Keep left of the road to follow a track that apparently heads towards twin masts on a rise ahead. Keep to the right of these to follow another track towards a house, then keep left to follow a path away from this last building. The long, broad crest is known as the **Lomo de las Nieves**.

The narrow, stony path leads further up the arid, scrubby slope to reach a small cairn shelter. Red and white paint marks may already have been noticed, and these can be relied upon to indicate the route for most of the way. Follow a more or less level path onwards, overlooking the valley, though it gradually shifts to the

Transport: Servicio Regular Gomera Bus 2 links Las Casetas with San Sebastián.

Refreshments: Plenty of shops, bars and restaurants in San Sebastián.

right and loses this prospect. Walk down a short, steep, stone-built ramp to reach a bare, rocky gap. There is a small rock shelter on this gap, with a view back to San Sebastián. A good path cuts across the rocky slope on the right, avoiding the crest of the rocky ridge. There is plenty of candelabra spurge, as well as dense growths of euphorbia. Large blocks of rock have been shifted to make the path. When it rises across a slope of scrub and prickly pears, watch carefully as it becomes narrow and rocky. Keep an eye on the red and white paint marks.

A pointed peak rises ahead, so keep to the right and pick up a path that contours along a soft, creamy looking layer on the rocky slope. Follow this feature and make a bit of a zigzag up towards some palm trees, then walk back down again. The path basically contours round a huge hollow in the mountainside around 500m (1640ft). After following the creamy contour path, watch out again for the red and white paint markers, which indicate a reddish, stony, zigzag path cutting up through old terraces. This path becomes rather vague at a higher

The path exploits a layer of softer rock on the mountain at Jaragón

The view down the valley to San Sebastián on the winding descent

level, so watch carefully while crossing the rugged shoulder of **Jaragán** around 625m (2050ft).

Swing to the right along another soft, creamy layer in the rock. This layer is on the steep and rocky face of Jaragán, roughly contouring across the face. There is a narrow path, strewn with rubbish, climbing up from the terrace part-way along. Don't follow it, but bear in mind that a goatherd lives up there, unlikely though it may seem. Dogs may kick up a racket, and you may see the goats being gathered at milking time. Keep following the terrace onwards. Be careful, blocks of rock may fall from the overhang above. When the far end of the ridge is reached, walk downhill using the steps scooped-out of a bright band of rock. A sign announces the Parque Natural Majona, and at that point another path heads off to the right, but don't follow it. Zigzag down from the ridge to reach a prominent bend on a dirt road, next to another sign for the Parque Natural Majona. The altitude is 599m (1965ft) and it is time to make a decision.

If things are going well, then it is possible to follow the dirt road away to the right and continue walking all the way to the distant Hermigua. If water supplies and energy are low, then turn left and follow the dirt road down to the main road to catch a bus back to San Sebastián. The dirt road is clear and obvious, with a large water pipe alongside. Following it down to the road involves skirting down around a huge hollow in the mountainside, then turn round a pronounced corner. The dirt road passes a few palms and continues down to the main road at Las Casetas, around 500m (1640ft).

To catch the bus back to San Sebastián, be sure to make yourself visible by the roadside at a point where the driver can see you and pull in safely. Just up the road is a tunnel mouth and the bus tends to hurtle out of it before flashing past the junction with the dirt road. If there is time to spare, walk up to the tunnel mouth and enjoy the view from the Mirador a Lazcano alongside. Towers of rock arranged around the head of the valley look quite remarkable.

WALK 15

Las Casetas to Hermigua

Transport: Servicio Regular Gomera Bus 2 links Las Casetas with San Sebastián and Hermigua.

Refreshments: Hermigua has a few shops, bars and restaurants at the end.

Distance:	18km (11 miles)
Start:	Las Casetas
Finish:	Cepsa filling station in Hermigua
Map:	1:50,000 Military Map Sheet 37-41/42
Terrain:	The whole walk can be accomplished on a broad, firm, clear dirt road. There is the option of a more rugged path at the beginning. Sparsely forested slopes give way to arid slopes on the way down to the cultivated valley at Hermigua.

Start at **Las Casetas**, on the main road close to a tunnel mouth and the Mirador a Lazcano. There is a decision to make at the beginning. Either follow the broad dirt road gradually uphill and cross a prominent gap in the mountains, or follow a rugged path over a higher gap almost directly above. The dirt road is so clear and obvious that there can be no doubt about the route. It is accompanied throughout by a large water pipe. If you choose to follow it, then after crossing the gap it leads to a large goat farm at **Enchereda**.

The rugged path is less obvious, but climbs uphill in stony zigzags from the junction of the main road and dirt road. It rises past a sign for the Parque Natural Majona and eventually reaches a fine little rocky gap with pine trees on either side. There is a view back to San Sebastián, as well as ahead to the forested slopes of Majona. The path is nicely engineered across a rocky slope covered in cistus and tree heather. Follow it through a little rocky notch, then down steeper and more rugged zigzags to reach an area of terracing. Continue down to the dirt road and turn left to follow it. The road contours across a slope, passing a few sparsely planted pines, before descending to the goat farm at Enchereda at 600m (1970ft).

The goats at Enchereda are penned and their milk is used to make cheese. There are also some free-range pigs and a few sheep. Follow the dirt road past some palm trees and rise up across a scrubby slope. The road moves through thick pine plantations, passes a pumping station and climbs up from a rocky valley to bend around a ridge. Turn another corner on a ridge sparsely planted with stunted pines. Walk gently downhill into the Barranco de Galión, which is full of old terracing. The ruins of the **Casas El Helechal** lie below the road. Walk gently uphill and round into the next valley, walking gently downhill among tree heather and laurels. There is another pumping station in the bouldery Barranco de Juel, on a bend of the road. Walk onwards and gradually upwards amid sparse heather and laurels. All of a sudden there is a broad, stone-paved road winding further uphill, with a small viewpoint overlooking the rugged coast along the way. A gate amongst taller trees is reached at over 700m (2300ft).

The walk from Las Casetas to Hermigua can be completed by either walking along a broad, firm, clear dirt road the whole way, or starting with a more rugged path climbing across a mountain gap. Either way, the dirt road, or Camino Forestal de Majona, is followed for most of the day. Although there is sparse forest cover in the early stages, the trees thin out and, as the dirt road loses height, the surroundings are distinctly arid. Please refer to the map on p. 94. Hermigua comes as a complete contrast at the end of the day, as banana plantations fill the valley floor and all manner of fruit and vegetables are grown on the terraces.

The stone-paved road goes through a cutting and the dirt road that continues downhill has been carved from the cliff face. There are a series of bends as the road slices down the wooded slope, with one bend surfaced in concerete offering a sheer drop. After passing through rock-cuttings, there is a view ahead that seems to take in a network of dirt roads, but in fact there is really only one long, looping road with a few short spurs. Most of what you see is what you actually walk along. Zigzag down past a whitewashed ruin and pass a stone block with the water pipe running through it. Walk downhill and round a couple of little valleys full of palms and cane, then swing round to the right to enter a big valley where the dirt road can be seen ahead, slicing across the arid slopes.

A couple of houses are seen far below the dirt road. As the road is remarkably bendy, overlooking the same valleys time and time again, these pop up in the view from time to time. Two valleys are passed with one containing palm trees and the other planted with pines. A small roadside memorial is passed on the way round a bend, then the road descends and the last few trees peter out on the slopes. Swing round a huge bend overlooking the houses again, then continue round another arid valley. Peeping over a gap to the left reveals lush, green cultivated slopes around Hermigua. Continuing on you will reach a road junction on a bend. Here it is possible to look one way down to the beach at Hermigua and the other way down to the beach at the Playa de la Caleta. Turn left to follow the road down to Hermigua, though it is also possible to walk steeply down a zigzag path to reach the pebbly **Playa de Hermigua**.

Follow the road as it drops steadily into the valley, and it is worth studying the layout of paths and tracks in the banana plantations in preparation for your walk across the valley. Wait until a road junction is reached, signposted back uphill for Playa de la Caleta, and turn right. Just before reaching a telephone, turn left down concrete steps and walk between tall walls through banana plantations. Just before reaching the bottom, turn

A glimpse of the sea down the valley before the descent to Hermigua

left and follow a path across a footbridge, then follow the path up steps to the main road at the Cepsa filling station in **Hermigua**. Either turn left to reach the church in the middle of town where the greatest number of shops, bars and restaurants are situated, or turn right to walk down to the beach. Alternatively continue with the next stage of the route.

ATLANTIC OCEAN
Roques de los Organos
Buenavista
564m
Ermita de Nuestra Señora de Coromoto
Parque Maritimo
Walk 17
Walk 17
Ermita de Santa Clara
735m
VALLEHERMOSO
600m
Embalse
Walk 17
Walk 16
Walk 16
760m
Roque Blanco
700m
Chorros de Epina
Walk 18
Monumento Natural Lomo de Carretón
Punta de Tejeleche
618m
550m
Parque Nacional Garajonay
Ermita
Arure
800m
La Laguna Grande
1260m
Arroyo de El Cedro
960m
1280m
Walk 21
Walk 18
La Mérica
835m
Walk 19
Walk 20
Parque Rural Valle Gran Rey
Walk 19
Chipude
1180m
1485m
Garajonay
Pajarito
1340m
Ermita
700m
Gerián
1232m
La Fortaleza
Walk 21
Walk 19
VALLE GRAN REY
Argaga
LA GOMERA
Walks 16–21
SCALE
0 1 2 3 kms
0 1 2 miles
1000m
500m
sea level
N

WALK 16
Hermigua to Vallehermoso

Distance:	14km (8¾ miles)
Start:	Cepsa filling station in Hermigua
Finish:	In the middle of Vallehermoso
Map:	1:50,000 Military Map Sheet 37-41/42
Terrain:	Road walking gives way to paths climbing steeply uphill. There is a road-walk in the middle of the route, then tracks and paths lead downhill towards the end of the day. Most of the walk is through cultivated country.

This day's walk could be completed in two parts if required. This would allow plenty of time to look around the national park visitor centre, or Centro de Visitantes Juego de Bolas, above Las Rosas. The bus services on the main road below can return you to town. The route involves some initial road-walking as well as some steep climbs. The middle parts are quite easy and there is a long descent to Vallehermoso at the end that is not too difficult. Anyone trying to complete the whole of this walk while relying on bus services to and from San Sebastián would be advised to keep an eye on the time. Please refer to both the map on p. 94 and that on p. 102.

Leave **Hermigua** by following the main road out of town in the direction of Vallehermoso. The road descends gently through the valley, then reaches a junction where you climb steeply uphill, turning round a zigzag bend at a higher level, with a viewpoint along the way. The road clings to a steep slope overlooking cultivation terraces and the sea, then reaches the village of **Agulo** at 200m (655ft). Walk past the bus stop and turn right along a narrow stone-paved road. This leads down and up through the village, aiming for the low, white dome of the church. Continue uphill, downhill, then up the cobbled road to the cemetery. Take an old stony road rising to the left, and look back at Agulo tucked in beneath the cliffs. The village is in three parts, though the divisions are not so clear when you walk through it.

The path turns round the rocky nose of the headland and climbs to the main road at a point where it emerges from the Túnel de Agulo. Beware of traffic coming from the tunnel, and turn right uphill round a bend on the road. Watch out for an old cobbled road rising to

Transport: Servicio Regular Gomera Bus 2 and 5B serve Vallehermoso.

Refreshments: Shops, bars and restaurants at Hermigua and Agulo. Bar restaurant near the national park visitor centre, and another one at Roque Blanco. Shops, bars and restaurants at the end around Vallehermoso.

the left and continue walking uphill. The line of the old road is excellently engineered, though it is a bit rough and narrow at one point. A level red-earth track passes a palm tree to reach the foot of a cliff. The path zigzags onwards and upwards, with fine views back along the route. Eventually a cottage situated among terraces is reached. Behind the building is a signpost. Follow the path zigzagging further uphill, as signposted for La Palmita. The steep slope is sparsely planted with heather and laurels, with a few pines. The stony surface gives way to bare earth and bare rock in places, then keep left of an eroded groove to continue across a broad crest. The ground is trodden reddish and grey, and after slicing across the crest a track rises further across a slope to around 700m (2300ft). Simply follow the track straight on to the **Centro de Visitantes Juego de Bolas**. This may be busy with coach parties and motorists, though it is closed on Mondays. There is a bar restaurant available if food and drink are required.

A break at the visitor centre is highly recommended, and if walkers can include a visit early in their explorations of La Gomera, then so much the better. There is plenty of information and a full translation in English can be supplied. Of particular interest are the gardens, where endemic plants of La Gomera can be studied. The importance of the 'laurisilva' forests on the higher parts of La Gomera is explained, both from the point of view of their ancient history and their importance in keeping the island's water-table supplied through drip-feeding. If the centre is to be explored for any length of time, and it is no longer feasible to walk all the way to Vallehermoso, note that the main access road runs down to the little village of Las Rosas, where the bus can be caught beside the Bar Casa Luis.

To continue to Vallehermoso, walk through the large car park beyond the visitor centre to reach a fork in the road. Keep right as signposted for Laguna Grande. At the second gap in the roadside barrier, exit to the right and follow a path through to another road. Cross the road and follow a path down a groove, keeping to the right of a clearer track that has a fence alongside. Cross a streambed and walk up steep, broken steps past a handful of buildings and a slope of vines. The path drifts to the right at a higher level, crossing a crest of red earth dotted with clumps of heather. Keep just to the left of two pylons and follow the path across a slope of heather and laurel to reach another pylon on a nearby ridge. The path swings right downhill and is rough and stony.

A tiny reservoir lies hidden deep in the valley above Vallehermoso

Turn right down a concrete road, which turns to a dirt road. When a flight of concrete steps lead off to the left, from a house, drop down to the dam of a small reservoir at 600m (1970ft). If you turn right along and up a road from the dam, you can quickly reach the Bar Restaurante Amalagüigue. To continue with the walk, however, cross the reservoir dam then turn left. The reservoir is depressingly empty, containing only a small pool of water. Follow the road gradually up through the valley. There are a few houses and cultivation terraces, with 'laurisilva' forest rising above. The road climbs and turns a bend above a campsite called the Campamento Garabato. There is a sudden view down into the valley towards Vallehermoso, though only a few houses are in sight below. If food and drink are needed, head for the Restaurante Roque Blanco.

There is a viewpoint around 760m (2495ft) overlooking the steep-sided valley at **Roque Blanco**, and the track that leads down across the valley side is plainly in view. Follow this track across a steep slope of 'laurisilva', and note also the palms and chestnuts, as well as the terracing around the few houses further down. Stay on the main track, avoiding the little spurs to the right. At an apparent dead-end, a path drops down onto a terrace to reach the last little house. Drop down from the house onto a narrow ridge and follow a stony path further downhill. There is a disused concrete water channel alongside, as well as views down to a tiny reservoir and ahead to Vallehermoso. The path sticks to the ridge, passing a fine juniper tree and plenty of malfurada scrub. As the ridge steepens, the path zigzags and eventually lands on a broad track.

Turn left to follow the track down through the valley. Note the towering form of the Roque El Cano dominating the scene. The track makes a sweeping zigzag across the lush terraces that rise from the valley floor, then a narrow tarmac road leads onwards downhill. After passing several houses, watch out for steps on the left that allow a quick descent to Vallehermoso by avoiding the final zigzag bends on the road. You arrive on the main road beside a curious sculpture play-park at around 200m (655ft). Turn left to walk up into the middle of town, where the bus stop is just off an ornate roundabout. There are shops, bars, restaurants and taxi services.

WALK 17

Vallehermoso to Chorros Epina

Distance:	15km (9½ miles).
Start:	Vallehermoso
Finish:	Bar Restaurante Los Chorros de Epina
Map:	1:50,000 Military Map Sheet 37-41/42
Terrain:	Mostly easy walking along a valley road and a broad, high-level track, but there is also a steep and rocky path between them.

Most of this day's walk is quite easy, beginning with a road walk and ending with a long walk along a dirt track. However, there is a steep climb along a narrow path on an arid slope that should be taken at a gentler pace. Please refer to the map on p. 102. It is also possible to combine this day's walk with that to Arure, though if you do this the walking at the end of the day is tougher. Otherwise ending at Chorros Epina can be problematic, as the bus service back to Vallehermoso is limited. If you think you may miss the bus, take the phone number of a taxi driver from Vallehermoso.

Leave **Vallehermoso** by following a road signposted for the Parque Maritimo, away from the central roundabout. The road runs down through a valley and the buildings seem to peter out, though there is another area of settlement near the valley mouth. There are plenty of palm trees and an interesting botanic garden, with great views up to the Roque El Cano. When you reach the houses further down the valley, look carefully uphill on the left to spot one called Cuadrado. Just a little further down the road, also on the left, two flights of concrete steps rise from the road to a few more houses. Go up the first flight of steps, and climb straight up a rugged *barranco* when you reach a palm tree.

The route is waymarked with blue arrows and red dots painted on the rock. The path later leaves the *barranco* and slices up across a steep, scrubby slope. There is a fine view down to the Parque Maritimo and its swimming pool, close to the Playa de Vallehermoso. Euphorbia scrub is dotted with dark green clumps of juniper. The path zigzags higher and higher, offering increasingly good views along the rugged north coast of La Gomera. There are also a few stunted pines on the

Transport: Servicio Regular Gomera Bus 2 and 5B serve Vallehermoso. Servicio Regular Gomera Bus 4 links Chorros Epina and Vallehermoso.

Refreshments: There are a handful of shops and bar restaurants at Vallehermoso. Chorros Epina has a bar restaurant.

slope as the path forges straight up the rocky ridge. After shifting to the left of the ridge, the path rises easily to the crest, passing more pines and joining a dirt road. A right turn leads to the nearby viewpoint of **Buenavista**, where there are a few wind-blasted pines at 564m (1850ft). Although you are close to the celebrated **Roques de los Organos**, these can only be seen properly from boat trips around the coast.

From Buenavista return to the path and simply follow the dirt road onwards. Grassy slopes are sometimes flowery and dotted with clumps of juniper and heather. The dirt road climbs gently and if there is no mist, then you can catch a glimpse of Vallehermoso from a couple of gaps on the high crest. At a junction, where the road to the right leads down to the tiny settlement of Casa Chigueré, keep left, moving uphill. The dirt road passes the Ermita de Nuestra Señora de Coromoto. The land around the *ermita* is rapidly eroding, leaving bare subsoil and boulders. The road continues rising and weaves about on a bare part of the crest, with views of the sea on one side, and the valley inland on the other. A few laurels and heather trees are dotted about the road beore it continues its gradual ascent, passing a house and an area of cultivated terraces. After following the road gently uphill and around a hollow in the hillside, the **Ermita de Santa Clara** is reached at 735m (2410ft). There's a parking area and fine views over the remote village of Arguamul. The Montaña de la Caldera, swathed in 'laurisilva' rises beyond the *ermita*.

The dirt road shifts onto the steep slopes of Montaña de la Caldera, overlooking the coast, rising gently uphill, then running downhill across the foot of a cliff. Although there is plenty of 'laurisilva' on the high slopes, it quickly peters out below the dirt road, where there are old terraces. When a junction is reached, keep walking downhill, with a view over the village of Tazo. A scrubby slope is dotted with palm trees and there's a goat pen at a junction with another dirt road at 640m (2100ft). This other road serves Tazo and Arguamul only, so turn left to continue away from these villages.

The new botanic gardens are seen on the way down from Valleheroso

There is more vegetation as the road climbs to eventually reach a junction with a narrow tarmac road. Turn left through a gap in the rugged crest, then right to follow the road onwards. At the next junction, the main road is signposted for Vallehermoso and Valle Gran Rey. Turn right, as if for Valle Gran Rey, and the road leads you the short distance to the Bar Restaurante Los Chorros de Epina at 700m (2300ft). If you have any time to spare before you catch your bus, you can enjoy food and drink, or the view from a nearby mirador.

The rugged north coastline of La Gomera

WALK 18

Chorros Epina to Valle Gran Rey

Distance:	16km (10 miles)
Start:	Bar Restaurante Los Chorros de Epina
Finish:	Valle Gran Rey
Map:	1:50,000 Military Map Sheet 37-41/42
Terrain:	A lengthy road-walk near the start, but also steep and rocky paths that can be quite exposed at times. An arid slope later gives way to a steep and rocky descent to Valle Gran Rey.

This day's walk starts easily enough on a path wandering downhill. There is then a stretch along a level road, followed by a chance to make a detour to the spiky Punta de Tejeleche. The next paths along the Lomo del Carretón are narrow, rocky and exposed. These paths require care, but they are well worth walking along as the rock scenery is awesome. It is possible to break the journey at Arure, where there is food, drink and buses, but the continuation to Valle Gran Rey is fairly easy and leads to a greater range of services. Paths are clear and gently graded towards the end, but the final stage of the descent is steep and rocky. Please refer to the map on p. 102.

Start at the Bar Restaurante Los Chorros de Epina at 700m (2300ft). Just up the road is a road signposted for Chorros Epina, next to a large sign for the Parque Nacional Garajonay. Follow the stone-paved road downhill through 'laurisilva' woodland to reach the Ermita de San Isidro at the road-end. A path continues down through the 'laurisilva' and there are boulders lying around that have fallen from the cliffs high above. As the path emerges onto an open slope there are a few pines and a small reservoir. You pass a sign for the Monumento Natural Lomo del Carretón. A narrow path covered in grass and flowers winds downhill, passing boulders and clumps of heather, dropping between old terraces and passing palms and scrub. When it reaches a road, turn left.

The road runs gently downhill and ultimately serves the village of Alojera, which is in view below. When a signposted junction is reached, however, turn left for Taguluche. The road contours around 550m (1800ft) across a steep, scrubby slope, with the cliffs of the Lomo

Transport: Servicio Regular Gomera Bus 4 links Vallehermoso with Chorros de Epina. Servicio Regular Gomera Bus 1 and 5A serve Arure and Valle Gran Rey.

Refreshments: Chorros de Epina has a bar restaurant, while there are a couple more shops and bar restaurants at Arure, and plenty others around Valle Gran Rey.

de Carretón high above and terraces falling towards Alojera and the sea. From a prominent road bend Alojera looks like a garden village, with plenty of colour and greenery. The eye is drawn towards the spiky crest of the Punta de Tejeleche, rising above Alojera.

To climb the Punta de Tejeleche, leave the road at the bend and follow a sparsely cairned path out onto the rocky headland. This narrow path weaves about and as it is gritty underfoot, be sure to plant your feet firmly. Remain on the Alojera side of the ridge to approach the higher parts. It is necessary to wrestle down past a couple of palms after one horribly awkward, eroded stretch, then the path becomes easier as it approaches the ridge, and is even buttressed in places. As you cross the ridge, note the monstrous tower of rock high above, as well as traces of old terracing where crops would once have been grown. Decide whether you want to go all the way to the main summit at 618m (2028ft), or simply want to wander around and enjoy the views from different parts of the ridge. Afterwards, turn around and retrace your steps faithfully back to the road at 550m (1800ft).

Once here take the steep, eroded, gritty path from a sign for the Lomo del Carretón, just off the bend. This is the way up to the village of Arure. The path leads up into a pulverised rocky groove, though the higher parts are stone-paved and zigzag up to the left of a bouldery buttress. There are a few pines, then the path swings across the top of the bouldery buttress and continues along the base of an awesome columnar cliff-line. Note the freshly detached slabs and boulders lying near the path and beware of rockfalls all the way along this cliff-line, . The rock scenery is impressive and there are views down to the village of Taguluche as well as across the sea to La Palma. The path undulates for a while, then begins to climb, and stone zigzags lead up into an area of pines. Watch carefully to spot a little pool collecting drips of water. A splendid terrace path finally leads to the **Ermita del Santo** around 800m (2625ft). There may well be more people milling around a new complex here, where there is a splendid *mirador* that is easily approached

On the path along the rugged ridge from Arure to La Mérica

from Arure. A stone-paved ramp leads uphill and under an arch, then down the other side to a minor road. A left turn leads into the village of **Arure**, which has a few shops, bars and bus services.

To continue to Valle Gran Rey is fairly easy. Instead of turning left to reach Arure, turn right to follow the road in the other direction. The end of the road comes suddenly and there is a view down Valle Gran Rey. Follow a dirt road up from the end of the tarmac, passing beehives and keeping an eye open for big trucks. Walk downhill and keep left at a fork. To the right is a tipping site, where all the trucks are heading. There is a sign for the Parque Rural Valle Gran Rey at the track junction. Walk downhill a little, then uphill, keeping to the right to walk up a stone-paved ramp. The path rises across a water channel and passes a goat pen. Cross a rocky notch and descend a little, overlooking the head of Valle Gran Rey. Zigzag uphill and pass a cave often used by goats sheltering from the sun. Keep climbing the broad path, enjoying views back along the crest towards Arure, as well as the forested uplands around Garajonay, and the rocky promontory of La Fortaleza.

The long descent to Valle Gran Rey starts with the path passing close to **La Mérica**, and there are a couple of short paths to the right leading to the 835m (2740ft) summit trig point. The ground underfoot is bright and chalky and is unbearably bright in the full sun. Old terraces alongside are long exhausted and even the scrub seems parched. Notice the view over the edge into the deep-cut valley while you pass a couple of ruined buildings alongside an old limekiln. The broad path drops gradually through the old terraces to pass another old building and a threshing floor. Keep walking downhill until a fork is reached.

Head down to the left, zigzagging on a steepening slope with fine views of Valle Gran Rey. The zigzags are often paved, but are also rugged and covered in loose stones, so do not rush down the path. It seems like an interminable switchback, but eventually you draw closer to the buildings at the bottom of the slope, and the last stretch has much better paving. A few steps finally drop onto a narrow road at La Calera. Turn right down the road, passing a musuem, church and a few shops. Pick a way down to the left to reach a couple of bar restaurants by the main road, where there are also taxis and bus stops. **Valle Gran Rey** comes in three or four parts. This part is La Calera, and close by is Playa del Valle Gran Rey and Borbalán, with Puerto de Las Vueltas further away at the end of the road.

WALK 19

Valle Gran Rey to Garajonay

Distance:	16km (10 miles)
Start:	Vueltas, Valle Gran Rey
Finish:	Pajarito, below Garajonay
Map:	1:50,000 Military Map Sheet 37-41/42
Terrain:	The ascent involves some exposed scrambling in a rocky valley, later giving way to narrow paths, then broader paths and tracks through cultivated higher slopes. Forest tracks and paths are easier towards the end.

It is possible to climb Garajonay in only a few minutes from a bus stop high on the mountain road at Pajarito. Walkers looking for a more challenging route can climb Garajonay starting from sea level at Valle Gran Rey. The route is remarkable, following a valley gradually uphill where contorted cliff faces look quite impassable to walkers. The route involves a lot of scrambling, exposed in places, but within the capabilities of most walkers. At a higher level there are easier paths and tracks, but if time is being lost, then the walk can be broken at Chipude. The last stretch, from Chipude to the top of Garajonay, is perhaps the easiest part of the route, and buses on the mountain road run until late at night to Valle Gran Rey. See map on p. 102.

Vueltas is the small harbour at the end of the road running through **Valle Gran Rey**. Buses turn at that point and there is a chance to obtain food and drink before embarking on the walk. There are also ferries from San Sebastián and Playa de Santiago. Follow a track round the little harbour, passing along the foot of a steep cliff from which boulders tend to fall from time to time. The coastal track crosses a *barranco* at a sign announcing the Parque Rural Valle Gran Rey. Another track immediately runs inland, up into a steep-sided valley. Although the track is marked as private property, with no public access, there is also a notice indicating that fit and well-equipped walkers wishing to climb to Gerian or Chipude are permitted. Note that there is no escape from the **Barranco de Argaga**, and a lot of scrambling on the ascent.

Only a short way up the valley track there is an invitation to visit a Tropical Fruit Garden. If you do drop in you need to keep an eye on the time. The track climbs past a few habitations, winding in such a manner that

Transport: Servicio Regular Gomera Bus 1 serves Valle Gran Rey, Chipude and Pajarito. Servicio Regular Gomera Bus 5A also serves Valle Gran Rey and Chipude.

Refreshments: Plenty of shops, bars and restaurants in Valle Gran Rey. There are a few bars in Chipude, as well as a small supermarket.

you cannot see ahead to gauge the full extent of the valley. Before reaching the last buildings, step down into the bouldery *barranco* and pick a way carefully upstream. The banks of the *barranco* are initially gritty and crumbling and need care; obviously, this is no place to be in wet or windy conditions. The route is marked by small blobs of red paint. After passing the last few buildings and plots, pass a small dammed pool, then climb over some substantial stone terraces that have a 'lost city' look about them.

Just above the terraces, cross another little dam and continue up beside the *barranco*. A tight squeeze is indicated down to the bed of the *barranco*, while red arrows show the way to climb up the other side. Scramble up past small terraces and pick a way up a gritty zigzag path. The path passes beneath a cliff that overhangs in places before steps and another gritty path lead back down into the *barranco* near a dry waterfall. Little cairns mark the way. Follow the rocky bed of the *barranco*, until another dry waterfall bars upward progress. Use a path leading up through small terraces to continue, then walk along the pebbly bed of the *barranco*. Looking further up the valley is enough to give a crick in the neck, and the way seems to be closed by awesome rock walls in all directions.

Watch carefully for the path and blobs of red paint, and scramble up out of the *barranco*. Hands will need to be used quite a lot as you pick your way up and across a very steep and rocky face. The route passes close to a water pipe, but zigzags to avoid it. While slicing up and across the cliff face again, the water pipe crosses the path, and as the route zigzags further uphill, crosses it again. Keep zigzagging, passing gingerly under a scooped-out cavern, then later climbing above it. Be sure to keep an eye peeled for the red paint blobs and small cairns while making upward progress. When you stop to take in the view, there is a glimpse of the sea far below. The path, if you can call it a path, moves back towards the *barranco* and picks its way across the cliff face high above a ravine. Literally stick to the cliff face and keep watching for those little cairns. Walk along an easier terrace, then climb up and around a buttress perched over the ravine. In this narrow defile a fence appears quite suddenly and the path climbs steeply uphill alongside it. Considering that anything grown here has to be carried out along the path it is amazing that anyone cultivates fruit and vegetables!

This walk can be combined with Walk 20 for a two-day coast-to-coast walk across La Gomera.

Easier zigzags lead uphill and the path runs along a terrace where there is a chance to breathe more easily. There are palm trees and the path is practically level in places. This cannot last and indeed it does not! The path begins to zigzag uphill again with a vengeance, and this part can be desperate in the heat of the day. The zigzags are loose and stony in places, but the line is well-engineered. Looking across a ravine, there are some pine trees arranged in a line on the steep slope. Keep climbing towards some palm trees at a higher level, where the path swings to the right. It remains quite steep and rugged, exploiting a worn, reddish, gritty layer in the bedrock. Beware of rockfalls from above. There are other paths on this rough slope, but the main path, that you need, is characterised by cairns and zigzags up and out of the valley, passing a sign for the Parque Rural Valle Gran Rey. A left turn leads quickly along the edge of the valley to the little village of Gerián at 700m (2300ft).

There is a bendy track running between the buildings, continuing away from Gerián. Use it if you've had enough and want to reach Chipude quickly. It is also possible to stay on the edge of the valley, where an old water channel contours across the slope. This feature can be followed for a while, but don't follow it round a rocky buttress. Instead, cut uphill to reach the prominent whitewashed **Ermita de Nuestra Señora de Guadalupe**. A statue in the *ermita* is taken down to the sea in a procession each year, and a fleet of fishing boats accompany it to San Sebastián. The *ermita* is perched on a natural viewpoint, allowing views back down and further up the valley to where the route proceeds next.

Follow a path back down to the old water channel, having avoided the rocky buttress, and simply let the

The Barranco de Argaga is steep and rocky throughout its length

line of the channel lead you up the valley. It clings to a steep and rugged slope and is often fractured and no longer capable of carrying water. Some short stretches are best avoided by using well-trodden paths either above or below it. The channel passes some old terraces and eventually swings in and out of a little side valley. There are a few little plots and palms at this point. Looking back down the valley, the *ermita* is now a small white dot. Follow the channel further up the valley, noting how the riverbed almost rises to meet it. However, before this point take the path branching away to the right, passing a prominent solitary palm tree.

It is important to watch carefully to spot this rather vague path heading to the right up alongside a *barranco.* This quickly crosses the bed of the *barranco* and starts zigzagging up a slope. Keep an eye open for a path junction at a higher level, where a sharp left turn is made. The path runs along the foot of a blocky little cliff and climbs uphill. There is a view of the village of El Cercado on the skyline, and after turning a corner on the valley side it is also possible to see the village of Chipude, with the forested Garajonay beyond. The path climbs up the valley side, passing old terraces and occasional palm trees. There is a clear view throughout the ascent. The path slices straight across a track and passes a few cultivated plots and a house. Watch out for a flight of steps rising to the right, leading up to a track where you turn left. Simply follow the track up to a road and turn left a short way downhill. Just before a bus shelter, turn right up a track and continue up a stone-paved road to reach Bar la Candelaria at the village of **Chipude** at the altitude of 1180m (3870ft).

Walkers who have had enough at this point can catch a bus back to Valle Gran Rey, or retire to one of the bars for food and drink. The Bar Sonia also offers accommodation and a full meal service. The village has a pleasant central plaza and the 16th century church of the Virgen de la Candelaria.

Walkers who wish to continue all the way to Garajonay can stop for food and drink, then nip behind the Bar la Candelaria and walk further up the steep, stone-paved road to leave Chipude. A track continues up past the last houses and over a rise, descending slightly to join a narrow tarmac road. Turn left to follow the road down and around a valley, and head for a small farming settlement called Los Manatiales. There is a path crossing this valley, but it is often overgrown, so it may be better to use the road.

At the end of the road, at 1220m (4000ft), turn sharply right to follow a path up across the valley side, passing terraces and a few palms. Further up the valley there are clumps of tree heather and the path becomes a good track. Turn right at a junction where there is taller, denser tree heather, then turn left as signposted for Alto de Garajonay. There is another junction only a short distance away, with a sign reading 'Pinar de Argumame'. Spare a moment to walk off the track into tall pines where there is welcome shade on a sunny day.

Keep following the track signposted for Alto de Garajonay, which winds uphill and is flanked by flowers and heather, with a few laurels. Although the slopes are largely forested, there are views back to La Fortaleza and ahead to Garajonay. There are a few more pines as height is gained. At a higher track junction there are views stretching away to the island of La Palma and the peak of El Teide on Tenerife. Keep straight on to the next track junction, then turn right and again follow the signpost for Alto de Garajonay. The track climbs up in a loop, keeping left at a junction and pass a building and a mast. Just beyond is the summit viewpoint where, encircled in a walled enclosure, a trig point marks the height at 1485m (4872ft). An information board details the view (clouds permitting) which stretches to Malpaso on El Hierro, the mountainous crest of La Palma, the peak of El Teide on Tenerife, and possibly the more distant Gran Canaria. The rolling uplands of La Gomera are often brushed by clouds where the water vapour is condensed, allowing water to drip to the ground and keep the island moist.

The sixteenth-century church of the Virgen de la Candelaria at Chipude

The summit of **Garajonay** had special significance for the original Guanche inhabitants of La Gomera. Their territorial boundaries met at the summit where arachaeological traces of a settlement have been found, comprising shepherd's huts and structures known as *aras* which are thought to have had a ritual or sacrificial use. Flint scrapers have also been discovered.

Walk down a handful of stone steps to leave the viewpoint and follow a rugged path along the crest. The path is smoother later, then a flight of log steps leads down to a gap. Climb up more log steps almost to the top of a subsidiary summit, but watch out for a path heading off to the right. A long flight of log steps leads downhill on the forested slope, then another flight continues down to a track. The track quickly leads to a road junction at Pajarito, at 1340m (4395ft). A late bus service passes this junction, heading back through Chipude and down to Valle Gran Rey.

WALK 20
Garajonay to Hermigua

Walkers who blanched at the thought of climbing Garajonay from sea-level at Valle Gran Rey might instead consider the long descent from the summit to sea-level at Hermigua. Buses run to the high forested slopes of the mountain, so an ascent from Pajarito is quickly accomplished. The descent is initially confined to the ancient 'laurisilva' forest, then there is a very steep descent into a valley to reach Hermigua. The last part of the walk down to the sea is quite easy. If you link this walk with the ascent of Garajonay from Valle Gran Rey, then it offers a splendid coast-to-coast walk across La Gomera. Please refer to the maps on p. 94 and 102.

Distance:	16km (10 miles)
Start:	Pajarito, below Garajonay
Finish:	Playa de Hermigua
Map:	1:50,000 Military Map Sheet 37-41/42
Terrain:	Good paths and tracks lead down the forested mountainside. Steep and rugged zigzag paths lead down into the valley. The walk ends with easy road walking.

The walk begins at a road junction at **Pajarito**, at 1340m (4395ft), unless you have already reached the top of Garajonay by another route, in which case you can omit the first paragraph. Close to the road junction, a track leads away from the road onto a forested slope. A right turn signposted Alto de Garajonay leads up a flight of log steps. Climb up these and climb up a longer flight of log steps to reach the crest of Garajonay. A left turn leads down a flight of log steps to a gap, then another flight of log steps and a path lead to the summit of **Garajonay**. The summit viewpoint has a trig point in the middle of a circular walled enclosure at 1485m (4872ft). An information board details the views that stretch from El Hierro and La Palma to El Teide on Tenerife, and possibly the distant Gran Canaria. The rolling, forested uplands of La Gomera are often brushed by clouds, so views may be obscured.

Walk down a handful of stone steps to leave the viewpoint and walk back along the crest of Garajonay, basically retracing your earlier steps across the gap. This time, continue straight past the path junction where you climbed up from Pajarito, to reach a subsidiary summit and to enjoy more of the view. Continue along the path, down more log steps. Take care here as the path is rather rugged in places. Turn right down a broader track, which later swings right to reach a parking space on the road below, at 1280m (4200ft).

There are information boards at the car park and signs indicate a path to El Cedro. The path begins as a groove through the tree heather, then is fenced as it drops down flights of log steps. It is waymarked as a nature trail, with numbered posts, and there is a mighty til tree at number three. In fact, the 'laurisilva' forest contains plenty of big trees, including tall heather trees at number 6, and more huge tils. There is a small viewpoint allowing a glimpse of a forested valley, with the peak of El Teide still in view on a clear day. Steps lead further down a steep slope into dark and dense forest where sunlight hardly penetrates. Cross a *barranco* and note the big, mossy boulders where the ground is always moist. An easier stretch of path leads through the dark forest, undulating gently and reaching another viewpoint where there is a view back up towards Garajonay.

The path drops steeply again through tall, dense forest, then the gradient eases a little. Between nature trail numbers 10 and 11 the trees are mostly laurels. There is another small viewpoint, this time limited to a peep into the Barranco del Cedro, where there may be a copious flow of water. The level path continues through the laurels, where the ground is usually damp and ferns flourish. A huge chestnut stands beside the path and a sign reads 'Campamento Antiguo' among tall heather and laurels.

Signposts pointing back to Alto de Garajonay and ahead to Arroyo de El Cedro are passed. Walk down through tall, dark forest to reach number 15 on the nature trail on the banks of the stream, where chestnuts grow among the heather and laurels. Use a ford just below a boulder dam to cross the stream. Head downstream among tall trees and cross a footbridge. At the next path junction keep going straight onwards. The only sign here is a symbol of a walking man pointing back

Transport:
Servicio Regular Gomera Bus 1 serves Pajarito. Servicio Regular Gomera Bus 2 and 5A serve Hermigua.

Refreshments:
There are shops, bars and restaurants at Hermigua.

Heather trees form the 'cloud forest' that covers La Gomera's mountains

along the path. A broad path running roughly parallel to the stream leads down past tall trees to reach a junction at a bend on a broad dirt road at 960m (3150ft). Here at **Arroyo de El Cedro Las Mimbras** there is an information board as well as signposts. There is a trickle of water available from a pipe if you don't fancy drinking from the stream.

Turn left to follow the dirt road uphill. It gradually climbs from the dense forest and levels out around 1040m (3410ft) on a slope with more heather cover. While walking along there are only a couple of glimpses down into the valley. A signpost points right for Caserío de El Cedro, but stay on the dirt road to descend more gradually for a short way. Turn sharply right at a junction and follow another track downhill. The track is flanked by heather and laurels, and although these sometimes offer shade, most parts are open to the sun. Descend past a couple of waterworks buildings and a house, then continue down to a bendier stretch of the track. At a junction on a bend there is a splendid view of El Teide on Tenerife beyond the valley mouth, as well as a sign reading 'Rutas Senderos Aceviños San Juan'. Walk down a few steps at this point and follow a path along the ridge. The path appears to head for the distant cone of

El Teide on Tenerife, and cuts out a broad bend from the track. Continue walking down the track and enjoy a fine view down to Hermigua far below. The altitude is around 700m (2300ft).

Zigzag steeply downhill, often on a paved path, which is sometimes flanked by handrails. There are some level stretches along terraces, passing a couple of ruined buildings, but for most of the time it is a steep and knee-jarring descent. Take it slowly and steadily and enjoy the bird's-eye view over Hermigua. After turning a prominent corner you can look up to the head of the valley, which has a serrated crest. Walk further downhill and cross a road-end near a small *ermita*. Continue down a rough stone path with steps, then concrete steps lead down to a road bend at a sign reading 'Rutas Senderos San Juan Aceviños'. Just across the road, more concrete steps and another steep and stony path lead further downhill, passing a few houses to land on a lower road. Turn left and walk a short way round to the end of the road, then walk down more steps and along a concrete and stone-paved street. This street winds down between buildings and finally lands on the main road at **Hermigua** at 110m (360ft).

Turn left to pass the Post Office and Ayuntamiento. The road continues past sports pitches, the Hotel Villa de Hermigua and a small botanic garden. When the church is reached in the middle of town, the road appears to split either side of the building. Keep left to pass the church, or take a break for food and drink, as there are shops, bars and restaurants hereabouts. The main road leads onwards, then it is simply a matter of keeping right and walking down to the Playa de Hermigua. Walk back up from the beach to the main road to catch a bus.

WALK 21

La Fortaleza and Garajonay

Distance:	16km (10 miles)
Start/Finish:	In the square at Chipude
Map:	1:50,000 Military Map Sheet 37-41/42
Terrain:	Hands-on scrambling is required to reach the top of La Fortaleza. The rest of the walk is mostly along good forest tracks and paths.

Chipude is one of the highest villages on La Gomera, around 1180m (3870ft). The rugged crest of La Fortaleza can be seen from the plaza and it is easy enough to reach the peak and continue to the forested Garajonay afterwards. Please refer to the map on p. 102. A fine circuit can be made by wandering through the ancient 'laurisilva' forest to La Laguna Grande, noting the sudden transition from native woodlands to cultivated slopes on the way back to Chipude. Although cloud often covers Garajonay, when it is clear the views can be surprisingly extensive.

Leave the village of **Chipude** by following the road uphill from Bar Tito. When the road bends right, keep walking straight onwards up a narrow, stone-paved old road. This crosses the main road at a higher level, keeping left of a bus shelter, then descends towards the village of El Apartadero. Turn left at the bottom, clipping a bend on the road, then follow the old road uphill again. The stone paving gives way to bare rock on the approach to a house on a rise. Descend again, but before reaching the road, climb again along another stone-paved road. Walk down to the tarmac road in El Apartadero and turn left to reach the little Bar Los Camioneros. Just across the road from the bar, a stony path drops into a valley, passing prickly pears and palms, then rises back up to the road. Turn left along the road, then right to walk up a broad, stone-paved lane through the crumbling little village of Pavón. Turn right at the top to reach the very last little house.

There is a sign for the Monumento Natural La Fortaleza and the rocky peak rises to the right. If you think it looks too difficult, then there is no need to climb it, as the route returns here later. To continue up, however, follow a path up a steep slope dotted with cistus bushes. There are more flowers and shrubs at a higher level. The path is white and dusty and a crude set of rock steps lead more steeply uphill into a tight little gully. There are plenty of holds for hands and feet and the exposure is slight. At the top, swing right along a rock ridge, cross a slight rocky gap, then emerge on the stony plateau of **La Fortaleza**. Turn around to take a good look at the rocky ridge as you will have to come back this way and reverse all your moves. A prominent white cross stands on the plateau, surrounded by cistus bushes.

The rolling, forested slopes of Garajonay can be seen in the middle of La Gomera, while out to sea are the islands of La Palma and El Hierro. Walk round the summit plateau, passing a trig point at 1232m (4042ft). There is also a remarkable rocky ridge to the south that is worth walking along for fine cliff views, but don't go too far and be sure to return to the plateau before making the next move. Though a complete circuit of the plateau can be made, retracing your steps to the little house above Pavón is the only one way down.

A path, boulder-paved in places, climbs beyond the little house rising to join a clear track. Keep heading gently uphill, passing waterworks buildings to join the main road. Turn right and follow the road to a prominent building, the Casa Forestal Las Tajoras. There is a large sign announcing the Parque Nacional Garajonay at this point. A track on the left leaves the road, then swings right and descends into a little cultivated valley. There are dense heather trees to the right and all the higher slopes are covered in 'laurisilva' forest. Walk down to a track junction and keep to the right, among tall pines and tree heather. Keep straight onwards as signposted for Alto de Garajonay. There is another junction only a short distance away, with a sign reading 'Pinar de Argumame'. Spare a moment to walk into tall pines just off the track at this point, where the shade is welcome on a sunny day.

Keep following the track signposted for Alto de Garajonay, which winds uphill and is flanked by flowers and heather, with a few laurels. Although the slopes are largely forested, with a few more pines as you gain height, there are views back to La Fortaleza and ahead

Transport:
Servicio Regular Gomera Bus 1 and 5 serve Chipude.

Refreshments:
There are bars at Chipude and El Apartadero at the start, as well as a bar restaurant at La Laguna Grande.

to Garajonay. At a higher track junction, the island of La Palma and the peak of El Teide on Tenerife can be seen. Keep straight on to the next track junction, then turn right as again signposted for Alto de Garajonay. Climb the track as it ascends in a loop, keeping left at a junction, to pass a building and a mast. Just beyond is **Garajonay's** summit viewpoint, where there is a trig point in the middle of a circular walled enclosure at 1485m (4872ft). An information board details the view, clouds permitting, which stretches to Malpaso on El Hierro, the mountainous crest of La Palma, the peak of El Teide on Tenerife, and possibly the more distant Gran Canaria. The rolling uplands of La Gomera are often brushed by clouds, and the cloud forest condenses the water vapour, allowing it to drip to the ground and keep the island moist.

The summit of Garajonay had special significance for the original Guanche inhabitants of La Gomera as their territorial boundaries met here. Archaeological traces of settlement comprising shepherd's huts and structures known as *aras* thought to have had a ritual or sacrificial use have been found here. Flint scrapers have also been discovered.

Walk down a handful of stone steps to leave the viewpoint and follow a rugged path along the crest. The path becomes smoother before a flight of log steps leads down to a gap. Climb up more log steps to reach a subsidiary summit and enjoy more of the view. (If time is pressing, before this summit there are steps leading down to the main road at **Pajarito**, allowing you to link with bus services). Continue along the path, down more log steps, where the path is rather rugged in places. Turn right down a broader track, which later swings right to reach a parking space on the road below. Just on the point of this last bend, however, leave the track on the left and a flight of log steps descend into dark, dense 'laurisilva' forest. The path is near the road and actually runs very close to it for a while.

A track leading down to the left, away from the road, is signposted for La Laguna Grande and El Cercado. Follow this track down through tall, dense 'laurisilva' to

Walkers on the summit of Garajonay, with a view back to La Fortaleza

reach a signposted junction. Turn right as signposted again for La Laguna Grande and El Cercado. Walk round a bend to reach yet another junction, and this time keep straight onwards to return to the road. Turn left, to follow a path running alongside the road, though tree heather and laurels screen you from traffic. The path later drifts down from the road to reach an open recreational area at **La Laguna Grande**. This can be busy at times when coaches and cars pull in, but it can also be nearly deserted. Facilities include a bar restaurant, toilets and water taps. The altitude is 1260m (4135ft).

There is a pleasant looped path, entirely enclosed by rustic fencing that offers an interesting nature ramble through the woodlands. The 'fayal brezal' is less dense than true 'laurisilva' forest, and the lower parts of the forest floor can be covered by Canarian geraniums in spring. Information signs point out the range of tree species, which is dominated by tree heather, but also includes laurels. At the top of the trail there is a view of the volcanic laccolith of Fortaleza de Cherelepín. Birds to watch out for include two types of dove or pigeon, one preferring the woodlands and the other the rocky cliffs. A bewildering tally of over 1000 invertebrate species have been recorded in the area.

Leave La Laguna Grande past the bar restaurant, toilet block and generator building. There is a viewpoint worth a moment's pause, then steps and a rugged path lead down into the 'laurisilva'. On the way, notice the huge eucalyptus tree trunks lying where they were felled. Eucalyptus are not native to the island and if left to flourish they would overwhelm the native 'laurisilva'. Thus hundreds of trees were felled and saplings vigorously uprooted to clear the eucalyptus from the national park. The path reaches a junction at the edge of the woodlands, and by walking straight onwards you leave the woods and national park at the same time.

Follow a broad track leading gently downhill, passing cultivated plots and terraces that overlook a small and virtually empty reservoir. Pass the dam, then turn left and follow a track in front of it, climbing up the other side of the valley. Ignoring tracks to left and right, keep to the main track that passes vines or overgrown patches on the valley side. A water pipe spans the track, then there is a descent towards small villages. Looking far across the sea from La Gomera, parts of La Palma and El Hierro might be spotted. Closer to hand, La Fortaleza can be seen to the left, and the rolling, forested slopes of Garajonay rise beyond.

Follow the track downhill until a tarmac road rises from the right. Note how a line of telegraph poles cross over the crest at this point, and turn left to find a rough, stone-paved track leading down to the road. Cross over the road and go through a gap in the crash barrier. Descend alongside palms and prickly pears, then climb back up to the road. Turn right and let the road lead uphill into the lower part of **Chipude**. Watch carefully beyond a bus shelter to spot a track rising to the left. This bends and becomes a stone-paved road. It cuts out a bend from the main road, leading directly up to Bar La Candelaria in the middle of the village. Bar Sonia provides accommodation and meals, while the Bar Navarro has a small supermarket.

WALK 22

Los Roques to Playa de Santiago

Distance:	20km (12½ miles)
Start:	Roque de Agando
Finish:	Playa de Santiago
Map:	1:50,000 Military Map Sheet 37-41/42
Terrain:	Steep wooded slopes lead down to Benchijigua. A rocky and arid ridge is crossed to reach El Rumbazo. A steep and rocky path leads up to Targa. A broad track descends an arid slope to reach Playa de Santiago.

Walkers who travel round the southern parts of La Gomera will be surprised from time to time to notice a handful of rocky peaks on the skyline. Walking opportunities around Los Roques are limited, but it is possible to start a walk and marvel at them, then head down to the quiet little village of Benchijigua. A rugged ridge walk leads to El Rumbazo, from where a remarkable cliff path climbs to Targa. The walk can finish with an easy descent to the sea at the Playa de Santiago. Please refer to the map on p. 94

Start on the main road beside the awesome Roque de Agando, around 1070m (3510ft). Wander around the Mirador de Los Roques to obtain varying views of the scenery. On a clear day the pyramidal form of El Teide can be seen on distant Tenerife. The information boards provided explain how these rugged towers are the remains of volcanic plugs. There is also a monument commemorating a number of people who died in a fire in 1984. A signpost points out the path descending to Benchijigua, and there is also a sign for the Reserva Natural Integral Benchijigua. A cobbly path and log steps descend among pines, tree heather and cistus. It is narrow and overgrown in places, with a small clearing and another sign below the monstrous tower of rock. Continue down among trees and shrubs to cross a concrete watercourse, enjoying the fine views down the valley as you go. Take an easy, almost level, path that cuts across the valley side, with fine views back to the rocks and ahead to the valley. There are plenty of palms on these slopes, before you take a steep and rough

Transport: Servicio Regular Gomera Bus 1 passes the Roque de Agando, while Bus 3 serves Targa and Playa de Santiago.

Refreshments: There is a bar at Benchijigua, but no food or drink available in the other little villages along the way. There are plenty of shops, bars and restaurants at the end in Playa de Santiago.

zigzag path that passes a watercourse among pines and eucalyptus. A dirt road is reached at **Benchijigua** at 600m (1970ft).

It is worth wandering along the dirt road just to see the pretty houses, then return to the little bar and maybe also have a look at the little *ermita* tucked in against a prominent outcrop of rock. Leave the village by following a track (which often has a chain across it) away from the bar, signposted for Imada. Walk gently down and along, then at a junction keep right . The track bends left around a small valley full of palms, then when the palms thin out, watch carefully for a narrow, but well-trodden, path off to the right. There is a house buried among greenery to the left, while the path to the right is marked with orange dots.

Follow the path as it turns a corner and descends a little, passing beneath a dry waterfall in a streambed. Climb past a couple of palms and turn round a corner to see one last building. Continue along the path, passing a few more palms in a little side valley. The path begins to zigzag up the steep, scrubby, rocky slope. It is a well-engineered route, but rather rough and narrow. Follow it faithfully and enjoy widening views over Benchijigua and its valley. Although you need to look carefully to spot a vague path heading off to the left, it is worth going to the top of the gap first, at 833m (2733ft). Here you see the little village of Imada at the head of another valley, as well as a few ruined houses immediately underfoot. If you visit the gap and then retrace your steps, the vague path you need to follow is now off to the right.

The path leads to a pole bearing a black and white marker. This narrow path becomes clearer as it leads across a steep and scrubby slope, passing a few palms and gradually drifting downhill. Enjoy the views back up to the rocks where the walk started, as well as down to the village of Pastrana, with the sea far beyond. The path usually exploits a band of soft, light rock, but then becomes a wriggly, rough and stony path that switches to the other side of the rough crest. Zigzag downhill,

The Roque de Agando is the most striking peak of all on La Gomera

then follow the path parallel to a road across a steep and rugged slope. There is a water pipe alongside the path, and a little water regulating hut is passed. A road is reached at a house called Casa Maria Angeles. Turn sharp right down the road, then sharp left, and follow the road down to a transformer tower. Turn right and follow the road down beside what is usually a dry riverbed at 200m (655ft). Turn right as signposted for **El Rumbazo**, where a short, steep road climbs to a little huddle of houses.

The road ends in front of the houses, so turn immediately right along a narrow path in front of the buildings. Cross a bouldery *barranco* and keep left at a junction, passing chicken coops and zigzagging uphill a short way. Walk along a level path, crossing another bouldery *barranco* and a few palms, then continue between terraces to reach a couple of small buildings. Start zigzagging uphill, past more palms, with cliffs rising ahead and above. The ascent looks impassable, but the zigzag path is well-engineered and rises up ramps of softer rock. After climbing a reddish ramp you will find a spur path to the right that offers a good view of the valley. Climb further uphill and cross a culverted watercourse. The zigzags become wider and there is a lot of scrub. Climb up and across a buttress, then pass a solitary palm and a tighter series of zigzags climb even higher. After slicing one last time across a buttress, and passing a cool cave, the path finally emerges on a high crest at 750m (2460ft). There may be a view of El Teide on the distant island of Tenerife. Walk down a few paces past a quarry to land on a minor road at the village of **Targa**.

If time is pressing, or the day is too hot to consider walking any further, then it is possible to bail out by turning right and following the road through the village to reach a bus shelter. Playa de Santiago can be reached in a few minutes by bus. If you wish to keep walking, then head left to reach the road-end, then continue along a track to reach a few prominent masts. The track bends at the last mast, but be sure to enjoy the view down into the valley first. Do the same at the next couple of bends as the track draws close to the edge. Note how the palm trees that grow in some number around Targa gradually thin out as the track descends the arid slope. The bendy track passes above and below a ruined farmhouse amid crumbling terraces. There is also a small reservoir in view as you cross a concrete watercourse. The track runs close to the edge for another view of the valley.

Follow the fairly straight track as it rises slightly. There is another concrete pipeline watercourse alongside that leads to a small reservoir. Enjoy the views over the edge again, as the track swings across the desert-like slope at Altamache.

You pass a couple of old houses and broken watercourses. The track continues to wind downhill, and the slope is so dry and broken that it looks almost as if it has been quarried, rather than simply terraced. There are good views over Playa de Santiago on the last set of numerous and very well-buttressed zigzags. As you arrive at the main road at the bottom turn left, then turn right as signposted for **Playa de Santiago**. Walk straight down the road to find a selection of shops, bars and restaurants. There is accommodation, as well as taxis and buses. There may even be ferries to San Sebastián or Valle Gran Rey.

The peak of El Teide seen across the desert-like terrain near El Portillo (on Walk 25)

TENERIFE

Tenerife is the largest and highest of the Canary Islands, and in fact the peak of El Teide is the highest point in all Spain at 3718m (12,198ft). It nearly always stands proudly above the sea of clouds and divides the green northern slopes of the island from the arid southern slopes. El Teide is in a national park and presides over a spectacular *caldeira* full of ancient lava flows. Further downhill, all the sides of the mountain are covered in Canary pines; the Corona Forestal. There are areas of 'laurisilva', which are best observed at Teno and Anaga, at the western and eastern ends of the island respectively. Many areas are barren and rocky, and there are some deep and spectacular *barrancos* to explore.

Tenerife has two airports, one is situated near the southern resorts and caters for most charter flights, and the other, near La Laguna and Santa Cruz de Tenerife serves most inter-island flights. Ferries to and from the islands of La Gomera, La Palma and El Hierro berth at Los Cristianos. Ferries from Santa Cruz de Tenerife head for Gran Canaria. The main resorts are Playa de las Américas and Los Cristianos, though some people

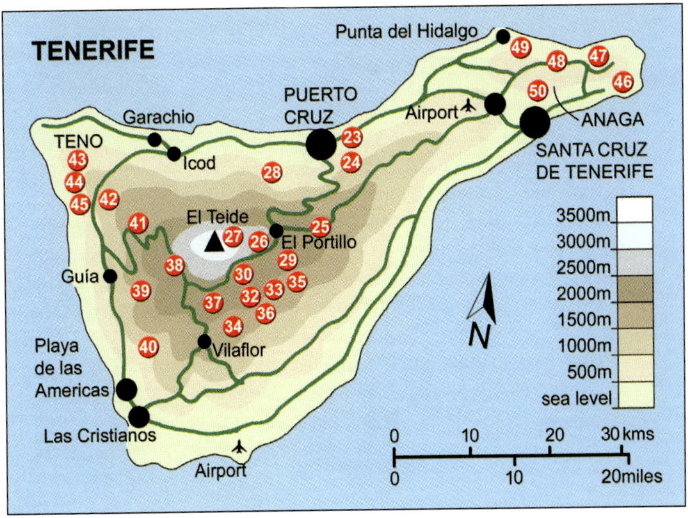

The popular Roques de Garcia (Walk 31)

stay in Puerto de la Cruz and Santa Cruz de Tenerife. Most walkers would be happy to give these big centres of population a miss, and most of the southern coast is barren and unattractive. Stay in quieter upland villages if you have a choice. The bus services around Tenerife are excellent and allow walkers to reach almost any place they care to walk. There is a great choice of walks and it can be useful to explore Tenerife and get a feel for walking in the Canary Islands before hopping to the smaller western islands.

Many walkers set their sights on the ascent of El Teide, which is laudable, but it is a high mountain where the air gets noticeably thinner. It is worth exploring Las Cañadas around the base of the peak before making a dash at the steep slopes. A four-day ascent of the mountain from sea-level at Puerto de la Cruz is suggested, as well as a dozen or so interlinked routes around Las Cañadas and the slopes beyond. The whole central area of Tenerife is a national park and the scenery is impressive, so it deserves to be explored thoroughly. Teno, at the western end of Tenerife, and Anaga, at the eastern end are two other areas that merit careful exploration. A three-day and four-day trek takes in these peninsulas, and there are other one-day walks available too. Walkers will find plenty of paths and tracks criss-crossing the island, but they are not always well signposted, so careful navigation is required.

ATLANTIC OCEAN
SCALE
0 1 2 3 kms
0 1 2 miles
PUERTO DE LA CRUZ
Walk 23
Cuesta de la Ville
300m
Walk 24
580m Pino Alto
LA OROTAVA
480m La Florida
Pinolere
Walk 24
N
Valle de la Orotava
1060m
Aguamansa
La Caldera 1180m
Icod el Alto
Mirador El Lance
540m
La Corona
Walk 28
El Asomadero
1100m
Choza Chimoche
Parque Natural Corona Forestal
Walk 25
Piedra de los Pastores
La Cumbrita
Choza J Ruis
Walk 28
Lomo La Burra
Izaña
2240m
Corral del Niño
2080m
Walk 28
El Portillo
Collada Degollada del Cedro
Roque de Peral
2050m
Walk 25
2290m
Llano de Maja
Siete Cañadas
Montaña de los Tomillos
3500m
3000m
Walk 26
2500m
Laderas del Teide
Parque Nacional del Teide
2000m
2500m
1500m
El Teide
3718m
Walk 26
Walk 27
1000m
TENERIFE
500m
2750m
Walk 27
Montaña Blanca
Walks 23–28
sea level

WALK 23

Puerto de la Cruz to Cuesta de la Ville

This walk can be completed in a morning or an afternoon. It is an easy enough walk, although it does include a steep climb that can be tiring in the heat and humidity. You are rewarded by a bar at the top offering refreshments and a wonderful view back to Puerto de la Cruz. Clouds permitting, you are also able to see the shapely cone of El Teide. For those walkers who like to rise to a challenge, this route combined with walks 24, 25 and 26 offer an ascent of El Teide from sea level. For those who don't want to climb all the way, each walk stands on its own merit as a simple day walk. Please refer to the map on p. 139.

Distance:	8km (5 miles)
Start:	Puerto Pesquero in Puerto de la Cruz
Finish:	Cuesta de la Ville
Map:	1:50,000 Military Map Sheet 39-39
Terrain:	Roads, tracks and cliff paths. The route is essentially coastal, climbing inland towards the end along roads..

Begin at the little harbour called Puerto Pesquero in **Puerto de la Cruz**. Follow the coast as closely as possible, walking round a sea wall defence where cannons are mounted. Turn inland a short way to pass the Ayuntamiento, then continue along the coast by following the Calle de San Telmo. This street runs downhill, then there are steps up to the Ermita de San Telmo, which dates from 1780. Turn immediately inland along the narrow Calle Aldea, then turn left up the Calle la Hoya. Cross a busy road and continue along the Calle la Hoya to reach a complex road junction, with a large shopping centre beyond. Keep to the right of the shopping centre, climbing up flights of steps beside small shops. At the top turn left up more steps to reach a road. Just to the left is the Mirador de la Paz, offering a splendid view over the town.

Exit to the right down another path equipped with steps. There is a restaurant along the way if you need refreshment at this point. Climb up steps beneath a prominent dragon tree. Continue on and pass behind the Hotel Semiramis. Turn left to follow the narrow Camino la Costa, keeping left in the suburbs, following a combined road and walkway that dips underneath the main coast road using a tunnel. A battered road continues through banana plantations. Follow a concrete road through the plantations, then walk down steps to cross a *barranco*. Climb up steps on the other side and turn left along a concrete lane. A sign says it is 300m (330yds) to the Bar Restaurante Bollullo, where a break can be taken.

Follow a cliff path with railings to an enormous painted sign reading 'Playa', but don't go down to the beach, though there is a café bar down there. Keep following the railed cliff path, then squeeze past thick, gnarled tamarisks that block the view down to the sea. Stay on the cliff path, avoiding steps going down to the beach. The railings end and there is an exposed bit, but this can be avoided by going through a hole in a wall to walk inside a banana plantation. Avoid another horribly fractured flight of steps to the beach and instead head inland on a path flanked by tall walls.

This path is overgrown in places and rises steeply passing bananas growing on the slope. There are broken concrete steps, bare rock and canes. You join a road and turn right to follow a concrete road through banana plantations. Walk all the way to the end of the road – most of the other turnings are marked as private. A good track runs onwards, descending to the last house, which is called Finca Ancon. There is no need to go down there, but if time can be spared then it is worth the trip for the view.

A path rises from the concrete road-end and is marked as 'café'. Simply follow the trodden path, where zigzags are often marked with red arrows. Towards the top, where houses rise above a tall retaining wall, a flight of concrete steps lead straight uphill. Turn left along a road, then at the road-end there are two choices. The Café Vista Paraiso is on the left, and a path on the right is marked 'bus' and leads up to another road. Most walkers will be happy to take a break at the café, and there

Transport:
Numerous TITSA Bus services operate between Puerto de la Cruz and Cuesta de la Ville

Refreshments:
There are plenty of shops, restaurants and bars in Puerto de la Cruz. The Bar Restaurante Bollullo is in the middle of the walk, and the Cafe Vista Paraiso is near the end. There are a few bars and restaurants in Cuesta de la Ville.

Picking a way along the cliff-line to the east of Puerto de la Cruz

are wonderful views from the terrace, looking back towards town and up to El Teide.

Leave the café and climb up steps to reach the Calle Vista Paraiso. Turn left to walk parallel to a busy main road, then turn right and right again as signposted for La Ortava. Walk up to the old main road, which is quite busy, in the village of **Cuesta de la Ville**, which is around 300m (985ft) high. There are a few shops, bars and restaurants, as well as frequent bus services running back to Puerto de la Cruz.

WALK 24

Cuesta de la Ville to La Caldera

Distance:	10km (6 miles)
Start:	Cuesta de la Ville
Finish:	La Caldera
Map:	1:50,000 Military Map Sheet 39-40
Terrain:	A series of steep roads linking villages. Cultivated slopes finally give way to forested slopes at a higher level.

There is no decent off-road route from Cuesta de la Ville up to La Caldera. For much of the way, the road used to be little more than a dirt track linking a series of hillside villages, but in recent years it was covered in tarmac. However, when the steepness is taken into account, some walkers might prefer to follow the roads, and have access to roadside bars from time to time. Take this stretch slow and easy, especially if the day is hot and humid, though often there is a bank of cloud clinging to the mountainside, cutting out the full glare of the sun. Once this stage is completed, walkers proceeding beyond La Caldera have more trees for shade. Please see the map on p. 139.

There are a handful of bars and restaurants along the main road in **Cuesta de la Ville**, around 300m (985ft) high. After leaving the bus, walk back along the road in the direction of Puerta de la Cruz, then turn left up a road that is blocked against traffic. This is the Calle Morales, and there is a fork just beyond the block, where you keep left to start climbing. Remain on this main street called the Camino los Morales, which is really steep, until you reach a main road at a higher level. Turn right to follow it further uphill, then swing round a sharp left bend to climb further. Walk up to a junction where a right turn is signposted for **Pino Alto**. Follow a steep concrete road then one with a gentler gradient, passing the Bodegon Eusebio. There is a viewpoint on a level stretch of road in the village, so take a break and look back down to the sea. The altitude is 580m (1900ft).

A tarmac road runs downhill through the village, passing the Restaurante California. Take a moment to observe the view on the way out of the village. The whole of the Valle de la Orotava is laid out, sloping steeply from the sea to the peak of El Teide. Your route hugs the villages to the left, climbing inexorably to the forested slopes at La Caldera. After reaching the skyline,

Transport: Numerous TITSA Bus services operate between Puerto de la Cruz and Cuesta de la Ville. TITSA Bus 346 serves La Florida and 345 serves La Caldera.

Refreshments: Bar restaurants are available at Cuesta de la Ville, Pino Alto, La Florida, Florida Alta, Pinolere, Aguamansa and La Caldera.

the route heads straight to El Teide, which you will follow if you are walking all the way to the summit of the mountain. You may already have noticed odd *Sendero Turistico* plaques along the way. These indicate that you are still on one of the old walking routes, even though the roads are now used by traffic. The old plaques are often battered and bent, but in any case are non-directional and simply indicate that you are still on course. Note the vines on the slopes as the road is followed steeply downhill. Walk uphill a little to reach a road junction at **La Florida**, at 480m (1575ft). The Bar Cafeteria La Palma is available at this point, otherwise simply turn left up the Calle La Palma to keep walking.

The road climbing through La Florida is very steep and the street is like a canyon, being narrow throughout its length with houses rising high on either side. The Bar y Viveres La Palma is passed on the ascent. Keep climbing uphill to leave La Florida and turn right up the Camino Florida Alta. An exceptionally steep road climbs to the Bar Florida Alta, where another break might be in order. The steep road leaves the top end of the village, eventually levelling out to offer a balcony view over the village. It then climbs again to the next village, which is **Pinolere**. On the way, note the vines and other fruit growing on the slopes. When walking up through the village, keep left of the church and note a recent development where peculiar thatched huts have been built. Turn right before the Bar Coromoto to climb up the very steep Calle los Cominos.

The slopes alongside the road are rather more overgrown, with less fruit and vegetables being propegated. Follow the Camino de Mamio as it rises past overgrown fields and occasional potato patches. There are a number of chestnut trees alongside the road and standing in clumps on the slopes. At a colourful little roadside shrine, turn right as signposted for Aguamansa. Later, at a crossroads, turn right again for Aguamansa. A bendy stretch of road crosses a couple of water-slips feeding a reservoir that is almost empty and full of tangled undergrowth. Looking uphill, there is a view of the columnar

Crossing a riverbed above a reservoir on the approach to Aguamansa

The little church at Pinolere on the long road-walk up to Aguamansa

cliffs of Los Organos. At a road junction, turn left up to the main road, and the bus stop and water tap. Turn left again to pass the Restaurante Aguamansa, and maybe take another break here if the need is great. The altitude is 1060m (3480ft).

The main road bends right around a trout farm, again with a fine view up to Los Organos. There is also a sign announcing entry to the Parque Natural Corona Forestal. Just behind a bus shelter on the left, a path is signposted for La Caldera. This rises rough and stony among tree heather and pines, passing a mighty pine on one bend. Cross a track and continue up the path. There is a water pipe alongside for a moment, then look out for a narrower path rising to the right. This leads up to a road bend. Keep left to walk up the road to reach **La Caldera**. There is a car park and bus stop, at 1180m (3870ft), as well as a mapboard. The road follows a circuit around a large depression, which is La Caldera, where you will find barbeque sites and children's play equipment. There is also a small bar restaurant, where a break can be taken while waiting for a bus.

WALK 25
La Caldera to El Portillo

Distance:	17km (10½ miles)
Start:	La Caldera
Finish:	Centro de Vistantes at El Portillo
Map:	1:50,000 Military Map Sheet 39-40
Terrain:	Forest tracks and paths give way to scrub-covered mountainsides. The route ends with an easy road-walk gradually downhill to El Portillo.

This walk negotiates a series of forest tracks and paths to emerge on scrub-covered mountainsides above. The strange shapes of the observatories on the high crest of Tenerife often draws attention away from the shapely cone of El Teide. Towards the end of this stretch, however, the mountain commands attention and the route eventually reaches El Portillo, the gateway to the Parque Nacional del Teide. Please refer to the map on p. 139.

From the bus terminus at **La Caldera**, at 1180m (3870ft), either visit the nearby bar restaurant for a drink and a snack, or simply walk along the road that makes a complete circuit around La Caldera. Follow the one-way signs, looking for a sign pointing to a *Zona Acampada*, or campsite, along a forest track. Follow the track past the campsite, where there are two pipes dispensing water. Continue more or less on the level among tall pines, a few laurels, and undergrowth of heather and guelder rose. At the junction at Pasada de las Bestias, turn right to keep following the main track, which is bendy and rises past a waterworks. At a higher junction there is a wooden shelter at **Choza Chimoche**, beside a tall eucalyptus tree.

Follow a path straight uphill through thickets of guelder rose and back into the forest. The path zigzags up a steep and stony slope of pines. At a junction marked as Pasada del Fraile, turn right and immediately left to continue climbing. A zigzag track rises steep and stony to a junction marked as Cuevitas de Limon. Turn left at this point and keep climbing. At the next junction turn sharp left further uphill, then at a higher level swing sharp right and keep climbing. Turn left steeply

Transport: TITSA Bus 245 serves La Caldera from Puerto de la Cruz. TITSA Bus 342 and 348 serve El Portillo from Playa de las Américas and Puerto de la Cruz respectively.

Refreshments: There is a bar restaurant at La Caldera and another one at El Portillo, with others located not far from El Portillo at the end of the day.

up a sparsely forested slope at a junction marked as **La Cumbrita**. There is a metal pole set in a stone base at this point. Climb steeply up the cinder track, zigzagging and enjoying increasingly wide-ranging views beyond the forest.

The pines are small, and the forest cover ends quite suddenly, though the cinder track climbs further uphill. The gradient eases as the track swings left across a barren slope devoid even of scrub. There is scrub later, and looking ahead you will see a wooden hut. Either head directly for the hut, or follow the track, which swings left, then right, to reach it. The shelter is called the **Choza J Ruiz José el de Izaña**. There is a view of the peak of El Teide, as well as a view across the sea to the island of La Palma.

Leave the shelter and simply follow the broad cinder track gently uphill. It has a few bends as it hugs the slopes and plays hide-and-seek with the peak of El Teide and the surreal observatory buildings on the crest above. There is a lot of broom and scrub on the weirdly eroded cinder slopes, and looking downhill you see a line of little volcanic cinder cones roughly arranged in a line across the slope. Follow the track up to a main road at a parking space called **Corral del Niño**. The altitude at this point is 2240m (7350ft).

Turn right down the road and enjoy a view of El Teide for a while. The road bends and there is a track off to the left. Walk past a barrier and head gradually uphill. There is a view of El Teide to the right beyond the gravel plain of **Llano de Maja** at around 2290m (7515ft). Watch carefully on the right for two boulders, and a path pushing through the scrub to reach the plain. Follow a narrow, cairned path to reach a larger cairn and a faded sign. Keep straight on, following the waymarked Sendero 2. This runs level, then gradually drops downhill, steepening as it reaches the rim of Las Cañadas. At the bottom the path is a vague line down through a shallow, bare, gravelly valley. A clear track is reached where you makea right turn. The track crosses the gravelly strip called **Siete Cañadas**, then rises over

Observatory buildings above the cinder slopes on the way to Corral del Niño

the bare shoulder of a hill. Walk down past a barrier to reach a junction with another track. Simply walk down into a dip and up to the main road beside the **Centro de Visitantes El Portillo**, around 2050m (6725ft). If there is plenty of time to spare it is worth finding out about the Parque Nacional del Teide.

For those who are climbing to the summit of El Teide all the way from sea level at Puerta de la Cruz, this is the last day's walk. A desert-like area is crossed shortly after leaving El Portillo, where even the scrub becomes remarkably sparse. A path through the desert links with a good track on the bare slopes of Montaña Blanca. This track, and the path that continues up the final steep and rugged slopes of El Teide, is the only permitted ascent for walkers. Please refer to the map on p. 139. There is a refuge high on the mountain, as well as a cablecar service offering a rapid descent. Bear in mind that a permit is needed to climb to the very top of the mountain. Details of how to obtain the permit are included in the introduction to Walk 27.

WALK 26

El Portillo to El Teide

Distance:	13km (8 miles)
Start:	Centro de Vistantes at El Portillo
Finish:	At the top Teleférico station
Map:	1:50,000 Military Map Sheet 39-40
Terrain:	Clear paths and a track all the way. Easy at first, but some steep and rugged slopes, with altitude possibly becoming a problem towards the end.

Start at the Centro de Visitantes **El Portillo**, at 2050m (6725ft), which offers plenty of information about the Parque Nacional del Teide, and providing a useful map covering the distance to the summit of El Teide. Follow a narrow path just to the left of the entrance lobby of the visitor centre, crossing a concrete water channel. Keep left at an intersection with the Jardin Botanico path, then walk through a gap in a fence. There is a slight descent with a fine view of El Teide ahead. The landscape looks remarkably desert-like. Cross a gravelly depression that is like a garden when the codesa is in bloom, then rise along a path marked as Sendero 1 and 6. Follow the path to a junction and turn left as marked Sendero 6, apparently away from El Teide. After a short walk there is another junction where a right turn leads further along Sendero 6.

The path rises gently and there is plenty of scrub. Later, the gradient steepens and the scrub begins to thin out. Cross a gentle gap and follow the path as it undulates, though the general trend is still uphill. The scrub almost vanishes, leaving only the bare slopes of Montaña Blanca and El Teide ahead. The summit cone of El Teide passes from sight, obscured by the mass of dark lava on its slopes. The path rises more steeply across the arid slopes to join a broad and obvious track on the slopes of Montaña Blanca around 2500m (8200ft). The track is marked as Sendero 7 and as it bends back and forth across the slope, it passes dozens of huge, dark, round boulders. These are *Los Huevos del Teide*, or 'The Eggs of Teide', and were formed when lumps of lava simply detached themselves and rolled downhill ahead of the dark lava flows seen higher up the slopes.

Keep climbing along the track and note the path branching off to the right, where there are a couple of signs amid clumps of yellow flowers at a snout of black lava. Bear in mind that the track could be followed for a few more minutes in a loop around the 2690m (8825ft) summit of **Montaña Blanca**. This is worth considering as there is a chance to see the summit cone of El Teide, which is not visible from the path junction. There is also a fine view around the rest of the national park.

A white, dusty, gravelly path leads in tight zigzags up a steep scree slope. Follow it faithfully and note the long black lava flows to either side of the slope. Looking towards the skyline, it is possible to spot a slender post that marks the position of the Refugio Alta Vista, which is only just out of sight. A clutch of large, dark boulders are reached, a few more of the 'Eggs of Teide'. Continue up a gritty, zigzag path on a slope of gravel, boulders and retama. The path rises onto a slope of reddish lava and is often on bare rock as it zigzags further up the steep slope. There is little vegetation apart from a few clumps of daisy-like plants, but yellow codesa indicates that the path is getting close to the Refugio Alta Vista.

Some walkers climb to this point and stay overnight, completing the ascent of El Teide the next morning. if you want to do so it is essential to book in advance, and at times the refuge may be closed, and only a simple shelter alongside is left open. The refuge has a common room, kitchen, toilets and enough space for 50 people. It stands at 3300m (10,825ft) up the mountain.

Transport: TITSA Bus 342 and 348 serve El Portillo and the Teleférico from Playa de las Américas and Puerto de la Cruz respectively. The Teleférico almost reaches the summit of El Teide, but is frequently closed during high winds.

Refreshments: Bar restaurant at the start at El Portillo. The Refugio Alta Vista sometimes runs out of water and seldom offers food. If using the Teleférico for the descent, food and drink are available at the bottom station.

Looking from the summit of Montaña Blanca towards the peak of El Teide

The path, climbing from the refuge and marked as Sendero 7, is flanked by masses of blocky lava and is gravelly underfoot. Off to the right is an old ice cave. The higher parts of the path are compacted boulders and cobbles. Though they are hard on the feet, they are much better than the huge, angular blocks of lava to either side. There are occasional views of the summit and the path rises through a rocky defile, eventually reaching a junction with another path. Only a few paces to the right is a viewpoint overlooking a fumarole, with a notice explaining how steam and sulphurous gases are emitted from vents on the mountainside. Plants such as *Gnaphalium teydeum* can survive near the fumaroles as the area remains warm and moist in the winter.

Continuing towards the summit, the rough, block-paved path is marked as Sendero 11, and is also known as La Rambleta. It undulates across a slope of blocky lava and squeezes between some immense rocks. Another path junction is reached close to the top station on the Teleférico, where Sendero 10, the Telesforo Brava path, leads to the summit of El Teide. Assuming you are early and aren't able to use your permit yet, continue along the path beyond the Teleférico, marked as Sendero 12. This leads across the slopes to a fine viewpoint overlooking the neighbouring Pico Viejo.

This is more of a wide crater than a peak, and was once filled with a lava lake that periodically overflowed, then subsided. Lava flows poured southwards in 1798, and before that, Teide erupted periodically through the Middle Ages. Looking in the direction of La Palma, Volcán Chinyero, which last erupted in 1909, can be seen. Enjoy the views across the western end of Tenerife, as well as to the islands of La Gomera, El Hierro and La Palma, then walk back past the Teleférico station. Note the gas sampling machine on the way, which checks the amount of carbon dioxide and sulphur dioxide being emitted from the mountain, and there is a distinct whiff of sulphur in the air.

Sendero 10, the Telesforo Brava path to the summit of **El Teide**, is normally roped off and guarded by a ranger. You need to present a valid permit and passport to be allowed onto the path, then simply follow it as it zigzags up the steep and rocky cone. The crater is blindingly white in the full sun, and tinged with green and yellow where sulphur crystals and other minerals are deposited around fumaroles. Again, the air smells sulphury. The path leads to the very highest point of the mountain, at 3718m (12,198ft), then there is no further access to the crater rim. Views are naturally extensive, though the sea of clouds can obscure lowland features. It is usually possible to see the islands of La Gomera, El Hierro, La Palma and Gran Canaria rising above the clouds, but the main attraction is the view over the Cañadas del Teide to the south. This is also the highest point in Spain, standing head and shoulders above anything in the Pyrenees or the Sierra Nevada.

There are only three options available to finish the walk. One is to walk down to the Teleférico station and descend by cablecar in a matter of minutes to the bottom station and the main road. If you aim to catch a bus, then timing will be crucial. Another option is to walk down to the Refugio Alta Vista for the night, and complete the descent the next morning. Finally, and inevitably, if the Teleférico and Refugio Alta Vista are both closed, is a complete reversal of the route back to El Portillo, or to the road at the foot of Montaña Blanca.

WALK 27

Ascent of El Teide

Distance:	10km (6 miles)
Start:	At a roadside car park below Montaña Blanca
Finish:	At the top Teleférico station
Map:	1:50,000 Military Map Sheet 39-40
Terrain:	Clear track and paths all the way, but some steep and rugged slopes, with altitude possibly being a problem towards the end.

To say this is the easiest ascent of El Teide is misleading. This route via Montaña Blanca involves climbing around 1370m (4495ft), with some of the steepest and roughest climbing coming high on the mountain. As the height ranges from 2350m (7710ft) at the roadside, to 3718m (12,198ft) on the summit, there are also the effects of the altitude to consider.

Start the walk at a small parking space beside a big stone mapboard for Montaña Blanca. The mapboard shows the line of a track that loops to Montaña Blanca, and towards the end there is a path leading off to El Teide. Even if you only get as far as Montaña Blanca, it is an interesting and scenic walk. Follow the track up past a barrier and pass a snout of blocky lava. There are only a couple of glimpses of the summit of El Teide, which is hidden from sight for most of the ascent. The crunchy white gravel track continues gently uphill to a junction. Keep to the left to climb gradually uphill, and do not short-cut any of the loops on the track. The route is marked as Sendero 7. When the track begins to bend back and forth across the slope, it passes dozens of huge, dark, round boulders. These are *Los Huevos del Teide*, or 'The Eggs of Teide', and were formed when lumps of lava simply detached themselves and rolled downhill ahead of the dark lava flows seen higher up the slopes.

Keep climbing along the track and note the path branching off to the right, where there are a couple of signs amid clumps of yellow flowers at a snout of black lava. Bear in mind that the track could be followed for a few more minutes in a loop around the 2690m (8825ft) summit of **Montaña Blanca**. This is worth considering as there is a chance to see the summit cone of El Teide, which is not visible from the path junction. There is also a fine view around the rest of the national park.

A white, dusty, gravelly path leads in tight zigzags up a steep scree slope. Follow it faithfully and note the long black lava flows to either side of the slope. Looking towards the skyline, it is possible to spot a slender post that marks the position of the Refugio Alta Vista, which is only just out of sight. A clutch of large, dark boulders are reached, a few more of the 'Eggs of Teide'. Continue up a gritty, zigzag path on a slope of gravel, boulders and retama. The path rises onto a slope of reddish lava and is often on bare rock as it zigzags further up the steep slope. There is little vegetation apart from a few clumps of daisy-like plants, but yellow codesa indicates that the path is getting close to the Refugio Alta Vista.

Some walkers climb to this point and stay overnight, completing the ascent of El Teide the next morning. if you want to do so it is essential to book in advance, and

The walk starts easily enough with a firm gravel track, but higher parts involve mobile scree and uneven blocky lava. Please refer to the map on p. 139.There is the Refugio Alta Vista at 3300m (10,825ft), but if you plan to use this, then make sure it is open and that your name is on a bed. Some people like to climb to the refuge at leisure during the day, then climb to the summit the following morning for sunrise. To reach the summit, you must obtain a permit in advance - see the details below.

Obtaining a permit for the Telesforo Brava

Before you start the ascent of El Teide, you need to obtain a permit to be allowed on the Telesforo Brava, the path climbing the last 150m (490ft) to the highest point on the mountain. To do so, you must go in person, on workday mornings only, to the following address: Parque Nacional del Teide, 4th Floor, Calle Emilio Calzadilla 5, Santa Cruz de Tenerife. Telephone 922-290129, Fax 922-244788. Take a photocopy of your passport, and be ready to tell the staff what day and what time you expect to be on the summit. The permit is issued free, and must be presented with your passport to gain access to the summit at the stated time and date. If your ascent is abandoned on that day, it is usually the case that you can show up at the same time the following day and be allowed to the summit. Beyond that, you need to apply for another permit.

Transport: TITSA Bus 342 and 348 pass the car park below Montaña Blanca and the Teleférico from Playa de las Américas and Puerto de la Cruz respectively. The Teleférico almost reaches the summit of El Teide, but is frequently closed during high winds.

Refreshments: None until you reach the bottom station on the Teleférico. The Refugio Alta Vista sometimes runs out of water and seldom offers food.

at times the refuge may be closed, and only a simple shelter alongside is left open. The refuge has a common room, kitchen, toilets and enough space for 50 people. It stands at 3300m (10,825ft) up the mountain.

The path, climbing from the refuge and marked as Sendero 7, is flanked by masses of blocky lava and is gravelly underfoot. Off to the right is an old ice cave. The higher parts of the path are compacted boulders and cobbles. Though they are hard on the feet, they are much better than the huge, angular blocks of lava to either side. There are occasional views of the summit and the path rises through a rocky defile, eventually reaching a junction with another path. Only a few paces to the right is a viewpoint overlooking a fumarole, with a notice explaining how steam and sulphurous gases are emitted from vents on the mountainside. Plants such as *Gnaphalium teydeum* can survive near the fumaroles as the immediate area remains warm and moist in the winter.

Continuing towards the summit, the rough, block-paved path is marked as Sendero 11, and is also known as La Rambleta. It undulates across a slope of blocky lava and squeezes between some immense rocks. Another path junction is reached close to the top station on the Teleférico, where Sendero 10, the Telesforo Brava path, leads to the summit of El Teide. Assuming you are early and aren't able to use your permit yet, continue along the path beyond the Teleférico, marked as Sendero 12. This leads across the slopes to a fine viewpoint overlooking the neighbouring Pico Viejo.

This is more of a wide crater than a peak, and was once filled with a lava lake that periodically overflowed, then subsided. Lava flows poured southwards in 1798, and before that, Teide erupted periodically through the Middle Ages. Looking in the direction of La Palma, Volcán Chinyero, which last erupted in 1909, can be seen. Enjoy the views across the western end of Tenerife, as well as to the islands of La Gomera, El Hierro and La Palma, then walk back past the Teleférico station. Note the gas sampling machine on the way, which checks the amount of carbon dioxide and sulphur dioxide being

El teide at sunrise seen from the neighbouring summit of Guajara

emitted from the mountain, and there is a distinct whiff of sulphur in the air.

Sendero 10, the Telesforo Brava path to the summit of El Teide, is normally roped off and guarded by a ranger. You need to present a valid permit and passport to be allowed onto the path, then simply follow it as it zigzags up the steep and rocky cone. The crater is blindingly white in the full sun, and tinged with green and yellow where sulphur crystals and other minerals are deposited around fumaroles. Again, the air smells sulphury. The path leads to the very highest point of the mountain, at 3718m (12,198ft), then there is no further

The Refugio Alta Vista at (3300m 10.825 ft) offers basic accommodation

access to the crater rim. Views are naturally extensive, though the sea of clouds can obscure lowland features. It is usually possible to see the islands of La Gomera, El Hierro, La Palma and Gran Canaria rising above the clouds, but the main attraction is the view over the Cañadas del Teide to the south. This is also the highest point in Spain, standing head and shoulders above anything in the Pyrenees or the Sierra Nevada.

There are only three options available to finish the walk. One is to walk down to the Teleférico station and descend by cablecar in a matter of minutes to the bottom station and the main road. If you aim to catch a bus, then timing will be crucial. Another option is to walk down to the Refugio Alta Vista for the night, and complete the descent the next morning. Finally, and inevitably, if the Teleférico and Refugio Alta Vista are both closed, is a complete reversal of the route back to the foot of Montaña Blanca.

WALK 28
El Portillo to Icod el Alto

Distance:	16km (10 miles)
Start:	Centro de Visitantes at El Portillo
Finish:	Mirador El Lance at Icod el Alto
Map:	1:50,000 Military Map Sheet 39-40
Terrain:	Undulating, arid scrub at the start. Forest tracks and paths are used for the descent. The roads at the end of the walk are very steep.

Here is a route for those who like to walk downhill with a vengeance. The walk starts at El Portillo and explores a small part of the Parque Nacional del Teide. Undulating terrain at the beginning obscures the broad, desert-like Cañada de los Guancheros and the cliffs of La Fortaleza, but both are seen at close quarters in due course. After crossing a gap, the route makes use of forest tracks and linking paths to drop nearly 1800m (5900ft), eventually reaching a road with a bus service at Icod el Alto. Please refer to the map on p. 139. Judging by recent work on some of the forest tracks, it wouldn't be surprising if most of this route was one day covered in tarmac, so walk it while it is still largely free of vehicles.

This walk can be started either at the Restaurante El Portillo, if food and drink are required, or from the national park visitor centre just up the road. If there is time, then explore the visitor centre to appreciate what the Parque Nacional del Teide is all about, and get an insight into the complexities of volcanic action in the area. Follow a path just to the left of the entrance ramp into the visitor centre, crossing a concrete water channel. Keep left at an intersection with the Jardin Botanico path, then walk through a gap in a fence. There is a slight descent with a view of El Teide ahead. The landscape looks remarkably desert-like. Cross a gravelly depression that is rather like a garden when the codesa is in bloom, then rise along a path marked as Sendero 1 and 6. Stone seats are available at scenic viewpoints along the way. Follow the path to a junction with a clear track and turn right as marked Sendero 1.

Cross a shoulder alongside the shapely **Roque del Peral**, then walk gently downhill. Cross a scrubby cañada and note the ranks of pines away to the right. The path climbs and undulates, then drops down onto the desert-like Cañada de los Guancheros, where very little grows. The cliffs of the Riscos de la Fortaleza rise

Transport: TITSA Bus 342 and 348 serve El Portillo from Playa de las Américas and Puerto de la Cruz respectively. TITSA Bus 354 serves Icod el Alto, linking with Puerto de la Cruz and Icod de los Vinos.

Refreshments: The Restaurante El Portillo is near the Centro de Visitantes. The Restaurante Mirador El Lance is at the end of the walk.

above it. Keep to the right and watch carefully for a path climbing uphill a short way, crossing a gap at the **Collada Degollada del Cedro**, where a few pines can be seen. There is a small shrine and shelter among the pines as well as a turning space in the bare gravel at the end of a dirt road. Take a last look back at the cone of El Teide, which will soon be lost to view.

Turn right to follow the dirt road away from the turning space. Watch out for a lesser track branching off down to the left, and follow it, though it has a corrugated surface and proves awkward underfoot. There are pines to the left while the slope on the right is covered in scrub. The track weaves about on the slope, then runs more directly down the **Lomo La Burra**, clipping a corner of the dirt road. Cross over and keep walking straight downhill. Keep straight on at a junction. The track drops down into the pine forest, almost clips the dirt road, then swings to the right and almost runs along the level for a while.

Looking through the trees to the right, you will be aware of a steep drop into the broad Valle de la Orotava. Continue steeply downhill, sometimes on a bendy course, but generally near the steep edge, though without much of a view. You will pass a wide and scrubby swathe and a tiny wayside shrine alongside the track. Little clumps of heather feature in the undergrowth. A junction is reached with a bend on the dirt road at the **Piedra de los Pastores**, where there is also a shelter. There are signposts pointing in all directions, but you simply continue straight downhill, as indicated, towards Chanajiga.

The dirt road winds downhill, and you should keep following it, this time avoiding the path signposted for Chanajiga. While 'improving' the track, forest workers have planted a variety of little trees and shrubs alongside, including a few arbutus. From time to time the other dirt road is seen off to the left, but whenever there is an intersection, keep right and keep winding downhill. The pine forest begins to feature a 'laurisilva' understorey of laurels and tree heather. When a complex

Underground entrance to the National Park Visitor Centre at El Portillo

junction of dirt roads is reached, Los Llanadas and Los Realejos are signposted to the right, leading further downhill. As usual, keep to the broad dirt road and keep winding, noting the transition from pines to 'laurisilva', then sparse 'laurisilva' and bracken. Some of the undergrowth has been cleared and the margins of the dirt road have been planted with a greater variety of trees and shrubs. When a signposted junction is reached, any traffic is likely to head left, as marked for the Pista General Icod el Alto.

Walk straight downhill from the junction, following a narrow path. A lot of this route was once a narrow path, before being widened to accommodate vehicles. When other tracks and dirt roads are reached, always keep to the right, noting tall eucalyptus among the other trees on the crest. Head towards a prominent transmitter mast on a hill-top at **El Asomadero** along a concrete access road to where there are lovely views over the green and well-settled Valle de la Orotava. The view stretches all the way from the sea at Puerto de la Cruz up to the summit of El Teide, and so it makes a great vantage point for anyone considering the full ascent as described in Walks 23, 24, 25 and 26.

Keep walking down steep tracks and keep to the right at intersections, always aiming to walk roughly parallel to the steep edge. However, do not turn right into

A storm and rainbow seen from the Mirador El Lance at Icod el Alto

another stand of transmitter masts, but keep walking downhill towards yet another series of masts at **La Corona**. There is a shrine and a splendid viewpoint just to the right, and for the adventurous, a steep and winding rocky path leading down to the road far below. It is better to backtrack a little from the shrine to reach a nearby car park, then walk down the minor road. Turn right at a junction, following an empty road that becomes crowded with houses. It is called the Calle El Lance and by degrees it becomes steeper and steeper. Turn right down another steep road to land down on a busy main road at **Icod el Alto**. Turn sharp right and beware of the traffic on an awkward bend. There is a lay-by and bus stop at the **Mirador El Lance**, as well as the Restaurante Mirador El Lance. While waiting for the bus, enjoy a drink and a snack and take in the wonderful views over the Valle de la Orotava.

WALK 29

Las Cañadas

Distance:	17km (10½ miles)
Start:	Centro de Vistantes at El Portillo
Finish:	Parador Cañadas del Teide
Maps:	1:50,000 Military Map Sheets 39-40 and 39-41
Terrain:	An easy gravel track rises gently through desert-like terrain in the high mountains.

Transport:
TITSA Bus 342 and 348 serve El Portillo and the Parador from Playa de las Américas and Puerto de la Cruz respectively.

Refreshments:
The Restaurante El Portillo is near the Centro de Visitantes. The Cafeteria Los Roques is alongside the Parador.

This walk can be started either at the Restaurante El Portillo, if food and drink are required, or from the national park visitor centre just up the road. If there is time, then it is worth exploring the visitor centre to learn about the Parque Nacional del Teide. The walk starts on the other side of the main road, where a track is signposted for Siete Cañadas. The altitude is 2050m (6275ft).

TENERIFE
Walks 29–35
Parque Natural Corona Forestal
El Portillo
2050m
Centro de Visitantes
Walk 35
Cerrillar
Llano de Maja 2290m
Siete Cañadas
Walk 29
Walk 35
Laderas del Teide
El Teide
3718m
Teleférico
Parque Nacional del Teide
Cañada de Diego Hernandez
Cañada de las Pilas
Risco Verde
Las Cañadas
Walk 30
2194m
Montaña Majua
Los Aljibes
Walk 29
Mesa del Obispo
Walk 35
Walk 30
Walk 31
Roques de Garcia
Walk 29
2200m
Topo de la Grieta
Roque de la Grieta
Parador
Walk 32
Montaña Pasajiron
2414m
Degollada de Ucanca
2715m
Guajara
N
Walk 34
Walk 33
Walk 33
Valle de Ucanca
Paisaje Lunar
Walk 34
Parque Natural Corona Forestal
1580m
Pista Forestal
1500m
VILAFLOR
SCALE
0 1 2 3 kms
0 1 2 miles
3500m
3000m
2500m
2000m
1500m
1000m
500m
sea level

Two waymarked routes follow this track, gently downhill, then gently uphill. They are Sendero 2 and Sendero 4. Keep to the right at a junction, still rising gently and following these markers. There is a slight descent to **Siete Cañadas**, then the track undulates gently. Enjoy views of El Teide, as well as the slopes to the left, which gradually become higher and more and more rugged as the walk proceeds. The track across Las Cañadas to the Parador is Sendero 4.

The track makes its way across the **Cañada de Diego Hernández**, gradually pulling away from the main road, which is glimpsed only occasionally. Look out for a prominent cave on the left; the Cueva de Diego Hernández. The rocky prow of Risco Verde rises ahead, as the track passes reddish, spiky rocks as it turns around the foot of the mountain. Big angular boulders lie on the slope, while the track makes its way across the **Cañada de las Pilas**. Beyond the gravel flats are what appear to be heaps of boulders dotted with retama bushes. Having passed a rocky bluff as you keep gently climbing , your attention is now drawn more to the prominent peak ahead, which is La Angostura, with the Cañada de la Angostura at its foot. After passing this peak and crossing the Cañada del Cogonito, the much larger Cañada de la Grieta comes into view. This broad, gravelly plain is dotted with small buildings, as are the rugged slopes of Topo de la Grieta. These were used by shepherds and their flocks as shelter when Las Cañadas was used for summer grazing.

When climbing away from the ruins, note the giant *tajinaste*, or echiums, on the rocky slopes. These plants were once sadly depleted, but have flourished since grazing in the national park was banned. Climb up through the narrow Cañada de la Camellita and cross a gap to face the rugged mountain called Guajara, which is the highest point on the rugged rim. Approach the foot of the mountain by walking across the Cañada del Monton de Trigo. The track runs past a buttress of rock where more *tajinaste* grow, then crosses a crest and reaches a junction with another track. Keep

This walk is ideal for anyone who wants to get a feel for the Parque Nacional del Teide with little effort. A fine gravel track works its way from El Portillo to the Parador Cañadas del Teide. The ascent is gradual and there is a chance to appreciate the scale of the shapely cone of El Teide that looms large over the desert-like landscape. This walk, coupled with one or two others in the area, can be used to acclimatise before tackling an ascent of El Teide. The whole area was once covered with a fine gravelly pumice, but eruptions of El Teide caused most parts to be filled with red, blocky lava and dark, ropy lava. The track followed on this walk includes views of lava snouts, which solidified before completely engulfing the gravelly plains on the southern side of Las Cañadas. Please refer to the map on p. 164.

The track passes awesome rock formations on the route to the Parador

straight on at this junction, although it's worth bearing in mind that you could turn right and walk all the way to the Teleférico on El Teide by using the other track. The altitude is 2200m (7220ft).

To reach the Parador, follow the track marked as Sendero 4, running down past towers of rock. The track wriggles and bends, but if you keep an eye open you can short-cut a prominent bend. Weird and wonderful rock outcrops buttress the lower slopes of **Guajara**, coming in vivid colours and strange shapes. There is a view of the Parador, a nearby chapel, and the remarkable peaks of the Roques de Garcia rising across the Cañada Blanca. The track lands on a road and you walk past a small building where a few cars are usually parked. Watch carefully for a path on the right, which is rough, stony and narrow. Follow it across a gentle slope of scrub and drift to the left, then later turn right to walk towards the **Parador**, at 2150m (7050ft). Of immediate interest is a cafeteria open to the public, and often quite crowded with visitors, but there is also an interesting little visitor centre that offers plenty of information about the national park and some of its most important features.

WALK 30

Montaña Majua

Distance:	11km (6¾ miles)
Start/Finish:	Parador Cañadas del Teide
Map:	1:50,000 Military Map Sheets 39-40 and 39-41
Terrain:	Undulating, dry, stony and scrubby slopes. The path can be vague at first, but quickly becomes clearer. The tracks are plain and obvious to follow.

A fairly level circular walk along a rugged path and good tracks can be enjoyed from the Parador Cañadas del Teide. Sendero 19 crosses the barren Cañada Blanca between the Parador and the foot of El Teide. After turning round the slopes of Montaña Majua near the Teleférico station, a good track marked as Sendero 16 leads through an awesomely rugged area of blocky lava flows around Los Aljibes. The track runs to the foot of Guajara, then another track marked as Sendero 4 leads back to the Parador. Please see the map on p. 164.

Start at the **Parador Cañadas del Teide**, at 2150m (7050ft). Walk a few paces along the road in the direction of El Teide, and Sendero 4 is marked off to the right. This quickly links with Sendero 19, which heads left, directly towards El Teide, and although vague at first, it is much clearer as it crosses the level, stone-strewn Cañada Blanca. The path is sandy, then a little more rugged as it hugs the margin of a lava flow. It gradually rises towards the foot of El Teide, and the lower Teleférico station makes a good reference point.

There is really only one intersection with another path, where you take the left turn to follow the waymarked path. The path is easier as it rises gently alongside the pumice slopes of **Montaña Majua**, and eventually it reaches a junction with a clear track. Walkers might like to nip up to the top of Montaña Majua at this point, a walk that takes only a couple of minutes. A sign warns of beehives in the vicinity. The summit at 2194m (7198ft) is completely dwarfed by El Teide.

Transport: TITSA Bus 342 and 348 serve the Parador from Playa de las Américas and Puerto de la Cruz respectively.

Refreshments: The Cafeteria Los Roques is alongside the Parador.

The route crosses lava flows between Guajara and El Teide

Turn right down the track, away from the main road, with blocky lava flows to the left and right. The track descends gently in a straight line, then rises a little, then descends again. Note the curious half-buried structures to the right, known as Los Aljibes, which are used for water storage. Avoid turnings to right and left, which are in any case marked 'Danger Bee Hives'. After turning round a pronounced corner the track rises again. It is all very straightforward and there are occasional markers for the Sendero 16 . The rugged mountain of Guajara is often seen ahead, except when obscured briefly by masses of jagged lava. Some sections of the track are quite bendy. Avoid lesser turnings that lead to a huddle of old buildings on the right or more bee hives. The track reaches a junction with another prominent track at the foot of **Guajara**, at 2200m (7220ft).

Turn right to follow the track marked as Sendero 4, running down past towers of rock. The track wriggles and bends, but if you keep an eye open you can short-cut a prominent bend. Weird and wonderful rock out-crops buttress the lower slopes of Guajara, coming in vivid colours and strange shapes. There is a view of the Parador, a nearby chapel, and the remarkable peaks of the Roques de Garcia rising across the Cañada Blanca. The track lands on a road and you walk past a small building where a few cars are sometimes parked. Watch carefully for a path on the right, which is rough, stony and narrow. Follow it across a gentle slope of scrub and drift to the left, then later turn right to walk towards the **Parador**. There is a cafeteria open to the public, as well as an interesting little visitor centre highlighting points of interest in the area.

WALK 31

Roques de Garcia

Distance:	4km (2½ miles)
Start/Finish:	Parador Cañadas del Teide
Map:	1:50,000 Military Map Sheet 39-41
Terrain:	A clear and fairly easy path, with a few short, steep and rocky parts.

Transport:
TITSA Bus 342 and 348 serve the Parador from Playa de las Américas and Puerto de la Cruz respectively.

Refreshments:
The Cafeteria Los Roques is alongside the Parador.

This walk can be started from the **Parador Cañadas del Teide**, or from the long car park across the main road. Either way, spend a few moments wandering round the various viewpoints first. Flights of steps and stone-paved stances may be crowded with visitors when coach tours

Sometimes it seems a continual procession of walkers encircles the Roques de Garcia, but it is possible to have the place to yourself early and late in the day. The curious rocky ridge is broken into buttresses and tall pinnacles, yet there is a path leading round the site that is fairly easy to follow. Please refer to the map on p. 164. Many casual visitors go no further than the viewpoints near the car park, then promptly retire to the nearby cafeteria at the Parador. This walk is short and easy enough to be attempted before or after other walks in the area.

roll in, but sometimes things are quieter. Some areas have been roped off to prevent erosion. There are notices offering explanations of the formation of the Roques de Garcia, and the separate little peak known as La Catedral. A flight of stone steps allow a good view of the curiously contorted, top-heavy pinnacle called the Roque Cinchado, among other names, with the massive bulk of El Teide rising beyond.

Follow a broad and gritty path away from the car park and viewpoints, passing below the Roque Cinchado and all the other buttresses and pinnacles. Walk slowly and observe how the rock formations seem to alter every few paces. The path is marked as Sendero 3 and it is a photographer's delight. The way becomes narrower and many casual explorers turn back to the car park. The rest keep shuffling forward, virtually on the level, despite the sheer rockfaces towering above. The Parador can be seen across the scrub-covered Cañada Blanca, but later it is lost to view. A wall of jagged, blocky lava is seen, but the path crosses darker tongues of ropy lava, which spewed from Pico Viejo in 1798. The path climbs and turns round the Torre Blanco, which is a gleaming bright tower of rock.

As the path starts to descend steep and rocky for a while, look back up to the Torre Blanco to see a dark lava flow that once poured through a gap. The path is rugged, but levels out and again features splendid views of the Roques de Garcia, which are taller on this side. Ahead rises La Catedral, with a curious polygonal buttress in front of the actual peak. Keep to the left of La Catedral to follow the path uphill. The line is vague in places, but still marked as Sendero 3 and leads back up to the car park.

The Roque Cinchado – the most curious of the Roques de Garcia

WALK 32

Ascent of Guajara

The third highest mountain on Tenerife rises rough and rocky from Las Cañadas, facing the noble cone of El Teide. At 2715m (8907ft) Guajara offers the chance to acclimatise before considering the ascent of El Teide, but it is well worth climbing for its own sake and many would agree that it was a finer mountain than its higher neighbour. The slopes are steep and rocky, with a danger of rockfall, so take care. A relatively straightforward circuit over the mountain can be enjoyed from the Parador, maybe leaving the rest of the day free for another walk in the area. Please refer to the map on p. 164.

Distance:	9km (5½ miles)
Start/Finish:	Parador Cañadas del Teide
Map:	1:50,000 Military Map Sheet 39-41
Terrain:	A rough and rocky path, exposed in places, with a danger of rockfall. The descent is less rough and rocky, but still needs care. Easy tracks and paths lead back to the start.

Start at the Parador Cañadas del Teide, at 2150m (7050ft), or from the parking space nearby. If there is time, explore the Centro de Visitantes attached to the Parador, which contains a lot of information about the area. A narrow and stony path leads away from a map-board near the Centro de Visitantes, in the direction of Guajara. Follow this path, turning left and right to reach a narrow road. Simply cross the road to find the path continuing for Guajara. Climb up a slope covered in scrub and swing right towards a bright, dusty path. This path proceeds up a blunt ridge covered in broom, apparently heading for a rock wall on the skyline. When the path reaches a rocky nose it climbs further, then slices up to the right to avoid the rock wall. Turning left, it reaches a high crest, where a short walk downhill leads onto a gap called the **Degollada de Ucanca**, at 2414m (7920ft).

Follow the path towards Guajara, threading a way between clumps of broom and passing a few little pines. The path doesn't aim directly for the summit, but cuts across slopes of boulders and blindingly white, gritty slopes. The route rises along a terrace beneath a cliff face prone to rockfalls. Note the black, glassy obsidian blocks lying around. Keep climbing, but watch out for a level shoulder where there is a splendid view over Las Cañadas. The last part of the ascent is over huge, angular boulders, then a network of paths converge on the summit of **Guajara** at 2715m (8907ft). There is a walled enclosure that should provide shelter whatever direction the wind blows. The broad slopes and shapely cone of El Teide dominates the view, then the eye takes in the levels of Las Cañadas, with southern Tenerife falling beyond. In clear weather the islands of El Hierro, La Palma, La Gomera and Gran Canaria can be seen. There may be daisy-like clumps of flowers around the summit.

Follow a gentle path down from the summit, heading roughly eastwards. It starts zigzagging and becomes, gritty, dusty and blindingly white underfoot. Cross a stony slope and drop down to a gap where soft white and ochreous rocks are eroded into weird shapes, with black obsidian nodules protruding. While it is possible to turn left down a path, the preferred route is around a hump and down to an adjacent gap before making a descent to Las Cañadas. The second path to the left offers a gentler descent, though it is still gritty, dusty and white underfoot. It leads down a rugged, scrubby slope to land on a clear track at the bottom. Turn left to follow the track and notice the fine *tajinaste* that grow alongside it.

The track crosses a crest and reaches a junction with another track at 2200m (7220ft). Keep straight on at this junction, although it is worth bearing in mind that you could turn right and walk all the way to the Teleférico on El Teide by using the other track. To continue towards the Parador, follow the track marked as Sendero 4, running down past towers of rock. The track wriggles and bends, but if you keep an eye open you can short-cut a prominent bend. Weird and wonderful rock outcrops buttress the lower slopes of Guajara, coming in vivid colours and strange shapes. There is a view of the Parador, a nearby chapel, and the remarkable peaks of the Roques de Garcia rising across the

Transport:
TITSA Bus 342 and 348 serve the Parador from Playa de las Americas and Puerto de la Cruz respectively.

Refreshments:
The Cafeteria Los Roques is alongside the Parador.

Climbing to Guajara with the flat and gravelly Llano de Ucanca in the background

Cañada Blanca. The track lands on a road and you walk past a small building where a few cars can be parked. Watch carefully for a path on the right, which is rough, stony and narrow. This path was followed at the outset, so simply retrace steps to return to the Parador.

WALK 33
Circuit of Gaujara

Distance:	13km (8 miles)
Start/Finish:	Parador Cañadas del Teide
Map:	1:50,000 Military Map Sheet 39-41
Terrain:	Steep and rocky slopes at the start, then gentler slopes on the southern side of Guajara. There is a steep and rugged descent before an easy end to the walk along good tracks and paths.

As Walk 32 covers the ascent of Guajara from the Parador, this walk omits the rock-bound summit and instead crosses the gaps to either side. It allows an exploration of the Valle de Ucanca and passes within sight of the Paisaje Lunar before climbing barren cinder slopes to return towards Guajara. For those whose only reason for not climbing Guajara was the thought of scrambling along an exposed terrace, there is the option to reach the summit by a much easier route on the way back to the Parador via the Degollada de Guajara. Please see the map on p. 164.

Start at the Parador Cañadas del Teide, at 2150m (7050ft), or from the parking space nearby. If there is time, explore the Centro de Visitantes attached to the Parador, which contains relevant information about the area. The Cafeteria Los Roques offers food and drink at the start. A narrow and stony path leads away from a mapboard near the Centro de Visitantes, in the direction of Guajara. Follow this path through arid scrub, turning left and right to reach a narrow road. Simply cross the road to find the path continuing for Guajara. Climb up a slope covered in scrub and swing right towards a bright, dusty path. This path proceeds up a blunt ridge covered in broom, apparently heading for a rock wall on the skyline. When the path reaches a rocky nose it climbs further, then slices up to the right to avoid the rock wall, passing a lonesome pine. Turning left, it reaches a high crest, where a short walk downhill leads onto a gap called the **Degollada de Ucanca** at 2414m (7920ft).

Cross over the gap and look carefully to spot the path running down the **Valle de Ucanca** on the far side. The path runs along the left-hand side of the valley and soon passes a *galeria*, from where a water pipe runs

Transport: TITSA Bus 342 and 348 serve the Parador from Playa de las Américas and Puerto de la Cruz respectively.

Refreshments: The Cafeteria Los Roques is alongside the Parador.

downhill. The path and the pipe pursue parallel courses down through the valley, but stop and look carefully whenever the line becomes vague. There is a peak in view ahead, the Roque del Encaje, which appears to block the valley mouth. Guajara rises steep and rocky to the left, in awesome tiered cliffs. There are plenty of *tajinaste*, or giant echiums beside the path. Pines are numerous, but rather scattered, offering little in the way of shade. A small water regulating hut is reached, where a draught of water might be obtained.

An old, narrow water channel leaves the hut and, though it is tempting to follow it, the path runs below it for a while before rising across the old channel, as marked by yellow arrows, and drifting uphill away from the channel. The ground is cindery underfoot and the path rises among pines, levelling out before descending. There is often a view of the steep and cindery slopes of Montaña de las Arenas to the left and a rough and jagged lava flow to the right. All of a sudden, the narrow path becomes a broad track, descending the steep and cindery, pine-covered slopes of Montaña de las Arenas.

As soon as the track levels out briefly at a break of slope, around 2000m (6560ft), exit to the left along a vague and narrow path. If you miss this turning, then as soon as you see the broken water channel again to the right, turn left immediately to pick up the path. Either way, turn left again up another path signposted for the Paisaje Lunar and Degollada de Guajara. Walk up the path a short way to reach another junction. At this point the **Paisaje Lunar** is down to the right, while the Degollada de Guajara is up to the left. Turn left up the rugged cinder path and it soon changes to finer cinders, which are soft underfoot. There is a small viewpoint off to the right that looks down on the curious, bright, fluted columns of the Paisaje Lunar. Follow the path up out of the pines and cross the bare, black, cindery shoulder of Montaña de las Arenas.

A *barranco* lies ahead, with pink rock walls exposed beneath the black cinders on either side. Follow the path down into the *barranco* and up the other side, crossing a

A view over the level Llano de Ucanca on the way up to Guajara

black cinder desert where hardly anything grows. The path is marked by parallel lines of short wooden stakes. When you reach a junction turn left and follow the path. The path is flanked by parallel lines of stones and climbs steadily up the slope of black cinders. Looking back down the slope, a number of little cinder cones can be seen towards the coast. Looking ahead, green pines and the pink rocky slopes of Guajara rise above, making a pleasing colour scheme. When the pines are reached, the path becomes rather rough and stony underfoot, but becomes clearer further uphill. Climbing above the pines, the path swings to the right to cross a bouldery little valley. Keep following the path and it descends slightly to reach a small metal post at a junction.

(A left turn at this point reveals the easiest path leading to the summit of **Guajara**. If this option is chosen, then the summit can be gained within 1km (½ mile), and the extra time it takes is repaid with a splendid view. If visiting the summit, then refer to Walk 32 for the descent.)

If not visiting the summit of Guajara, then turn right at the metal post and follow the path across an increasingly rugged slope, then let an easier path lead onwards to the gap called the Degollada de Guajara at 2373m (7785ft). Look out for a cairn on the gap, then turn left down a steep path. The path is gritty, dusty and white underfoot. It leads down a rugged, scrubby slope to land on a clear track at the bottom. Turn left to follow the track and notice the fine *tajinaste* that grow alongside it. The track crosses a crest and reaches a junction with another track, at 2200m (7220ft).

Keep straight on at this junction, following the track marked as Sendero 4, running down past towers of rock at the foot of Guajara. The track wriggles and bends, but if you keep an eye open you can short-cut a prominent bend. Weird and wonderful rock outcrops buttress the lower slopes of Guajara, coming in vivid colours and strange shapes. There is a view of the Parador, a nearby chapel, and the remarkable peaks of the Roques de Garcia rising across the Cañada Blanca. The track lands on a road and you walk past a small building where a few cars can be parked. Watch carefully for a path on the right, which is rough, stony and narrow. It leads across a rugged patch of scrub to the Parador. Watch for it bending to the left, then at a path junction, head right to reach the **Parador**.

WALK 34

Las Cañadas to Vilaflor

Distance:	20km (12 miles)
Start:	Parador Cañadas del Teide
Finish:	Vilaflor
Map:	1:50,000 Military Map Sheet 39-41
Terrain:	Mountainous, with a steep and rugged ascent at the start and gentler slopes beyond. The latter stages are along forest paths and tracks, giving way to a road-walk at the end.

Transport: TITSA Bus 342 serves the Parador and Vilaflor from Playa de las Américas. TITSA Bus 348 serves the Parador from Puerto de la Cruz.

Refreshments: The Cafeteria Los Roques is alongside the Parador. There are several bar restaurants in Vilaflor.

This walk runs from the Parador Cañadas del Teide, over a rugged gap beside Guajara, down to the historic little town of Vilaflor. It includes some splendid views of Las Cañadas, as well as a barren, black slope of cinders and a visit to an intriguing place known as the Paisaje Lunar. To be blunt, the slope of black cinders probably has more in common with the Moon's surface than the Paisaje Lunar. The latter part of the walk involves following a long forest road, looping around a handful of rugged valleys on the way to Vilaflor. Please refer to the map on p. 164

Start at the Parador Cañadas del Teide, at 2150m (7050ft), or from the parking space nearby. If there is time, explore the Centro de Visitantes attached to the Parador, which contains a lot of information about the area. The Cafeteria Los Roques offers food and drink at the start. A narrow and stony path leads away from a mapboard near the Centro de Visitantes, in the direction of **Guajara**. Follow this path through arid scrub, turning left and right to reach a narrow road. Turn left to follow the road to a small building where a few cars can be parked, then continue along a broad and clear track. There are weird and wonderful rock outcrops on the lower slopes of Guajara, coming in vivid colours and strange shapes. The track wriggles and bends, but if you keep your eye open you can short-cut a prominent bend. Continue along the track, passing towers of rock to reach a junction with another track, at 2200m (7220ft). Keep straight on here, past a buttress of rock where *tajinaste* grow, and walk downhill a short way.

Watch carefully to spot a path rising to the right, leading up the steep and rugged slopes, stony and dusty underfoot, aiming for a high gap. The gap is the Degollada de Guajara, and it is useful to keep to the left while climbing to it, avoiding paths climbing more steeply to the right. When the gap is reached, at 2373m (7785ft), turn right and follow a clear path that keeps to the left side of the crest. The path picks its way past yellow eroded rocks, then climbs alongside a valley called the Barranco del Río. The island of Gran Canaria sails into view in the mouth of the valley. A path junction is reached at a metal pole. A right turn here can be used to reach the summit of Guajara, otherwise keep left to descend from the mountain.

The path marked with paint blobs and arrows rises and is clear enough to follow. It swings to the right into a bouldery little valley, then continues left. Although the path has been dug from a slope covered in boulders, there are still plenty of boulders underfoot. It leads down onto a slope sparsely covered in pines. Looking ahead, a black and barren slope can be observed, and looking far ahead, little cinder cones can be seen near the coast. The steep and cindery slopes of Montaña de las Arenas rise to the right. The line of the path is marked with parallel lines of stones where it forges down a slope of black cinders. Looking back, the green pines and the pink rocky slopes of Guajara rise above, making a pleasing colour scheme. Looking down, the path runs straight into a pine forest, then drifts left and zigzags down a steep and stony slope.

Guelder rose grows between the pines. As the slope eases slightly, turn right along a path and drop steeply down into the *barranco.* Watch carefully for the line of the path, which is vague in places and very stony, though it later levels out and follows a cindery crest to a small ruin and a huge pine. At this point you can see the strangely fluted and light-coloured pumice columns of the **'Paisaje Lunar'**. Follow a path steeply down into the ravine from the huge pine. You will slip and slide on pumice and pine needles so, while hanging on to tree branches, watch out for tree roots. The path quickly leads into the ravine at the foot of the columns, giving another view of this feature.

Follow the path out of the *barranco,* uphill a little, then downhill. Take a rugged path to the right to stay close to the *barranco,* which you overlook from a cindery spur. A water pipe leads away from the *barranco* with the path alongside it. This is a useful feature to follow; before long a few cabins can be seen through the trees. The path drops down onto a track. Turn right just to clip a bend on the track, then follow a path more directly past the cabins to reach the site office. There are sheltered picnic tables and a water tap. The entrance/exit to the site is just below. The altitude is 1525m (5000ft).

Follow the dirt road away from the entrance and turn right for Vilaflor. A signposted junction with another broad road, the **Pista Forestal Madre del Agua**, is reached. Turn right to Vilaflor (though it is not signposted). The road gradually rises and there are glimpses of Guajara high above the pine slopes. On a bend at La

Rough and rocky terrain on the descent from the Degollada de Guajara

Florida there is a big sign for the Paisaje Lunar, the Valle de Ucanca and Degollada de Guajara. Follow the road a bit further uphill, then descend and keep left at a junction. At the municipal boundary there is a bouldery *barranco* and a fine view up to the mountains. The road crosses a gentle rise and passes between an old ruined farm and its former threshing floor.

The road bends in and out of prominent valleys, such as the Barranco de las Mesas. Rise across the valley side and pass a reservoir before turning into the next valley. Pass a ruin at the head of the valley and later overlook the cultivated area, also getting a better view of Vilaflor on the way out of the valley. Follow the dirt road round one last big valley, then turn a final bend to reach a junction with a main road on Lomo Blanco. Follow the main road, which is very bendy, down a steep pine-covered slope to Vilaflor. Buses travelling along here will only stop if it is safe to do so. Just before reaching Vilaflor there is a road bend with two notable big pines. The Pino Gordo is down to the left and the Pino de las Dos Pernadas is up to the right.

Parallel lines of stones mark the path down a soft slope of cinders

At a road junction turn left to **Vilaflor**, or Vilaflor de Chasna, to use its full name. It claims to be the highest village in Spain at 1500m (4920ft). Walking from the top to the bottom of the village you pass the Fuente Alta bottled water plant. You will then move into the old part of Vilaflor, founded in the 16th century by Pedro Soler de Padilla. The stout stone Santuario-Convento del Hermano Pedro has recently been restored and stands on the birthplace of Hermano Pedro de San Jose de Bethencourt. He was born in 1626 and died following extensive missionary work in Guatemala in 1667. The church of San Pedro stands at the top of a sloping plaza where there are a couple of bar restaurants. Keep walking down through the village to pass more bar restaurants, traditional craft shops, a *pension* and hotel. At the point where the road through the village rejoins the main road there are bus stops.

WALK 35
The Cañadas Rim

Distance:	24km (15 miles)
Start:	Centro de Visitantes at El Portillo
Finish:	Parador Cañadas del Teide
Maps:	1:50,000 Military Map Sheets 39-40 and 39-41
Terrain:	Fairly easy tracks and paths at first, though in the latter stages the mountain paths are rough and rocky. Easy tracks again towards the end. Most of the route is in the mountains and far removed from habitation.

Though Walk 29 is the regular walk from El Portillo to the Parador Cañadas del Teide, there is another along the rocky rim of Las Cañadas. There are broad tracks at this higher level, and even when these peter out, there are rugged paths leading over and between the peaks. The Parque Nacional del Teide used to stretch only to the high crest bounding Las Cañadas, but a recent extension has brought the southern slopes under national park protection. This route doesn't visit any summits on the high crest, but weaves between them, offering splendid views from the gaps along the way. Please refer to the map on p. 164. If aiming to complete this walk between bus services, keep a close watch on progress.

This walk can be started either at the Restaurante El Portillo, if food and drink are required, or from the national park visitor centre just up the road. If there is time, it is worth exploring the visitor centre to appreciate what the Parque Nacional del Teide is all about, and get an insight into the complexities of volcanic action in the area. The walk starts on the other side of the main road, where a track is signposted for Siete Cañadas. The altitude is 2050m (6725ft). Two waymarked routes follow this track, gently downhill, then gently uphill. They are Sendero 2 and Sendero 4. Keep left at a junction, still rising gently and following the markers for Sendero 2.

Easy loops rise on the arid, scrubby slopes of **Montaña Cerrillar**. A sign warns of bee hives and at times the track dwindles to a narrow path squeezing past clumps of retama. As the path swings round the slope and gains height, there are views down to the populated north coast, while El Teide's cone passes from sight. The path suddenly swings right across the slope, then left to pass a little rockface. The gleaming white observatory

Transport: TITSA Bus 342 and 348 serve El Portillo and the Parador from Playa de las Américas and Puerto de la Cruz respectively.

Refreshments: The Restaurante El Portillo is near the Centro de Visitantes. The Cafeteria Los Roques is alongside the Parador.

buildings on the high crest at Izaña are arranged along the skyline.

The path rises over a gentle gap and El Teide appears again, along with a fine view all the way round Las Cañadas. Guajara and neighbouring peaks are seen in the distance. Remember that the walk is going all that way too, so it is rather alarming to find the path drifting away from those peaks, and even turning its back on El Teide. A cairn is reached on the stone-strewn plain called **Llano de Maja**, and at this point there is a small marker for Sendero 2. There is a faded warning about proceeding directly ahead, but continue walking anyway, following a narrow, cairned path across the gravelly expanse. When the path pushes through scrub at the far side, it suddenly joins a broad and clear track.

Turn right to follow the track gently uphill, keeping left at a fork, to reach a broad and gentle gap at the Collado Degollado de Abreo. There is a wayside cross to the left and the altitude is 2314m (7592ft). Follow the track gently downhill and be sure to stay on the most obvious line, avoiding lesser tracks to left and right. The aim is to follow the rugged mountain rim of Las Cañadas, aiming for the highest ground ahead at all times. The track runs close to the rim and it is worth making short detours from time to time for a view over the edge. Following the high crest is like walking through a scrubby desert.

Rise gently to cross behind **Risco Verde**, a peak that appears quite innocuous from this side, but looks impressively rugged from the route of Walk 29. Descending gently, taking in the most rugged parts of the rim, the views across Las Cañadas get better all the time. If cloud starts billowing up then the walk becomes nothing more than a treadmill. A junction is reached where the main track descends to the left, but you should keep right, even though it is marked as *sin salida*, meaning no exit.

The track rises gently as it proceeds around the rim, passing a few *tajinaste*, or giant echiums along the way. Cross the shoulder of **Mesa del Obispo** and walk down to a gap. There is no need to worry about the awesomely rocky peaks rising ahead as the track outflanks them all. Climb up and around the slope to reach the next gap, and you will spot a crude drystone shelter tucked into the rock. The track descends gently to the next gap, where the sharp peak of **Topo de la Grieta** seems to rise so prominently, challenging the distant El Teide.

The track drifts downhill and round the back of the peak, keeping well away from the rocky ridge. There are views southwards down rock-strewn ridges and rock-walled *barrancos* where hardly anyone ever walks. The track is rough and stony as it climbs, then it makes a loop and descends across the slope. It becomes a rough and stony path as it passes a couple of pines and turns round the head of a valley.

At this point, white-painted arrows and dots show a steep and rocky path winding up the rugged, scrub-covered slopes of **Montaña del Pasajiron**. Follow these markers faithfully, even though they seem to lead aimlessly to and fro along the slopes. Once a shoulder has been crossed, take particular note of the markers; they show the way down a narrow pumice path, zigzagging to a rugged gap. Enjoy tremendous views on the way down to the Degollada de Guajara, where the pumice path levels out for a while at 2373m (7785ft). There are two options here. Either climb Guajara by reversing the high-level route description in Walk 32, or descend from the mountains and make your way to the Parador Cañadas del Teide.

The descent from the Degollada de Guajara is to the right, from a cairn. The path is still gritty, dusty and white underfoot. It leads down a rugged, scrubby slope to land on a clear track at the bottom. Turn left to follow the track and notice the fine *tajinaste* that grow alongside it. The track crosses a crest and reaches a junction with another track, at 2200m (7055ft). Keep straight on at this junction, following the track marked as Sendero 4, running down past towers of rock at the foot of Guajara.

The track wriggles and bends, but if you keep an eye open you can short-cut a prominent bend. Weird

Looking across the high gravel plain of Llano de Maja to El Teide

and wonderful rock outcrops buttress the lower slopes of Guajara, coming in vivid colours and strange shapes. There is a view of the Parador, a nearby chapel, and the remarkable peaks of the Roques de Garcia rising across the Cañada Blanca. The track lands on a road and you walk past a small building where a few cars can be parked. Watch carefully for a path on the right, which is rough, stony and narrow. It leads across a rugged patch of scrub to the Parador. Watch for it bending to the left, then at a path junction, head right to reach the **Parador**.

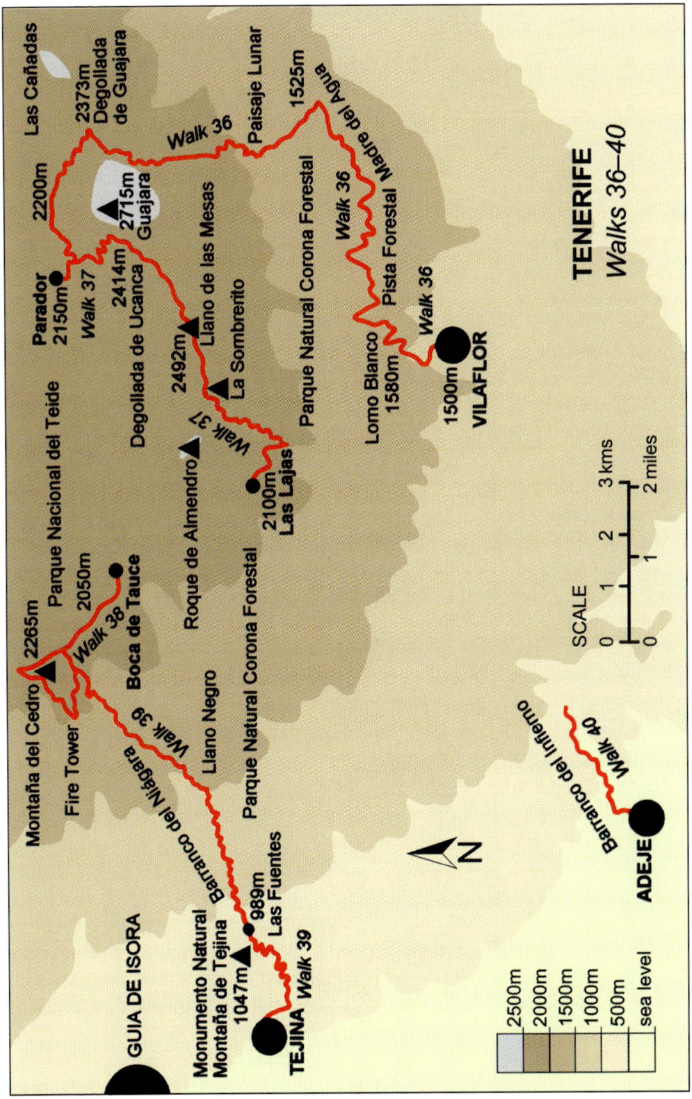
Las Cañadas
2373m
Degollada
de Guajara
2200m
Walk 36
Paisaje Lunar
1525m
Madre del Agua
2715m
Guajara
Parador
2150m
Walk 37
2414m
Degollada de Ucanca
Llano de las Mesas
2492m
La Sombrerito
Parque Natural Corona Forestal
Walk 36
Pista Forestal
Walk 36
Lomo Blanco
1580m
1500m
VILAFLOR
TENERIFE
Walks 36–40
Parque Nacional del Teide
Walk 37
Roque de Almendro
2100m
Las Lajas
2050m
Boca de Tauce
2265m
Montaña del Cedro
Walk 38
Fire Tower
Walk 39
Llano Negro
Parque Natural Corona Forestal
Barranco del Niágara
SCALE
0 1 2 3 kms
0 1 2 miles
Barranco del Infierno
Walk 40
N
989m
Las Fuentes
ADEJE
GUIA DE ISORA
Monumento Natural
Montaña de Tejina
1047m
TEJINA
Walk 39
2500m
2000m
1500m
1000m
500m
sea level

WALK 36

Valle de Ucanca

The walk from the Parador Cañadas del Teide over the top and down through the Valle de Ucanca is fairly simple. The initial ascent to the Degollada de Ucanca is the toughest part, yet it is soon completed and can be taken steadily. The descent is along a narrow path and a broader track, ending on the wide dirt road called the Pista Forestal Madre del Agua, which is open to vehicles. Towards the end you can either walk down a bendy road to Vilaflor, or intercept the bus coming down the road and save an hour. If you are staying in the historic village of Vilaflor, then of course there is no rush. Please see map on p. 187.

Distance:	16km (10 miles)
Start:	Parador Cañadas del Teide
Finish:	Vilaflor
Map:	1:50,000 Military Map Sheet 39-41
Terrain:	Mountainous, with a steep and rugged ascent at the start and gentler slopes beyond. The latter stages are along forest paths and tracks, giving way to a road-walk at the end.

Start at the Parador Cañadas del Teide, at 2150m (7050ft), or from the parking space nearby. If there is time, explore the Centro de Visitantes attached to the Parador, which contains a lot of information about the area. The Cafeteria Los Roques offers food and drink at the start. You begin on a narrow and stony path that leads away from a mapboard near the Centro de Visitantes, in the direction of Guajara. Follow this path through arid scrub, turning left and right to reach a narrow road. Simply cross the road to find the path continuing for Guajara. Climb up a slope covered in scrub and swing right towards a bright, dusty path. This path proceeds up a blunt ridge covered in broom, apparently heading for a rock wall on the skyline. When the path reaches a rocky nose it climbs further, then slices up to the right to avoid the rock wall, passing a lonesome pine. Turning left, it reaches a high crest, where a short walk downhill leads onto a gap called the **Degollada de Ucanca** at 2414m (7920ft).

Cross over the gap and look carefully to spot the path running down the **Valle de Ucanca** on the far side.

The path runs along the left-hand side of the valley and soon passes a *galeria*, from where a water pipe runs downhill. The path and the pipe pursue parallel courses down through the valley, but stop and look carefully whenever the line becomes vague. There is a peak in view ahead, the Roque del Encaje, which appears to block the valley mouth. Guajara rises steep and rocky to the left, in awesome tiered cliffs. There are plenty of *tajinaste* (giant echiums) beside the path. Pines are numerous, but rather scattered, offering little in the way of shade. A small water regulating hut is reached, where a draught of water might be obtained.

When an old, narrow water channel leaves the hut follow the path that runs below it for a while. More importantly, the path rises across the old channel, as marked by yellow arrows, then drifts uphill away from it. The ground is cindery underfoot and the path rises among pines, levelling out before descending. There is often a view of the steep and cindery slopes of Montaña de las Arenas to the left and a rough and jagged lava flow to the right. All of a sudden, the narrow path becomes a broad track, descending the steep and cindery, pine-covered slopes of Montaña de las Arenas. The track then descends more gently through somewhat denser pine. There is a gradual drift to the right, cutting across a rugged area of lava flows, slicing through a cutting in a softer bed of pumice. A ruined house is passed and the descent continues to reach a junction with a broader track, at 1800m (5905ft).

Cross over the track and follow a path marked with stones, leading further downhill. Cross over another track after a short while and look to the right to spot a series of caves cut into a rockface. Local people sometimes have picnics and barbecues here. The path continues away from the track and when the pines begin to thin out you will see that you are basically following a rounded, boulder-strewn crest. The path crosses a slight hump then winds down a stony slope. It becomes quite steep and stony before landing on a broad dirt road called the **Pista Forestal Madre del Agua**, at 1580m (5185ft).

Transport:
TITSA Bus 342 serves the Parador and Vilaflor from Playa de las Américas. TITSA Bus 348 serves the Parador from Puerto de la Cruz.

Refreshments:
The Cafeteria Los Roques is alongside the Parador. There are several bar restaurants in Vilaflor.

The mountain village of Vilaflor is the highest in Spain at 1500m (4920ft)

Turn right to follow this road, swinging round the deep Barranco de las Mesas. Rise across the valley side and pass a reservoir before turning into the next valley. There is a view far beyond a cultivated area of Vilaflor as a huddled collection of buildings. Pass a ruin at the head of the valley and later overlook the cultivated area, also getting a better view of Vilaflor on the way out of the valley. Follow the dirt road round one last big valley, then turn a final bend to reach a junction with a main road on **Lomo Blanco**. Follow the main road, which is very bendy, down a steep pine-covered slope to Vilaflor. If the bus comes it may stop if it is safe to do so. Just before reaching Vilaflor there is a road bend with two notable big pines. The Pino Gordo is down to the left and the Pino de las Dos Pernadas is up to the right.

At a road junction there is a turn to the left for **Vilaflor**, or Vilaflor de Chasna, to use its full name. It claims to be the highest village in Spain at 1500m (4920ft). Walking from top to bottom the Fuente Alta bottled water plant is passed first. The old part of Vilaflor was founded in the 16th century by Pedro Soler de Padilla. The stout stone Santuario-Convento del Hermano Pedro has recently been restored and stands on the birthplace of Hermano Pedro de San Jose de Bethencourt. He was born in 1626 and died following extensive missionary work in Guatemala in 1667. The church of San Pedro stands at the top of a sloping plaza where there are a couple of bar restaurants. Keep walking down through the village to pass more bar restaurants, traditional craft shops, a *pension* and hotel. At the point where the road through the village rejoins the main road there are bus stops.

WALK 37

Las Cañadas to Las Lajas

Distance:	10km (6 miles)
Start:	Parador Cañadas del Teide
Finish:	Las Lajas
Map:	1:50,000 Military Map Sheet 39-41
Terrain:	Rough and rocky mountain walking, often overlooking cliffs, but with very little sense of exposure and only a little scrambling. Paths are narrow and sometimes vague. The descent is on a slope covered in pines.

Although Guajara is quite often climbed, the mountains ranged westwards seem almost neglected. Maps show no paths, yet there is a narrow path trodden along the crest, and this has been flashed with paint blobs for the benefit of those few walkers who wish to walk that way. As the path tends to avoid the rough and rocky parts of the range, it misses most of the summits. Be careful with route finding in mist, especially when walking through featureless areas of scrub. The descent traces an old mountain path down a slope sparsely covered in pines. Please see the map on p. 187. The walk ties in with bus services to the Parador Cañadas del Teide and the recreational area of Las Lajas.

Start at the Parador Cañadas del Teide, at 2150m (7050ft), or from the parking space nearby. If there is time, explore the Centro de Visitantes attached to the Parador, which contains a lot of information about the area. A narrow and stony path leads away from a mapboard near the Centro de Visitantes, in the direction of Guajara. Follow this path, turning left and right to reach a narrow road. Simply cross the road to find the path continuing for Guajara. Climb up a slope covered in scrub and swing right towards a bright, dusty path. This path proceeds up a blunt ridge covered in broom, apparently heading for a rock wall on the skyline. When the path reaches a rocky nose it climbs further, then slices up to the right to avoid the rock wall. Turning left, it reaches a high crest just above a gap called the **Degollada de Ucanca** at 2414m (7920ft).

Turn right to start following a narrow, stony path alongside the rocky crest. Follow the blobs of paint and occasional small cairns, so avoiding confusion with other trodden paths to either side. Avoid being drawn up the path which follows the very crest of the ridge. A serious-looking peak on the ridge has a rocky little notch on its left-hand side, and the path passes through it. An easier pumice path crunches along the crest beyond and views across Las Cañadas to the peak of El Teide are magnificent. The ridge becomes quite rocky, but there is little sense of exposure. Keep to the left of another rocky peak, squeezing between the rocky slopes and a few pines that grow to this height on the mountain. Beware of rockfalls as all the buttresses are shattered. An easier path continues close to the crest, missing the summit of Montaña de la Corona, to reach a gentle gap.

Climb uphill along the crest, which is rocky for a short while. The path then weaves about on a boulder-strewn crest. Follow the path as it drifts to the left to avoid a rocky peak rising ahead, crossing an awkward slope covered in large, jammed, angular boulders. Watch carefully for the line of the path, looking for helpful paint blobs and small cairns until the crest is reached and the walking becomes easier again. The crest is a broad, gently sloping area of retama scrub, through which the path weaves, making its onward continuation at times vague. This stretch could be awkward in mist, so keep watching for those paint blobs and cairns. The retama has been burnt over a wide area, though it will regenerate in time. The broad crest, called **Llano de las Mesas**, becomes quite bouldery though there are plenty of painted arrows indicating the easiest way forward. The highest point on the broad crest is anyone's guess, but reaches 2492m (8176ft). The ridge becomes rockier and narrower, with one short stretch requiring an easy scramble. The path then runs easily down to a broad gap.

Follow the path over a little rise and down to another gap. At this point another path heads off down to the left, aiming for the flat, cliff-girt summit of **La Sombrerito**. Don't walk that way (unless you want to include the summit) but keep to the path along the main ridge. As a shoulder is crossed, take a peek to the

Transport:
TITSA Bus 342 and 348 serves the Parador from Playa de las Américas and Puerto de la Cruz respectively. TITSA Bus 342 also serves Las Lajas.

Refreshments:
The Cafeteria Los Roques is alongside the Parador. Las Lajas is a recreational area with a restaurant.

After passing this rocky peak you can turn around and admire the view

right to spot a steep and stony zigzag path leading down to the gravelly flats of Llano de Ucanca. Keep following the roller-coaster ridge, enjoying some of the roughest and rockiest views of the day with relative ease. All of a sudden, a painted asterisk on a rock marks the end of this splendid ridge walk. Looking ahead to the Roque del Almendro and La Cachucha, most casual walkers will realise that those pathless peaks are too dangerous to negotiate.

The paint-marked path turns left downhill and is clearly flashed with blobs and arrows. Keep to the right at a couple of path junctions, following the marked path down a steep and gritty slope. The gradient eases for a while when a slope of pines is reached. The narrow, well-marked path moves to the left of a rounded ridge called Lomo de los Pegueros. Walk past a couple of drystone shelters and notice a couple of enormous pines dripping with resin. There are signs of a forest fire in the recent past. The path zigzags dozens of times down a steep and stony nose, so keep to the marked route and avoid taking short cuts that might result in you losing the trail .

When the slopes breaks, the line of the path becomes a bit vague. It then drifts off to the right as the ground steepens again. A few more zigzags lead the path close to the main road, then rather oddly, it begins to climb in order to reach a couple of ruined buildings on a road bend near a bridge. Follow the main road uphill and around a bend to reach the mountain campsite and recreational area of **Las Lajas**, at 2100m (6890ft). This is a handy place to wait for the bus as it can pull into the entrance, and if there is any time to spare, you can visit the small restaurant on site.

WALK 38
Boca de Tauce

This is a fairly easy walk that offers a chance to study Las Cañadas, the different types of lava flow, scrub, and forest with a circuit around one of the mountains. Views are spectacular, although they are confined to a small area, with both the towering cone of El Teide dominating the scene, and the nearby peaks and pinnacles attracting attention. The walk can be completed as a simple there-and-back along almost level paths and tracks, but it is also worth making a circuit around Montaña del Cedro. By referring to Walk 39, you can enjoy a longer walk from Boca de Tauce, over a gap beside Montaña del Cedro, then down slopes of forest and scrub to reach Tejina. Please refer to the map on p. 187.

Distance:	11km (6¾ miles)
Start/Finish:	Boca de Tauce
Map:	1:50,000 Military Map Sheet 38-41
Terrain:	Mountainous and rocky, but the paths and tracks used are fairly simple and straightforward.

There is a road junction at **Boca de Tauce**, where two main roads meet. Buses often pull in at a lay-by so passengers can enjoy views across barren, blocky, spiky lava flows. Take a moment to look at the information boards that explain the difference between the rugged *aa-aa* and smoother *paehoehoe* lava flows. Walk back along the road in the direction of Vilaflor, noticing a national park building off to the right. Before reaching the building, step down from the road onto a small area of scrub and gravel. This is the Cañada del Pinito and a narrow path runs across it, passing a couple of pines. Continue through a narrow gap between a dark, blocky lava flow and the mountain rim of Las Cañadas. The rugged range to the left exhibits the most bewildering array of pinnacles, spires and leaning towers of rock. Stand still to look at them, or risk tripping over the stones that litter the path! The general altitude is around 2050m (6725ft).

The lava flow reached the base of a pointed tooth of a peak before solidifying, so the path is forced to climb over the old flow. It is remarkably cindery and it is rather like walking on spilled sacks of coke. The path eventually drops off the lava and is rough and stony as it continues through retama scrub and pine. Watch carefully for the line of the path, as it is often necessary to squeeze through the scrub. There is a low gap away to the left, while to the right a few patches of ropy lava are exposed, with the black, blocky lava now some distance away. El Teide and Pico Viejo, the two highest mountains in the whole of the Canary Islands, rise beyond.

Pass a sign warning 'Danger Bee Hives' and continue across the broad and gravelly Cañada de Chavao. You may spot a path on the left, which is actually your return route. Continue straight onwards, passing another sign warning of bee hives. By this time the path has become a track, and at a wire barrier it joins an even broader vehicle track. Turn right and follow the track, noting that it could be followed all the way to a junction with a main road. To make the circuit around Montaña del Cedro, however, follow the track only until it starts to rise and bend round to the right.

There is a boulder just to the left of the track and maybe a small cairn or two, marking the start of a narrow, stony path that doubles back sharply and squeezes through retama scrub as it climbs uphill. The path heads directly for **Montaña del Cedro**. As it climbs there are splendid views back along the route you have come. The path slices up across the steep slope and crosses a rocky little gap at the top at around 2150m (7055ft). Contour roughly around the rocky, pine-covered mountainside, passing a *galeria* full of water with a tiny shrine perched above it. The path continues round the mountainside, then descends gently. If the day is clear, and clouds haven't yet billowed up, you should spot a **fire tower** away down a rounded, forested ridge. The path runs towards this tower in due course and on reaching it, links with a clear forest road.

Follow the dirt road downhill and round a series of bends. Turn left uphill at a junction, watching El Teide and Pico Viejo rise to fill the gap ahead. The peak of Guajara can later be seen through a gap to the right. On reaching the gap directly ahead, leave the track and descend to the right along a narrow path to reach a broader one at the bottom. Simply turn right and follow this path, which was used on the outward journey. It crosses the blocky lava flow and returns to the road

Transport:
TITSA Bus 342 serves Boca de Tauce from Playa de las Américas.

Refreshments:
None

A leaning pinnacle hanging over the path near Boca de Tauce

junction at **Boca de Tauce**. Be sure of the bus timetables and make sure that the driver can see you to stop the bus.

Walkers who want to sample the scenic highlights of this short walk, but wish to enjoy a much longer route can refer to Walk 39. This offers the chance to walk downhill from Montaña del Cedro to the little town of Tejina.

WALK 39
Boca de Tauce to Tejina

Distance:	14km (8¾ miles)
Start:	Boca de Tauce
Finish:	Tejina
Map:	1:50,000 Military Map Sheet 38-41
Terrain:	Mountainous and rocky at the start, but the paths and tracks used are fairly simple. The middle stretches are rough and rocky, giving way to farm tracks and roads towards the end.

This walk starts amid spectacular scenery at Boca de Tauce in the Parque Nacional del Teide, then crosses a gap and heads downhill from 2080m to 560m (6825ft to 1835ft). The top part of the route is largely confined to pine forest, using a broad path marked by parallel lines of stones. Further downhill, a broad, rocky, scrubby ridge is followed, with views down into rugged barrancos. Although downhill most of the way, the path can be very rough and uneven. The Montaña de Tejina is a landmark on the descent, with tracks and quiet roads finally leading down to the village of Tejina. Please refer to the map on p. 187.

Near a road junction at **Boca de Tauce** there is a lay-by where buses often pull in so passengers can enjoy views across barren, blocky, spiky lava flows. Take a moment to look at the information boards that explain the difference between the rugged *aa-aa* and smoother *paehoe-hoe* lava flows. Walk back along the road in the direction of Vilaflor, noticing a national park building off to the right. Before reaching the building, step down from the road onto a small area of scrub and gravel. This is the Cañada del Pinito and a narrow path runs across it, passing a couple of pines. Continue through a narrow gap between a dark, blocky lava flow and the mountain rim of Las Cañadas. The rugged range to the left exhibits the most bewildering array of pinnacles, spires and leaning towers of rock. Stand still to look at them, or risk tripping over the stones that litter the path! The general altitude is around 2050m (6725ft).

As the lava flow reached the base of a pointed tooth of a peak before solidifying, the path is forced to climb over the old flow. It is remarkably cindery and it is rather like walking on spilled sacks of coke. The path eventually

Transport: TITSA Bus 342 serves Boca de Tauce from Playa de Las Américas. TITSA Bus 416 and 460 serve Tejina, linking with Guía de Isora and Icod de los Vinos in one direction and Playa de Las Américas and Granadilla in the other direction.

Refreshments: There are a handful of bar restaurants at Tejina.

drops off the lava and is rough and stony as it continues through broom scrub and pine. Watch carefully for the line of the path, as it is often necessary to squeeze through the scrub. There is a low gap away to the left, while to the right a few patches of ropy lava are exposed, with the black, blocky lava now some distance away. The Canary Islands two highest mountains, El Teide and Pico Viejo, rise beyond. Pass a sign warning 'Danger Bee Hives' and continue across the broad and gravelly Cañada de Chavao. Watch out for a path rising to the left and follow it up to a gap called Boca de Chavao at around 2080m (6825ft).

Slice down to the left, along a forest path marked with lines of stones, as a broad dirt road crosses the gap. Further downhill on the steep slope, the path is quite rugged, but it soon lands down on the forest road. Walk down around a bend on the forest road to reach a building at a junction. Turn left here, then swing right and pass a barrier. Next, look out for a path rising to the right of the forest road, marked by parallel lines of stones. The forest road pursues a parallel course, but the path is more direct, being less bendy. This path is clear at first, but becomes vague for a short while, then it is clear again. Rise a little, then continue gently downhill. Slice through a bend on the road and keep walking downhill. There are a few stone steps as the path drops down to clip another bend on the forest road.

Gradually, the path becomes narrower and steeper, as well as being more stony underfoot. There is a lot more flowery scrub between the pines, instead of the uniform layer of pine needles. Having clipped another bend on the forest road, you reach a junction of dirt roads. Turn right down the narrower one, which is steep and stony, overlooking the deep-cut **Barranco del Niágara** from time to time. Follow the dirt road downhill, but watch out for the path with parallel lines of stones reappearing on the right. It runs along the edge of the big *barranco* to reach a drystone wall at the bottom edge of the pine forest.

Turn left and follow the path across a couple of

A view of Pico Viejo and El Teide from the Boca de Chavao gap

bends on the dirt road. Keep right to follow a major water pipeline over a gentle rise, then follow the path again, which is now distinctly rough and stony, though clear and obvious throughout. Although there is one pine surrounded by stone seating, there are now great expanses of bushy scrub. The slope is rough, rocky and savage-looking, and it would be almost impossible to walk down it without the path. Large boulders have been shifted aside to create a passable route. Eventually, the path zigzags to the right of the ridge and overlooks the Barranco del Niágara again. It follows a rock ridge with rugged *barrancos* on either side, then passes between a ruin and a little hut bristling with water pipes. A sign points back uphill for the Casa Juan Evora and Los Poleos.

Continue along the rough and rocky crest, with the broad path flanked by low stone walls. There is an ankle-twisting descent along a very badly eroded track. Even when old terraces and ruined houses are reached at **Las Fuentes**, the track is still very awkward underfoot. Eventually it levels out as you reach vineyards, where even vehicles can negotiate the path. A sign pointing to the right indicates a walking route to Acojeja, but keep walking straight onwards towards the prominent Montaña de Tejina, passing one last cluster of houses. The landmark hill has been designated as the **Monumento Natural Montaña de Tejina**.

The track drifts to the left of the hill and climbs a little, then descends in loops past old terraces. A fine stretch leads through the rock-walled Barranco de las Carreras. There are more loops as the track works its way down through terraces often covered in prickly pears. When a road is reached at the bottom, keep left of the little hilltop village. After passing this settlement, turn left at a road junction well below it and later pass the church of the Virgen del Rosario on the little Plaza de Tejina. Keep walking down the road, which is the Calle Virgen del Rosario, eventually reaching a busy main road. Turn left for immediate access to bus stops on either side of the road. There is also the Cafeteria Bar Tejina, Cafeteria Achimaye and a supermarket close to hand. Just down the road is the Bar Terraza Pizzeria Aveti.

WALK 40

Barranco del Infierno

Distance:	7km (4½ miles)
Start/Finish:	At the church in Adeje
Map:	1:50,000 Military Map Sheet 38-41
Terrain:	A fairly easy path slices across steep and rugged slopes. Later, the path is narrow and often wet, flanked by rampant vegetation.

Transport: TITSA Bus 416 serves Adeje, linking with Guía de Isora, Playa de Las Américas and Granadilla. TITSA Bus 473 links Adeje with Playa de Las Américas and Los Gigantes.

Refreshments: The Bar Restaurante Otelo overlooks the *barranco* and there are many other places offering food and drink in Adeje.

Start at the church at the top end of **Adeje**, where the Barranco del Infierno is signposted along an almost level road. A right turn leads up the steep Calle de Molinos and the road ends at the Bar Restaurante

A clear path leads deep into the Barranco del Infierno

The Barranco del Infierno is one of those places where you meet all kinds of walkers. Everyone has heard of the place and they all want to have a look at it. The deep-cut, rock-walled valley is protected as the Reserva Natural Especial Barranco del Infierno. The only approach is from the little town of Adeje, following a clear, obvious, well-built and solidly buttressed path. The path picks its way along the valley side to reach the floor where there is almost always running water. It is like a jungle trek as the narrow path is tightly hemmed in by lush green vegetation. When the route reaches a rock-walled impasse you have to retrace your steps to Adeje. Please refer to the map on p. 187.

Otelo. There is a fine uninterrupted view along the length of the *barranco,* taking in some nearby towers of rock and the more distant sloping summit of Conde. A clear and obvious stone-paved path drops below the viewpoint and clings to the steep and rocky northern side of the valley. The path becomes rough and rocky underfoot, though it remains clear and easy to follow. Prickly pears and candelabra spurge grow on the rocky slopes and there are little viewpoints along the way.

The path is like a roller-coaster as it swings around a hollow to cross the smaller Barranco Chavor. A couple of aqueduct bridges can be seen. The path later rises to cross a water channel, only to drop down and cross it again on the way to the floor of the **Barranco del Infierno**. There may be a little log bridge to cross, and looking up at this point it is possible to spot a peak pierced through with a hole that looks like a blue eye. The path climbs and pushes its way further up into the *barranco,* crossing the streambed again and passing a point where water pours in from the left at La Cojudera. Cross and re-cross the streambed, pushing through dense vegetation, taking care of trailing brambles, and either step across or bend under fallen trees. There are a handful of little footbridges, though only one stout pipework bridge is really necessary. At a higher level there are no bridges, though there is nearly always running water. Several chestnut trees flourish in the moist ground.

The rock walls are either sheer or ominously overhanging, and the vegetation cover ends when the cliffs rising high above almost close in and block out the sun. A cave-like recess with only a tiny bit of sky overhead features a slender waterfall cascading into a broad pool, and this is as far as you can walk. Take a break and enjoy the coolness of the place. When the time comes to leave, simply retrace steps back down the path and out of the *barranco* to return to Adeje.

A slender waterfall and pool – you now have to turn around

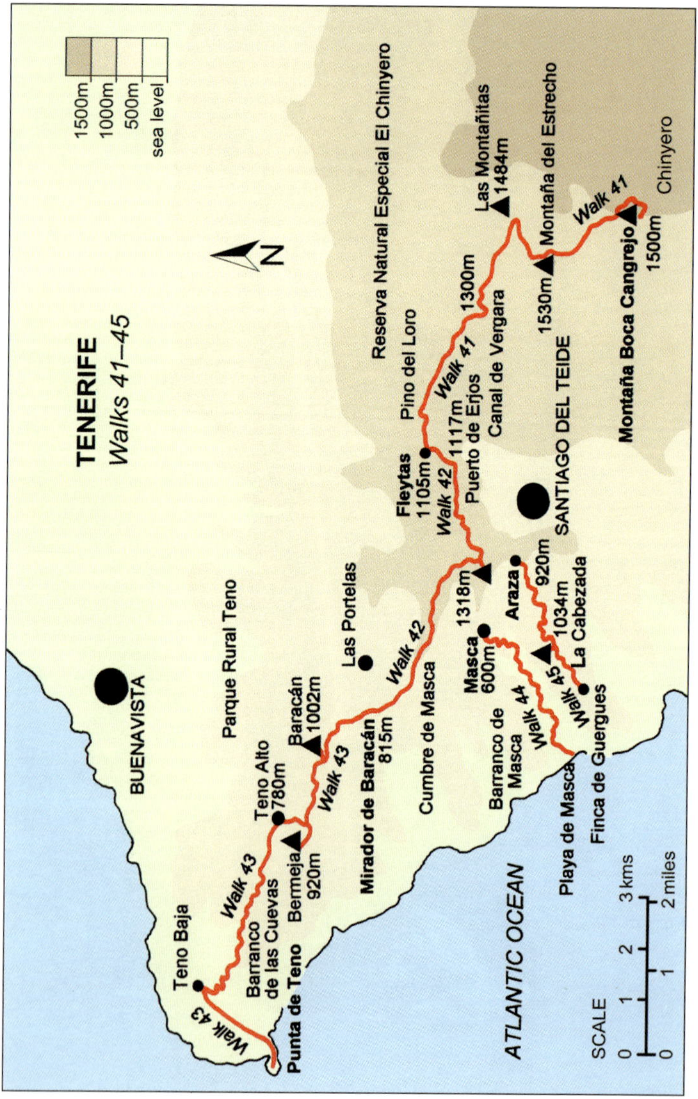

TENERIFE
Walks 41–45
1500m
1000m
500m
sea level
N
BUENAVISTA
Parque Rural Teno
Las Portelas
Reserva Natural Especial El Chinyero
Teno Baja
Walk 43
Barranco de las Cuevas
Punta de Teno
Bermeja 920m
Teno Alto 780m
Baracán 1002m
Mirador de Baracán 815m
Cumbre de Masca
Walk 42
1318m
Masca 600m
Barranco de Masca
Walk 44
Walk 45
Araza 920m
1034m La Cabezada
Finca de Guergues
Playa de Masca
ATLANTIC OCEAN
Fleytas 1105m
Pino del Loro
1117m Puerto de Erjos
Walk 41
Canal de Vergara
1300m
SANTIAGO DEL TEIDE
Las Montañitas 1484m
1530m Montaña del Estrecho
Montaña Boca Cangrejo 1500m
Chinyero
SCALE
0 1 2 3 kms
0 1 2 miles

WALK 41
Chinyero to Fleytas

Distance:	10km (6 miles)
Start:	Chinyero on the road above Chío
Finish:	The Restaurante Fleytas
Map:	1:50,000 Military Map Sheet 38-40
Terrain:	Cindery and forested slopes, with good paths and tracks. The lower slopes are gentler, with broad tracks crossing cultivated land.

The north-western end of Tenerife, known as Teno, presents an interesting variety of landscapes. One of the best ways to appreciate the changing features of the landscape is to walk through it. An interesting three-day walk can be considered, though each of the three stretches make fine one-day walks in their own right. The first stretch is from Chinyero, high on the road to Las Cañadas, taking in bleak and cindery volcanic landscapes. The last eruption here was in 1909. The slopes are mostly covered in pines, with good tracks leading down to Fleytas, a rich farming landscape. Please refer to the map on p. 206

There is no public transport up the main road from Chío to Las Cañadas, and the nearest place with taxis is Guía de Isora. The mountain road climbs in broad bends and is equipped with prominent kilometre markers. This walk can be started where a large sign announces 'Chinyero', but it is worth going just a little further up the road to start just before the 14km marker and a sign for **Montaña Boca Cangrejo**. The altitude is 1500m (4920ft) but the roadside sign says 1450m (4755ft). Rising steeply from the roadside are crumbling cinder slopes which are part of the **Reserva Natural Especial El Chinyero**. Climb up from the roadside and swing right, walking gently up a cindery path. To the left are the steep, bare and cindery slopes of **Montaña Boca Cangrejo**, sporting only a few pines. Follow vague cinder tracks around the slopes of this volcano, gradually swinging left, rising across a gap on the far side, then descending. The track appears to vanish in a stand of tall pines, but reappears beyond and drops steeply. It intersects with a broad dirt road beyond a pine tree.

The main road is not far away to the left, but keep walking straight onwards and turn right. When a junction is reached, keep left and walk gently downhill,

Transport: Use a taxi from Guía de Isora to reach Km14 on the road above Chío. TITSA Bus 325, 360, 392 and 460 pass the Restaurante Fleytas, serving points as distant as Puerto de la Cruz, Icod de los Vinos and Playa de las Américas.

Refreshments: The Restaurante Fleytas is at the end of the walk.

and note the dark, blocky lava flow seen beyond a screen of pines. The track eventually crosses the lava flow with surprising ease, considering how broken and jagged the surface is. Continue across a forested dip, then rise between the lava flow and the steep slopes of **Montaña del Estrecho**. There is a fine view looking up towards El Teide, with the intervening slopes covered in old lava flows and studded with volcanic cones.

The track swings round the slopes of Montaña del Estrecho in a loop, then descends from one junction to another. El Tanque is signposted to the right and you follow the track in that direction. Leave the forest to cross more jagged, blocky lava flows. Keep left at a junction, where the track to the right is signposted as no exit. Don't worry about the slight ascent along the way, or the fact that El Teide is still in view, or **Las Montañitas** are rising ahead. When you reach a well signposted junction turn left, as marked for the Canal de Vergara and Los Partidos de Franquis.

The track runs alongside lava flows and descends easily. The blocky lava contains more and more hollows filled with fine, black cinders, and there are more and more pines able to grow on the surface. The track descends in gentle loops, but simply keep on the clearest line and avoid lesser tracks to the right and left. Keep an eye open to spot the slab-covered watercourse called the **Canal de Vergara**, but bear in mind that it is closed to walkers to avoid accidents and contamination. The track loops down to a signposted crossroads, where you simply walk straight across. The bendy track leads down from pine forest into a scrubby woodland.

Notice a cinder quarry away to the right, but keep following the clearest track straight ahead. At a crossroads the track leaves the Reserva Natural Especial El Chinyero and immediately enters the Parque Rural Teno. The track passes fields, more small areas of scrubby woodland and a farm, then drops downhill with pines and tree heather alongside. A busy road is reached beside a large and ancient pine called the **Pino del Loro**.

Turn left along the road, then at a bend turn right along a track, then left down another track that quickly becomes narrower. Look ahead across a terraced valley to spot the continuation of this track, which leads up to a whitewashed building on the far side. The building stands at a road junction where there is a bus stop and shelter, as well as the Restaurante Fleytas. Keen walkers who started early enough in the day could continue with the next part of the route.

The track appears to head for Las Montañitas before suddenly turning left

WALK 42

Fleytas to Mirador de Baracán

The walk through the Parque Rural Teno continues from the Restaurante Fleytas to the Mirador de Baracán. This day's walk is along a ridge that starts with pine forest, switches to 'laurisilva' woodlands along the Cumbre de Masca, then finishes with rather scrubby and bare slopes. Walkers who are tempted to add this day's walk to the walk from Chinyero to Fleytas should be aware of the limited bus service along the road at the Mirador de Baracán. The only way to avoid being stranded at that point is to walk down the bendy road to Las Portelas to link with a bus service in the village. Please refer to the map on p. 206.

Distance:	10km (6 miles)
Start:	The Restaurante Fleytas
Finish:	Mirador de Baracán
Map:	1:50,000 Military Map Sheet 38-40
Terrain:	Roads give way to tracks and rugged paths on the initial ascent. The Cumbre de Masca is well wooded and served by good paths.

Start at the road junction near the Restaurante Fleytas, where there is a bus stop and shelter. You might like to avoid the first bit of road walking by staying on the bus that continues up the road to the gap called Puerto de Erjos, on the way to Santiago del Teide. The bendy road quickly climbs from the restaurant to the gap at **Puerto de Erjos**, at 1117m (3665ft). Take a right turn up a narrow minor road. The road is quite rough and serves a mast high on Montaña Jala. There are fine views overlooking Santiago del Teide, with the peak of El Teide rising far beyond. Old terraces are cut into the slopes below the road, and there is heather tree scrub, gorse and brambles. Further along the ridge are pines as the road runs level for a while.

Watch out for a clear track heading off down to the left of the road. Follow this track gently downhill and round the little valleys and spurs on the side of Montaña Jala. The pine cover is sparse and thins out even more as a rough and rocky path rises from the end of the track. Aim for a high gap called the Degollada de la Mesa and turn left to climb up a rocky nose. The path passes only a solitary pine, the rest of the vegetation cover being tree heather, cistus and arid scrub. The ridge narrows as it approaches a rocky little summit of broken blocks at

1318m (4324ft). There are magnificent views down the Barranco de Masca, while the wider vista takes in everything from El Teide to Teno, with La Gomera out to sea. There is obviously no way forward, so carefully retrace steps back down to the Degollada de la Mesa.

Follow a path slicing off to the left, which is fairly broad and contours across the slopes of Montaña Jala among bushy scrub. The path leads gently downhill to reach a junction where there are signposts, but keep left and walk down to a broad gap where there are a couple of ruined buildings. Signposts abound here, pointing back to Puerto de Erjos, or down a track for a quick exit via Las Portelas, and almost straight along the Cumbre de Masca for Teno Alto. Take this last one, following a broad and easy path shaded by heather and candleberry trees and flanked by cistus bushes.

When a path junction is reached, a short diversion left leads to a fine viewpoint from a rocky stance, but the fork to the right is the way to continue. The path is narrow and shaded, confined to dense 'laurisilva' woodland, but it eventually returns to a narrow and rocky part of the ridge. Drop off to the right again, then later return to the ridge. After an ascent, the path drops off to the right. There is another stretch along the rocky ridge, after which the path slips off to the left, onto an arid, scrubby slope. When the path crosses back over the ridge it reaches a signposted path junction. Teno Alto is straight along the Cumbre de Masca, while left leads down to Masca and right leads down to Las Portelas, if you want alternative descents.

The path roughly follows the rocky crest, crossing it a couple of times. The tree heather has been burnt and is regenerating, but in the meantime masses of aromatic fennel and prickly pears flank the path. The path finally drops down to a road bend, suddenly swinging right down a steep set of bouldery steps. Be careful how you land on the road bend as motorists may not see you. Carefully cross the road to reach the **Mirador de Baracán**, at 815m (2675ft). There is an information board to read while waiting for the bus. A path leads to a nearby viewpoint if there

Transport: TITSA Bus 325, 360, 392 and 460 pass the Restaurante Fleytas, serving points as distant as Puerto de la Cruz, Icod de los Vinos and Playa de Las Américas. TITSA Bus 355 serves the Mirador de Baracán, linking with Buenavista and Santiago del Teide.

Refreshments: The Restaurante Fleytas is at the beginning of the walk.

The Cumbre de Masca is a fine ridge largely covered in heather trees

is plenty of time to spare. If the bus has already gone, then you can walk down the bendy road to Las Portelas. If you take this option, there is also a quieter bendy road off to the left that could be used for a rapid descent.

WALK 43

Mirador de Baracán to Punta de Teno

Transport: TITSA Bus 355 serves the Mirador de Baracán, linking with Buenavista and Santiago del Teide. A taxi or pickup needs to be arranged at the Punta de Teno.

Refreshments: The Bar Los Bailaderos is at Teno Alto.

Distance:	15km (9½ miles)
Start:	Mirador de Baracán
Finish:	Punta de Teno
Map:	1:50,000 Military Map Sheet 38-40
Terrain:	Mountainous at the beginning, but with good paths and tracks. After passing through a farming landscape there is a rough and rocky descent to the coast. A road is followed towards the end.

Start on the road bend at the **Mirador de Baracán**, between Las Portelas and Masca. There is an information board and a short path leads to a fine viewpoint. Looking down towards Buenavista, you can see the little volcano of El Mocán, with its three big gashes on its slopes. The volcano once blocked the valley and caused a small lake to form. On the other side of the high gap, La Gomera can be seen neatly filling the sea. Pass a sign for Teno Alto and start climbing up the ridge path. There are zigzags and the path is clear, but take care to keep to the right at an apparent junction, as left leads to an impasse. Scrubby slopes give way to greener heather and laurel cover later.

There is only one good path on the slopes of **Baracán**, and it seems to omit the summit, but there is a spur to the right, from a battered signpost, allowing you to climb to the top. A trig point stands at 1002m (3287ft) and a wonderful view stretches around the Parque Rural Teno, from coast to coast, with the chance of seeing El Teide rising far beyond and the neighbouring island of La Gomera out to sea. It is also interesting to note how the lush 'laurisilva' growing on the northern slopes of the mountain, ends abruptly upon reaching the ridge.

Walk back down to join the main path and turn right to follow it back up to the ridge. A surprisingly easy path follows the crest, then descends gently alongside old terraces dotted with cistus, and boulder-strewn slopes. Enter a dense forest of heather trees and continue following the path gently downhill. you will exit rather abruptly onto an open slope again dotted with cistus, onto a winding path down to a concrete road. If time is limited, then turn right for Teno Alto, but if there is time to spare, then turn left for a short detour.

The concrete road leads up to a reservoir, and a short walk beyond leads up to a gap. Turn right along a track on the shoulder of **Bermejo** and follow it until it seems to expire. There are splendid views around the north-western end of Tenerife, though the Punta de Teno remains hidden from sight. The surrounding

The Parque Rural Teno covers the north-western part of Tenerife and anyone walking through it, especially along its high crest, will be struck by the ever-changing nature of the landscape. The Mirador de Baracán, between Las Portelas and Masca, offers views of rugged ridges and deep *barrancos*; generally arid and covered in scrub. Anyone climbing Baracán, however, will find themselves walking through 'laurisilva' woodlands and dense heather trees. After a break at the little village of Teno Alto, the route continues past little goat farms, down exceedingly rough and rocky slopes, and ends on the crumbling, cindery point of Punta de Teno. Please refer to the map on p. 206. Note that there are no bus services to Punta de Teno, so arrange for a taxi at the end.

Baracán is climbed from a road at a gap by the Mirador de Baracán

slopes are covered in flowery scrub, and dotted with occasional clumps of heather trees. Retrace your steps and walk back down the concrete road, which becomes tarmac as it winds down to the little village of **Teno Alto**. The Bar Los Bailaderos is immediately to hand, and there is also a little chapel, *bodegon* and souvenir shop.

If refreshment is not required, then simply turn left to leave the village, following the road signposted downhill for Teno Bajo. The tarmac runs out and the road becomes stony instead. Just as a gentle rise is being crossed, fork right and pass a tall cairn bristling with signposts. The dirt road running downhill is signposted for Jabuche, and there is a goat-pen up to the left. Follow the dirt road as it curves down and round a terraced hillside. Either turn right at the next junction, or clip the corner and drop down onto the lower dirt road (the one with a pylon line marching down to a narrow tarmac road).

Cross the tarmac road and slice off to the left as indicated, passing a cairn and following a narrow path. There is a water pipe alongside, running along the top edge of the rocky **Barranco de las Cuevas**. There are masses of prickly pears in the *barranco,* and the terraces alongside. When you reach the tarmac road again, follow it downhill through a goat farm. Head down to the left and follow the line of the path again, still with the water pipe alongside. Pass a couple of little buildings on the rugged slope and aim for the next little farmstead seen below, now the only habitation in sight. Though the path becomes very rough and rocky and sometimes it doesn't seem to be a path at all, the water pipes are a sure guide throughout.

Just before reaching the buildings, head off to the left, down to a concrete road-end in the bed of the Barranco de las Cuevas. Follow a stony track uphill and across the slope. At a fork, go down to the right, as marked by yellow blobs of paint, and through a gate. Walk to a turning space at the end of the track, where there is a stone shelter and a view down to the Punta de Teno and its lighthouse, or *faro*. Also in view are cultivation tents and a windfarm, while out to sea the islands of La Gomera and La Palma can be seen.

A stony zigzag path, well-engineered in its time, but now covered with rubble, winds down a steep and rocky slope covered in candelabra spurge and prickly pears. Take the descent slowly and steadily and aim for the road at Las Casas, where a building surrounded by cultivation tents can be seen. Once the road is reached, turn left to follow it gently downhill to Punta de Teno. Masses of scrub flank the road, and at Teno Baja there is also another area of cultivation tents and old greenhouses. A narrow isthmus is crossed and cars are often parked alongside as the road to the lighthouse is closed to traffic.

The **Punta de Teno** is composed of loose and crumbly beds of cinders, so take care if exploring close to any cliff edges. There is a wooden walkway and a couple of other paths on the point, and splendid views along the cliff coast to Los Gigantes. A small harbour accommodates a few boats, but access to the lighthouse is barred by tall gates. There is no bus service to

An attractive cliff coastline stretches away from the Punta de Teno

Punta de Teno, so if you haven't arranged to be collected by taxi, then have a chat with one of the motorists at the road-end with a view to securing a lift back along the road to Buenavista. The drive along the road is spectacular, with sheer cliffs and tunnels, but it is also prone to rockfalls.

WALK 44

Barranco de Masca

Distance:	8km (5 miles)
Start/Finish:	At the church in Masca
Map:	1:50,000 Military Map Sheet 38-40
Terrain:	The path is often steep and rocky. Some short sections require basic scrambling.

Despite being steep, deep and rocky, the Barranco de Masca attracts dozens of walkers every day. The usual approach is to walk from the village of Masca, at 600m (1970ft), down to sea level at the Playa de Masca, then turn round and walk all the way back up again. Please refer to the map on p. 206. Obviously, the second part of the walk is more demanding. Some walkers pre-book a boat from Los Gigantes, so that they can enjoy the walk down the *barranco,* then simply meet the boat at the Playa de Masca. Note that this service must be pre-booked! The distance given above assumes that you will be walking both ways.

Masca is a little village clinging to a steep slope. There is a church on a tiny plaza and a handful of little bar restaurants to choose between. The walk drops down from the road to the church, where there is a view down the *barranco,* taking in a tiny wedge of the sea. Continue down a stone-paved road to the Restaurante Bar La Fuente, then cut off to the right down a stone-paved path, passing the Restaurante Chez Arlette. This cuts a bend from the road, landing on a level stretch that is followed only for a short way. The Bar Blanky is seen ahead, but turn left down steps, as signposted for the **Barranco de Masca**. A steep and rugged path leads downhill, passing exotic plants along the way. A sign announces that you are entering an Especio Natural Protegido. You will lose sight of the sea while squeezing between some huge boulders, made of a boulder agglomerate.

Cross a footbridge and climb a little, then continue along narrow, rocky and often slightly exposed paths. There are some terraces, and the path crosses the *barranco* and traverses another narrow rock ledge. Cross back over the *barranco* where there are dense growths of cane. There is low headroom passing under a big boulder, then a rocky rib with small pools alongside leads down to a concrete dam. Note how a water channel is

Transport: TITSA Bus 355 serves Masca from Buenavista and Valle de Santiago. If you wish to leave by boat, be sure to pre-book and take careful note of the arrangements for being collected at the Playa de Masca.

Refreshments: There are a handful of little bar restaurants in Masca.

diverted off to the left from the dam. The other *barranco* joining here is the Barranco Madre del Agua.

Weave about on the broad and bouldery floor of the **Barranco de Masca**. Cross to the right to avoid a dry waterfall, which is more like an enormous boulder-choke. There is really only one path down from here, along the floor of the *barranco* or just to one side. The rock walls are sheer, or even overhanging, as well as often being bare of vegetation. Looking up, jagged rocks often protrude, and there are no signs of habitation, though there may be cats sitting at strategic points, obviously waiting for handouts from passing walkers!

The floor of the *barranco* is either stony or littered with huge boulders, sometimes thick with lush green vegetation and there may sometimes be a trickle of water. Keep winding down as the gorge narrows, passing huge boulders jammed in the bed of the *barranco.* Occasionally, the path is buttressed on one side and is quite easy. Keep an eye open to spot a flying buttress of a rock arch up to the left. The *barranco* narrows even further to make it appear that progress may come to a halt. however, a bouldery ramp up to the right leads the path up the steep and rocky side of the *barranco.* Be sure to remember this feature for the return trip.

A little further down the *barranco,* on the left-hand side, there is a short scramble along a rocky rib. Apart from this, keep weaving from side to side and follow the path faithfully, admiring deep, green rock pools and maybe tiny trickles of waterfalls. A stretch of path on the right-hand side of the *barranco* gives way to a stretch of path on the left-hand side. By listening carefully, you should be able to hear the sea, providing that there are breakers down on the beach. Climb uphill a little, then zigzag down a few terraces. After another odd little upward manoeuvre, a tiny portion of the sea can be spotted.

You will find that more light seems to enter the *barranco,* suggesting that the mouth is close to hand. However, there are still a couple of interesting little scrambles necessary to pass a couple of dry waterfalls,

The Barranco de Masca features a few green pools near the bottom

either side of a huge boulder jammed overhead. The bouldery *barranco* continues all the way down to the sea, where there are ragged tamarisk bushes and other knots of vegetation. There is a little house almost obscured by a clump of trees at the base of a cliff. There may be a roving gang of cats waiting for more of your food! You can walk a little further from the Playa de Masca by following a concrete walkway out to a solitary rock in the sea. This is popular for swimming and sunbathing, though space is limited. The island of La Gomera is further out to sea.

Sunbathe or swim from a rocky islet at the mouth of the Barranco de Masca

If a boat pick-up has been pre-booked, then simply wait until the appointed hour to be collected and ferried to Los Gigantes, then tie in with bus services at that point. If not, then at some point you must head back into the rock-walled *barranco* and climb back up to **Masca**. Make sure you have enough energy and water for the task, and bear in mind that the afternoon sun may now reach the floor of the *barranco* and make things uncomfortably warm.

WALK 45
La Cabezada

Distance:	7km (4½ miles)
Start/Finish:	On a road bend near Casas de Araza
Map:	1:50,000 Military Map Sheet 38-40
Terrain:	A mountainous ridge, steep and rocky in places, but mostly equipped with a good clear path. The latter parts are covered in scrub.

If for any reason you head for Masca and the walk down the Barranco de Masca is unsuitable, there is always a fine roller-coaster ridge walk to the peak of La Cabezada to consider. This rises high above the Barranco de Masca and, although the terrain is mountainous, the walk is actually easier than that down the *barranco*. See map on p. 206. There is a good path starting on a bendy stretch of road at Araza, between Masca and Santiago del Teide. Walkers may wonder, why this well-built path was built along the mountain ridge. After climbing La Cabezada, the reason becomes clear, as the ruins of old farms are seen ahead at Los Parajes and the Finca de Guergues.

Spotting the start of this walk from the bus is crucial. There is a very bendy minor road between Masca and Valle Santiago and a particularly tight bend on the Masca side of the highest point. Here a track with a chain barrier is marked 'Private No Trespassing' in a number of languages. The altitude is approximately 950m (3115ft). This is the start but, obviously, this track to the **Casas de Araza** is not to be followed. Instead, follow a narrow path away from the track, down to a gap, where another path is joined. Keep right at this junction, following the path to the left of the rugged ridge, cutting across the slope to reach another gap. This is a particularly good viewpoint overlooking Masca and the head of the Barranco de Masca.

The path climbs up a stone-built ramp, then crosses a rough and rocky face, following a series of small cairns. Walk down to another gap and enjoy more wonderful views into the valley. Climb up another stone-built ramp, which gives way to a narrower, boulder-paved path, then the route crosses bare red rock where narrow volcanic dykes have cut through. Pass a cool little cave just before regaining the ridge. The rough and rocky crest of the ridge narrows near some

A view of the head of the Masca valley from near the Casas de Araza

towers of rock. The paved path zigzags down to a gap to outflank these obstacles, then rises to a gate in a fence.

Dogs are forbidden beyond this point, but walkers can continue up the path. Simply follow the zigzags up around a corner, passing three little caves separated by volcanic dykes. Another stack of zigzags lifts the path further uphill, touching the ridge at one point and offering even more spectacular views over the Barranco de Masca. As the ridge rises, so the *barranco* falls, increasing the sense of depth all the time. A rough and rocky line slices up across the slope, continuing across the ridge, where the path is substantially buttressed on the side overlooking Masca. Zig-zag back up across the ridge, then consider a slight detour to the right to reach the summit of **La Cabezada**. There is a cairn at 1034m (3392ft). Magnificent views encompass Masca and the higher parts of the Teno region of Tenerife, with rugged ridges and deep *barrancos* slicing from the wooded central crest down to the cliff coast.

From the summit of La Cabezada it is possible to see the ruins of Los Parajes a short way down the arid, scrubby slopes, with the ruins of Finca de Guergues further away on a lower gap. The whole slope was terraced when the farms were inhabited, and these terraces are now covered in bushy scrub. The walk down to the ruins isn't quite as easy as it looks, but is accomplished by following a vague, narrow path with a few little cairns along the way. Only the first building reached at Los Parajes still has a roof, and it stands next to an old threshing floor. The path, marked by small cairns, can be followed to Finca de Guergues. A building with a roof is passed, then roofless ruins are reached at **Finca de Guergues**. After exploring the buildings, turn round and retrace steps faithfully back to the road near the **Casas de Araza**.

Transport:
TITSA Bus 355 passes close to the Casas de Araza between Masca and Valle Santiago.

Refreshments:
None.

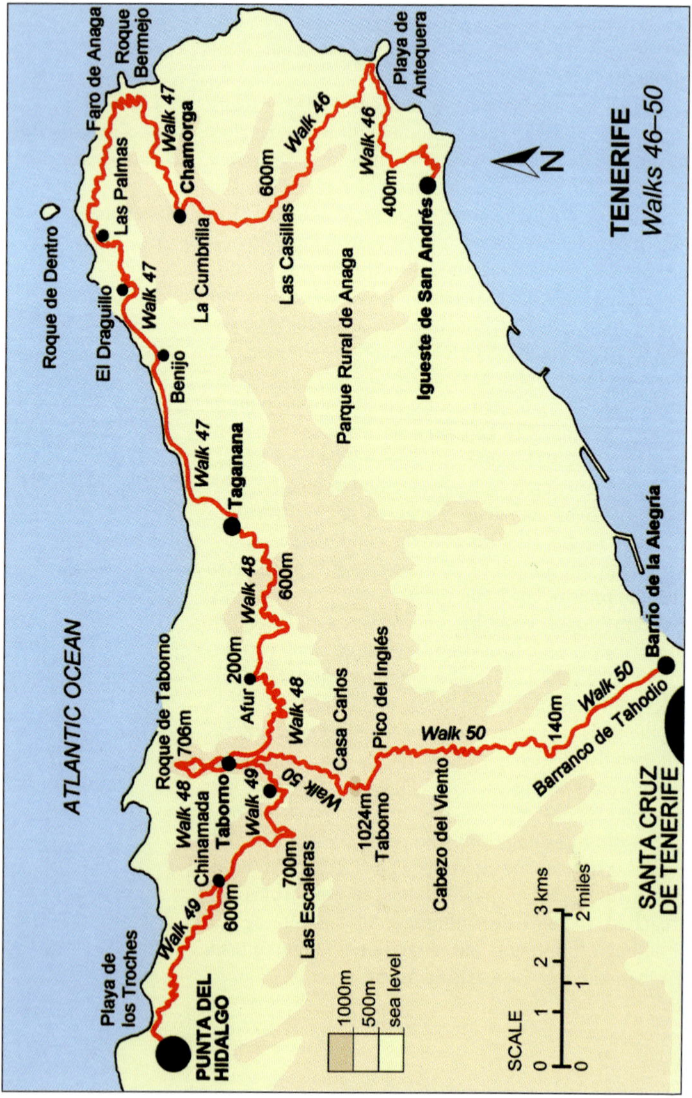
TENERIFE
Walks 46–50
ATLANTIC OCEAN
N
Faro de Anaga
Roque Bermejo
Playa de Antequera
Walk 47
Chamorga
Walk 46
Walk 46
600m
400m
Igueste de San Andrés
Las Palmas
La Cumbrilla
Las Casillas
Parque Rural de Anaga
Roque de Dentro
El Draguillo
Walk 47
Benijo
Walk 47
Taganana
Walk 48
600m
200m
Afur
Walk 48
Roque de Tabomo
706m
Casa Carlos
Pico del Inglés
Walk 50
140m
Walk 50
Barrio de la Alegría
Barranco de Tahodio
Walk 48
Chinamada
Tabomo
Walk 49
Walk 50
1024m
Tabomo
Cabezo del Viento
SANTA CRUZ DE TENERIFE
700m
Las Escaleras
600m
Walk 49
Playa de los Troches
PUNTA DEL HIDALGO
1000m
500m
sea level
SCALE
0
1
2
3 kms
0
1
2 miles

WALK 46
Igueste to Chamorga

Distance:	13km (8 miles)
Start:	Igueste de San Andrés
Finish:	Chamorga
Map:	1:50,000 Military Map Sheet 40-39
Terrain:	Paths vary from being very clear to rather vague, often on steep and scrubby slopes where care is needed. Towards the end there is an easy, wooded road walk.

Start from the bus terminus at **Igueste de San Andrés**. If you need any refreshment before starting the walk, then get off the bus before it reaches the turning space at the road-end. Walk past the church on the Plaza San Pedro and continue up steps and along the Calle del Carmen. Walk up and down more steps, then turn left along the Paseo Cementerio. Note that this is the paved path, and not the concrete one just below it, as the street sign would seem to imply. Before reaching the cemetery, take a left turn marked by a blue painted arrow on the paving. Follow a good, clear track up a steep and rocky slope. The track is often carved from solid rock and is substantially buttressed as it zigzags uphill. Views become increasingly interesting as the track climbs, and after passing a big stump of rock it is possible to look far along the coast, and inland to El Teide.

The track eventually levels out, and even runs downhill a short way to reach an old semaphore station, though you need to leave it before it levels out. Just before the track levels out, turn sharp left as indicated by cairns to follow a rough and rocky path. The path is vague in places, and you will have to scramble a little

The Anaga mountains look very rugged when seen from Santa Cruz, with spiky summits arranged along steep-sided ridges. In fact, this end of Tenerife is smaller than it looks, though it is an amazing place to explore. It is worth spending three or four days making a circuit around the peninsula, climbing the mountains, then dropping back to the sea, over and over again. Small villages and a patchy series of bus routes can be linked, but look very carefully at the bus timetables to break this journey at the relevant points. The first stage of this walk runs from Igueste de San Andrés to Chamorga. Like the other stages it can stand on its own merit as a one-day walk. Please see the map on p. 224.

Transport: TITSA Bus 245 serves Igueste de San Andrés. TITSA Bus 247 serves Chamorga.

Refreshments: There is the odd bar at Igueste and Chamorga, so be sure to take enough food and drink on the walk.

on the rock at times, but there should be no real problem reaching a cairn on a gap at 400m (1310ft). Drift to the left and continue a little further up the rugged, rocky ridge to reach a ruined building. This was once an *ermita* and its barrel-vaulted roof remains intact. Sheep and goats use it for shelter.

Cross a bright, limey patch on the ground and follow the path as it begins to zigzag downhill. Do not follow the path along the crest, but use the one that cuts across the head of the valley. This is narrow, but reasonably clear, contouring across the slope, sometimes squeezing between the scrub. Watch carefully for a little cairn that marks a turn-off down to the right once the path runs level. Another narrow path, vague at times, zigzags down the rugged, scrubby slope. After crossing a couple of little *barrancos*, let the path lead across the main *barranco*. Small cairns mark the path and the crossing places on the barrancos. Watch carefully for another important junction, where one path continues down alongside the *barranco,* while another path rises up the valley side towards a couple of prominent caves to the left. Walk up to the caves, which contain small drystone enclosures.

When leaving the caves, scan the slope to be sure of following the right path. Although a path runs across the slope, you need to start climbing onto a higher path, and the correct route is again marked by small cairns, so keep an eye peeled for them. Do not be tempted down the valley to the sea. The cliff path (or at least a path on a very steep and rocky slope) finally turns out of the valley and offers a splendid view of the beach at the **Playa de Antequera**. Take the steps leading up through a prominent dyke, then simply follow the path across the steep slope and finally zigzag down a rocky nose to the beach. This beach is often fairly quiet as it can only be reached on foot or by boat, though weekends see everyone with a boat in Santa Cruz descending upon the place! Walk along the black sand to the buildings on the far side.

Follow a path leading inland from the buildings, passing between a small house and an outbuilding. The

A view down the long and rugged valley towards the Playa de Antequera

path then rises above another small house. Basically, the path zigzags up into another *barranco,* passing old cultivation terraces, moving through a gap in a drystone wall to continue across scrubby slopes. The ascent is initially gentle, with a slight descent to cross the *barranco* before continuing up past a few more old terraces. After crossing a rock bar, cross the *barranco* again, only to cross back over it later. This crossing and re-crossing continues over and over again, with the ground getting quite bouldery and noticeably steeper in places. Sometimes the path is trodden down to bare rock, and as it climbs, it moves close to rock walls where heather trees grow. Stone steps and zigzags finally lead up to a rocky gap where there is suddenly a view down the other side to Igueste.

Turn right at the rocky gap to follow a vague path along the crest, zigzagging a little at first, then following a line of telegraph poles. The path crosses a steep slope, then climbs to cross a narrow, rocky ridge. Continuing onwards, a handful of old, derelict buildings are passed, at **Las Casillas**. The path undulates on or beside the ridge, and is gradually swallowed up into 'laurisilva' woodland.

A tiny chapel stands on the tiny plaza near the road-end at Chamorga

Follow a well-trodden path, avoiding spurs to left and right, passing close to a couple of buildings as you move around the head of a valley. Sometimes the path is in the woods, and at other times it is on an open slope, rising and falling as it curves round the valley head. A flight of earth steps finally leads up a wooded slope to emerge suddenly at a road junction, with a signpost pointing back to Igueste.

The road immediately to the right is a dead-end, leading to a small, overgrown cemetery. The road ahead drops downhill ahead leads to Chamorga. Follow it round bends and past a couple of houses, with a couple of cultivated plots hidden among the trees. A junction is reached where another dead-end road leads to the village of Las Bodegas. Climb uphill from the junction leads to a bus stop at a tunnel mouth, where the tiny village of **La Cumbrilla** is perched high above on a rocky gap. The tunnel is spacious and short, but take care if there is any traffic about. The road continues in broad loops down the wooded slope and finally reaches the lovely little village of **Chamorga**. The transition from 'laurisilva' to terraces full of potatoes is swift. Pass the tiny plaza and chapel to reach the road-end. The bus turns round close to the bar Casa Alvaro Chamorga. Looking round the huddled settlement, several dragon trees can be spotted.

WALK 47
Chamorga to Taganana

Distance:	16km (10 miles)
Start:	Chamorga
Finish:	Taganana
Map:	1:50,000 Military Map Sheet 40-39
Terrain:	Rugged valley and coastal paths, often broad and clear, but sometimes stony and narrow. The last stretch is along roads.

This tour of the Anaga mountains continues from Chamorga with a descent through a rugged and attractive valley to reach the coastal settlement of Bermejo. The route climbs an old zigzag road to reach the lighthouse called Faro de Anaga, then basically hugs the coast to reach Taganana. The slopes are quite steep and rugged, and the path is rather narrow and stony in places, passing the little farming enclaves of Las Palmas and El Draguillo. A dirt road leads to Benijo, where there are bar restaurants, and a coastal road continues past the Roque de las Bodegas, turning inland to reach Taganana. Please refer to the map on p. 224.

Start at the end of the road at Chamorga, where the bus turns round at the bar Casa Alvaro Chamorga. Walking routes down the valley, such as the Roque Bermejo and Las Palmas de Anaga, are signposted. Walk down off the end of the road and continue along a stony track leading down through the valley. The track narrows and a sign reading 'Camino Roque Bermejo' is passed . Walk down the path, avoiding the concrete path descending to the right. Pass a solitary building beyond the cultivated plots and walk down into the wilder recesses of the valley. The path is generally boulder-paved, but does cross bare rock, and occasionally just earth and grit. It is accompanied by telegraph poles, which you will eventually realise are carrying a power line to the lighthouse, the Faro de Anaga.

The path descends, though there are occasional short ascents, as it moves along the left side of the valley. There is plenty of candelabra spurge and prickly pears. The *barranco* features a few slime-green pools, cane thickets and trees. The path passes a couple of ruined buildings, then goes down past cultivated plots and finally reaches a prominent signposted junction. Although the track to the Faro is off to the left, it is worth

Transport: TITSA Bus 247 serves Chamorga. TITSA Bus 246 serves Taganana.

Refreshments: There is a bar at Chamorga. There are bar restaurants at Benijo, bars along the coast road and bar restaurants at Taganana.

a few minutes to detour to the right to the little coastal settlement of **Roque Bermejo**. Go at least as far as the little Ermita, where palms, tamarisk and dragon trees grow. There are great views of the rugged coast below.

Double back up the track and keep right to cross a waterspill. The track climbs up a scrubby slope in long and lazy loops. It is well-engineered, though crumbling in places, and leads finally to the lighthouse. Walk round the top end of the lighthouse enclosure, to find a signpost for Las Palmas de Anaga. Take the lower fork on the path, across a slope covered in scrub. The path cuts under a lip of rock, which occasionally features a small waterfall. Fennel grows abundantly among the scrub for a while, as the path works its way around the steep and rugged slope. It passes the Fuente del Junquillo where a trickle of water is piped away. Continue along and down the path, passing a huge boulder at Los Orobales, which has a small mill, buildings and caves constructed in hollows all around it.

Follow the path down and round a bouldery ravine, then continue across a slope of old terraces with a view out to sea to the **Roque de Dentro**. The sea is actually quite shallow between the slope and the rock, and a submarine ridge can be discerned just beneath the waves. The path drops down into a *barranco* full of cane, then zigzags up to the little farming settlement of **Las Palmas de Anaga**. Keep between the sea and all the buildings, but be careful where the path is crumbling. After the last building, the path meanders around a couple of little ravines, where prickly pears have the height and bearing of small trees. Zigzag up old, arid terraces and cross another ravine. Zigzag further uphill until the path starts to contour across the steep and rugged slope. It can be rather narrow and stony in places before you descend across a steep slope of scree. A flight of steps finally leads down to the little village of **El Draguillo**, where you can see an old dragon tree above the path.

Follow the concrete road out of the village, around a ravine and a headland, where it becomes a rough dirt road called the Pista El Draguillo. The dirt road runs

On the way down from Chamorga, look ahead to the Roque Bermejo

mostly downhill, but there is one slight ascent, to give you splendid views ahead. A couple of little houses are passed, which are tucked into the hillside. The dirt road ends at the Restaurante El Fronton, and a right turn leads down a tarmac road to pass the Restaurante El Mirador. Both places offer food, drink and wonderful views.

Follow the road down from the village of **Benijo**, round a series of bends and bouldery headlands, to reach a bouldery bay. This is the Playa de Benijo with a small bar/shack above the beach. The village of Almáciga can be seen perched precariously on another bouldery headland. Either follow the road below the village, or follow a clear, paved, zigzag path up to the village, then descend to the coast road to continue. There are buses along the road, though it is also pleasant to walk. Take in the view of the Roque de las Animas, with its fluted columns, towering above the coast road. The road drops gently to the Roque de las Bodegas, where there are a couple of bar restaurants. A paved path with railings leads out onto the rock, which is like a huge boulder in the sea. The road rises gently and offers great views of the mountains beyond, then

A strikingly scenic coastal road leads along the cliff foot to Taganana

cuts inland to reach the village of **Taganana**. Either follow the road round a bend at the Bar Restaurante El Puente to climb into the village, or cut off down a narrow road marked as no entry, then use a path on the left to climb into the village to avoid the road bends. You can catch a bus at Taganana.

WALK 48

Taganana to Taborno

Distance:	12km (7½ miles)
Start:	Taganana
Finish:	Taborno
Map:	1:50,000 Military Map Sheet 40-39
Terrain:	The route crosses from valley to valley, using clear paths and tracks on wooded or cultivated slopes. The circuit round the Roque de Taborno is on narrow and exposed paths, with some short stretches of scrambling.

It may look like a short day's walk from Taganana to Taborno on the map, but this walk also includes a substantial diversion. Walkers with a head for heights and a sure foot can complete a circuit around the Roque de Taborno. Though it looks like a simple diversion, the *roque* is more like a mountain and is surrounded on all sides by precipitous slopes. Plenty of time needs to be set aside for that part of the walk, so it makes sense to end the day at Taborno afterwards, where there is a little bar and a bus service. Walkers who omit the Roque de Taborno may continue to Punta del Hidalgo. See map on p. 224.

This day's walk starts at **Taganana**. If arriving by bus, the stop is at the Bar Restaurante Xiomara and the road rises past the Bar Restaurante Casa Picar. Turn left down a cobbled road past the church, then left again at the Viveres Santa Catalina, as signposted for the Farmacia, which is on the Camino Cruz de Limera. Turn left up the Camino Portugal, climbing steeply up the nicely cobbled street, then turn left at the top. A road leads gently up and down to Los Naranjos, where a right turn along a cobbled path is signposted for Monte de Las Vueltas, Afur and La Cumbrecilla. Take this cobbled path to rise above the last couple of houses at Taganana, and climbs alongside a lushly-vegetated *barranco* filled with cane.

Transport: TITSA Bus 246 serves Taganana. TITSA Bus 076 serves Afur. TITSA Bus 075 serves Taborno.

Refreshments: There are a few bars and restaurants at Taganana. There is a small bar restaurant at Afur and a small bar at Taborno.

When a junction is reached, turn right up the path for Afur. When a stone-paved road is reached, turn left uphill, then left again along another narrower stone-paved road. Vines fill nearby terraces and also grow among a heap of big boulders in the valley. Turn right up a few steps to continue up a narrow path. The roughly-paved path climbs up the valley into 'laurisilva' woodland filled with birdsong. This area of woodland contains candleberry, or wax myrtle. A high gap is reached, at 600m (1970ft), with two pylons and a bizarre arrangement of rocks high above. Take in the views back along the rocky coast as it will quickly pass from sight.

There is also a complex junction of paths and tracks on the gap. The way to Afur is straight down the footpath rather than the vehicle track, which also runs downhill. The path is grooved and worn into rock or red earth as it makes its way down through the woods, passing a couple of cultivated plots. It is flanked by bracken and brambles and eventually runs to a farm perched on an edge. Turn right down the concrete farm road and follow all its loops down to a road bend and bus shelter. Turn right down the road for Afur, enjoying the lush green valley dotted with darker clumps of heather. The road bends downhill and there are steps and paths leading down onto terraces. Watch out for a flight of concrete steps to take a path equipped with street lights, which leads down beneath an undercut cliff to the little village of **Afur**. There is a lovely little church, while the Bar Restaurante Casa Jose Canon incorporates a well stocked little shop. A bus service links Afur with La Laguna.

Just above the little church is an electricity transformer tower rigged with cables. A concrete path passes it and steps zigzag down into the valley. Cross a footbridge and keep right to rise a little and cross another footbridge where there is usually a green pool. Big boulders lie on the valley floor and the scenery is quite charming. Follow the concrete zigzag path up a ridge, lined with street lights, enjoying the views as you ascend

The long zigzag path linking the little village of Afur with Taborno

from the valley. Just before some houses are reached, fork to the left and keep zigzagging up the concrete path.

There is a flight of steps at the end, but don't climb them. Instead, turn left along a rocky path, reaching a gap high above the houses. At this point there is another fork, where you need to keep left again, along a path rising with street lights, steps and rocky zigzags. The path slips off the ridge and runs level across the slope for a while, then lots of stone steps lead up past a couple more houses to regain the crest at a higher level. The path passes interesting outdoor laundry tubs and there is a view down to the beach and up to the mountains.

Follow a path across the slope, passing a few houses, to link with a new road. Walk along the narrow and quiet road as it dips down and around a valley, passing a few terraces and 'laurisilva' woodland. The road rises to the village of **Taborno**, with the last few loops being concrete. The plaza, a little chapel and the Bar Abigai sit on a gap, and there are fine views back along the route, as well as ahead.

At Taborno there is an option to make a circuit around the impressive Roque de Taborno, but bear in mind that the paths are narrow and exposed, and there are parts where scrambling is required. Set off by facing the chapel. Walk up the ramp to the right of it. Continue along a concrete path with railings and fine views, and keep to the right at junctions with other paths. Eventually, steps lead downhill among laurels, and it is worth making a short detour to a splendid viewpoint. The tall laurels thin out and the path runs down steps, then climbs a little to reach a gap on a rocky ridge where there are awesome views of the Roque de Taborno. Pass a water tap and follow the rocky path up above a house, moving beyond goat pens, to go through a gate. The path runs down onto another rocky gap, then cuts across the slope to yet another gap. The path forks, and whatever direction is chosen, the idea is to return to this point. It is probably better to take the right fork.

The path leads gently downhill, but soon starts clinging to narrow rocky ledges, picking a way across crum-

The village of Taborno with the Roque de Taborno rising prominent beyond

bling bits, up and down steps, to reach a pronounced rocky corner. Climb straight uphill to the left, aiming to follow the rocky ridge, even if it involves scrambling at times. The idea is to climb until roughly on a level with a goat cave, which can be seen off to the left, but you don't approach it. Meanwhile, the **Roque de Taborno** towers menacingly overhead. Turn right to follow a narrow path that contours across the steep slope, then when a ridge is reached, walk down it. At a junction of paths, it is worth making a short detour to the right for the view, but return and contour further round the slope to reach another ridge. A route marked with small cairns leads down the rocky ridge, but keep a lookout on the left as there is a sharp left turn along another terrace path. This path is narrow and crumbling, leading just below another prominent goat cave. Head inland and follow the path to another rocky ridge, where a descent leads back to the path junction where the circuit round the Roque de Taborno commenced.

Follow the ridge path back past the house and goat pens to reach the water tap on the rocky gap. Take a path off to the right from the tap, brushing across a slope of heather, then climb towards Taborno. A concrete path with railings leads back to the church, plaza and Bar Abigai. The bus cannot get into the village, so follow the road a short distance out of the village to find the turning space and bus stop.

WALK 49

Taborno to Punta del Hidalgo

Distance:	13km (8 miles)
Start:	Taborno
Finish:	Punta del Hidalgo
Map:	1:50,000 Military Map Sheet 40-39
Terrain:	Wooded valley sides with easy paths from village to village, then a steep and rocky path down a dry and scrubby *barranco*.

The walk from Taborno to Punta del Hidalgo completes the circuit around the Anaga mountains. The route involves crossing a wooded valley from Taborno to Las Carboneras, then crosses a wooded gap and descends to Chinamada. This little village is noted for its cave dwellings, some in ruins, and others converted to include all the modern conveniences. A splendid, rugged path runs down into a rocky *barranco* to bring the route to a close at Punta del Hidalgo (see map on p. 224). If you walk all the way round the Anaga mountains you will realise that they have a character quite distinct from the rest of Tenerife.

Start where the bus turns round in **Taborno**, unless you want to walk down into the little plaza and visit the little Bar Abigai, which is also a shop. Leave Taborno by following the road downhill from the bus stop, passing a wide gap in the roadside barrier where a path drops down to the right. Avoid this path, which leads nowhere, and continue along the bendy road a short way to find another narrow gap in the barrier with a path dropping down to the right. This one leads towards a pylon, and is stony underfoot. Just before reaching the pylon, you will find a little alcove tucked into a corner on the left, containing a small wooden cross.

The path drifts to the left to start traversing round the wooded head of the valley. At first it can be rather narrow, flanked by bracken and brambles, but in the 'laurisilva' woodlands the path is wide and well trodden. The woods contain laurel, candleberry and tree heather. The path descends steadily, then climbs up through a winding groove full of crumbling steps. The path levels out, then climbs again on a more open slope, passing a few plots and terraces. A track finally leads up to a road at the Bar Valentin in the village of Las Carboneras. Turn right to visit the little Plaza de San Isidoro and the Bar Restaurante Tesegre. The bus turns around beside the little chapel, if an early escape from the area is needed.

Walk back past the Bar Valentin and follow the road past the last house to leave Las Carboneras. Watch out on the right for a flight of stone steps leading up to Las Escaleras. The path is well trodden and rises and falls gently across a sparsely wooded slope, accompanied by a half-buried water pipe and a line of telegraph poles. A water tap is passed before a gap is reached at around 700m (2295ft). Pause and enjoy views back to Taborno and ahead into a deep valley. The village in view is Batán, while Punta del Hidalgo remains hidden. A sign points the way towards Chinamada.

The path is initially in 'laurisilva' and runs gently down across the slope. There is only one junction, where you keep to the right, gently uphill. The path crosses a more open slope to reach a white building which is usually unoccupied. Turn round the far end of the building to continue roughly contouring across the slope. There is a glimpse of Punta del Hidalgo, with its distinctive white tower by the sea. The slope is sparsely wooded and a tangle of scrub. After passing a small cliff, the path descends through tree heather with a wayside cross to the right, to emerge on a rocky ridge with a view of Chinamada. Turn left down the road to reach the little Plaza San Ramon at **Chinamada**. There is a water tap, but no shop or bar. Many houses are glorified cave dwellings, and this draws many visitors. Old caves stand alongside houses half-built into caves, which are complete with water supplies and solar panels!

Just behind the plaza is a sign pointing to the right for the Mirador de Aguaide. This is off-route, but is a highly recommended detour to a fine viewpoint. It also allows more cave-houses to be studied at close quarters,

Transport:
TITSA Bus 075 serves Taborno and Las Carboneras. TITSA Bus 105 serves Punta del Hidalgo.

Refreshments:
There is a small shop/bar at Taborno, a couple of small bars at Las Carboneras, a water tap at Chinamada and a number of bar restaurants at Punta del Hidalgo.

and takes less than an hour to complete the return trip. Follow the path across bare rock, up and down a few carved steps, passing above a house. A little further along, there is a fine old cave to the left, then the path continues over the top of another house. After crossing a shoulder, the path drops down to a fenced-off viewpoint, where the cliff coastline can be seen in all its majesty, with Atlantic breakers far below. You can see the built-up Punta del Hidalgo, which looks odd in such a wild and rugged setting, and the island of La Palma can be seen out to sea. Retrace your steps to the plaza in Chinamada.

Just up the road behind the plaza is a signpost for Punta del Hidalgo. A rugged path drops down to the left, and a small sign draws attention to a rocky little peak called the Roque de los Pinos. A few pines cling to the sunny side of the rock, well outside the usual pine zone on the island. The endemic *Cistus chinamadensis* also grows on the rock. The path, either hammered out of the rock, or crossing a couple of cultivation terraces, continues across the steep and rocky slope. Prickly pears and other scrub cover these slopes, with the path having exploited the rock's soft layers. The path has undercut the rock so much in places that it sometimes overhangs the path from above. A fine viewpoint is reached at a prominent corner, with Punta del Hidalgo in view far below.

Uneven rock steps twist and turn the path taking you directly down the valley sides, where candelabra spurge grows abundantly. The rockfaces are pitted with dozens of caves and even the crest of the ridge is pierced from side to side in places. The path briefly runs along the very crest, then passes to the seaward side of an odd-shaped rocky peak. Some walkers might find this short stretch unnerving. The path zigzags down into the steep-sided *barranco,* exploiting more soft layers of the rock., creating dramatic rock overhangs. At the bottom of the path, just to the right, is a deep shaft. There is also a notice informing you of the Parque Rural de Anaga, and the easy access to the bouldery beach at the **Playa de los Troches**.

Splendid rugged coastal scenery seen at the end near Punta del Hidalgo

Taking a break above Chinamada; a village full of intriguing cave-houses

Cross the *barranco* using a log bridge and walk towards a derelict pumphouse full of rusting machinery from Birmingham. A track and concrete road climb from the building, and there are fine views back towards the twin peaks of Dos Hermanos and the ridge so recently descended. Turn left at the top of the road, where markers point back for the various walking destinations. Just uphill is a turning area and viewpoint, along with a sculpture of the Canarian folklorist, Sebastian Ramos, known as El Puntero. The bus stop is close to hand, but the nearest bar restaurants are some distance along the road, clustered around the church in **Punta del Hidalgo**.

WALK 50

Taborno to Santa Cruz

Distance:	12km (7½ miles)
Start:	Taborno
Finish:	Barrio de la Alegría
Map:	1:50,000 Military Map Sheet 40-39
Terrain:	Wooded ridges lead uphill and downhill. The latter stages of the descent are through a scrubby *barranco.*

This is a fairly straightforward walk across the Anaga peninsula. Though not quite coast to coast, it at least takes you from the little mountain village of Taborno to the Barrio de la Alegría in the suburbs of Santa Cruz. It can be accomplished in a day, though it can also be broken into two easier walks by linking with bus services on the mountain crest. The beginning can be made more adventurous by incorporating part of Walk 48 around the towering Roque de Taborno, which is often in view in the early stages of the walk. The higher parts of the route are covered in 'laurisilva', while the latter stages are down a scrub-filled *barranco.* Please refer to the map on p. 224.

Start where the bus turns round at **Taborno**, unless you want to walk down into the little plaza and visit the little Bar Abigai, which is also a shop. For a more adventurous start, refer to Walk 48, following the circuit described around the Roque de Taborno. To leave Taborno, however, simply climb up a steep, stone-paved path directly opposite the bus shelter. The paving quickly gives way to a more rugged path flanked by 'laurisilva'. A small concrete reservoir is passed on the ridge, fed by a water pipe that is often seen beside the path. Also in view from time to time is a line of telegraph poles. Although there is good woodland cover on both sides of the ridge, the ridge path itself is often bare, so that there are fairly good views.

There is a rounded hump ahead on the Lomo Alto, but the path neatly and easily contours round the wooded slope to reach a gap on the far side. A path to the left is signposted steeply downhill for Afur, but don't go that way. Instead keep straight on and down across the slope to reach another gap. As the path winds up crudely cut steps to the next part of the ridge, there are remarkable views into both the Afur and Taborno valleys. There is another rounded hump ahead

Transport: TITSA Bus 075 serves Taborno and also runs close to Casa Carlos. Several TITSA Bus services link Barrio de la Alegría with Santa Cruz.

Refreshments: There is a small shop/bar at Taborno, a bar restaurant at Casa Carlos, and a few bars around Barrio de la Alegría.

and the path rises gently to one side. Note the invasive eucalyptus that is out-growing the native 'laurisilva' as you move towards the next gap.

Keep climbing up the winding path through the dense woodland. A small building is reached, and as the path climbs above it, there is a splendid view back along the ridge to Taborno. Keep winding uphill, passing street lights attached to the telegraph poles. Pass a house and follow a concrete road up to a bend on the main road that runs along the high *cumbre*. Immediately to hand is the Restaurante Casa Carlos, offering food and drink; bus services pass here if you wish to break the walk at this point. Walk a short way up the road to a junction where the Taborno bus service can be used too.

Just above the junction you can see how water is piped away from a tiny wooded valley. To continue the walk take a narrow path rising steeply from the roadside onto the wooded slope. This path is like a jungle trek. If the day is misty, you will quickly appreciate the mechanics of the cloud forest as the heather trees catch every tiny droplet and shower them onto the path below. Many heather trees lean over the path, so you need to be nimble to get past them without getting too wet. When a fence is reached in the dense woodland, keep to the left and a narrow, though obvious path leads to a road. Turn left to follow the road, passing the derelict Restaurante Cruz de Afur, to reach a turning point. A short path leads to the Mirador Pico del Inglés at 960m (3150ft). The view is one of the best on Tenerife, embracing most of the rugged Anaga mountains, and the urban sprawl from Santa Cruz to La Laguna, then leading the eye to the pyramidal peak of El Teide, which often has a girdle of cloud around its lower slopes. Gran Canaria, frequently seen with a cap of clouds, lies out to sea.

Returning to the turning space you will find a signpost pointing downhill to Barrio de la Alegría. Take this rough and stony path to drop below a derelict building, then run through 'laurisilva' to pass another

Looking back down the forested ridge to Taborno and the Roque de Taborno

derelict building. After following the high crest, the path swings right to drop downhill. Keep right at a junction and walk down past a small building and cave. Keep to the most obvious path along the wooded crest, and walk straight onwards when you reach a junction. The ridge path is like a roller coaster ride, and although it is often rocky, it is not particularly difficult. Occasional glimpses to either side take in adjacent valleys, and the 'laurisilva' holds a couple of stands of eucalyptus. One of these stands is on a rounded hump on the ridge, but the path cuts off to the right to continue its descent. As the heather trees thin out, there are views down to the docks at Santa Cruz where the peculiar shape of the auditorium can be seen.

The path becomes rather rocky on the **Cabezo del Viento**, where it swings left and descends in boulder-paved zigzags. Tree heather gives way to prickly pears. When a path junction is reached on the descent, keep right, following a rocky zigzag groove (which is stone-paved at times) down towards a couple of pantiled buildings. A couple of cave entrances are passed on the last bend before these buildings. Keep always to

The Roque del Agua is seen on the descent from the Pico del Inglés viewpoint.

the right of the buildings to zigzag further downhill. The path later turns right at a junction, then heads left towards a solitary farmhouse and caves. Walk below the house and at the next path junction take the path signposted right to Barrio de la Alegría.

Zigzag down a slope of prickly pears and cross the Barranco de Valle Luis. Walk below another small house, keeping to the most obvious path, moving downhill alongside the *barranco.* Cross a broken water pipeline on a slope covered in candelabra spurge. The path passes a small dam where a channel leads off around the slope. This is connected by a tunnel to a small reservoir in a valley to the west. Do not follow the channel, but keep to the path running down through the *barranco.* Cross over the bed of the *barranco,* then a little later cross back again. Note the resistant dykes that stand like walls in the riverbed to become waterfalls in times of high water flow. There are a few old terraces along the way, then the path crosses back over the *barranco,* passing a small hut and more little terraces. After crossing the *barranco* yet again, the path remains clear and obvious though the rock walls, covered in candelabra spurge rise steep and tall. The valley makes a pronounced curve to the right and the path crosses the *barranco* one last time. There are houses in view and the path eventually zigzags down to the access road.

Turn left to walk down the road. One of the first buildings has a public telephone. There are plenty of buildings in the **Barranco de Tahodio**, but the place seems rather scruffy, though there is a neat little tennis club along the way. The road crosses a bridge and eventually reaches a school where there is a turning space for buses. A number of bus services turn here before running back to Santa Cruz. It is worth catching the first one you see, as the road needs to be followed for some time before the first little bar appears.

APPENDIX: TOPOGRAPHICAL GLOSSARY

Apart from a few placenames which are derived from original Guanche words, most names on the maps are Spanish. Several words crop up time and again and are usually very descriptive of particular types of landforms, colours and sizes. The following list of common words helps to identify what some of the places on maps or signposts mean.

Agua .... water
Alto/alta .... high
Arenas .... sands
Arroyo .... stream
Asomada .... promontory
Bajo/baja .... low
Barranco .... ravine
Barranquillo .... small ravine
Blanco/blanca .... white
Boca .... gap
Cabeza .... head
Caldera .... crater
Calle .... street
Camino .... path/track
Cañada .... gully
Canal .... watercourse
Carretera .... road
Casa .... house
Casa forestal .... forestry house
Collada/degollada .... col/gap/saddle
Colorada .... coloured
Corral .... farmyard/corral
Cruz .... cross/crossroads
Cuevas .... caves
Cumbre .... ridge/crest
De/del .... of the
El/la/los/las .... the
Embalse .... reservoir

Era .... threshing floor
Ermita .... chapel/shrine
Estacion de guaguas .... bus station
Fuente .... fountain/spring
Galeria .... water gallery
Gordo .... fat/giant
Grande .... big
Guagua .... bus
Hoya .... valley
Ladera .... slope
Llano .... plain
Lomo .... spur/ridge
Montaña .... mountain
Morro .... nose
Negro/negra .... black
Nieve .... snow
Nuevo/nueva .... new
Paso .... pass
Pequeno .... small
Pico .... peak
Piedra .... rock
Pino/pinar .... pine
Playa .... beach
Plaza .... town square
Puerto .... port/pass
Punta .... point
Risco .... cliff
Roja .... red
Roque .... rock
San/santa .... saint
Sendero .... route/path
Valle .... valley
Verde .... green
Vieja/viejo .... old
Volcán ....volcano

NOTES

NOTES

LISTING OF CICERONE GUIDES

NORTHERN ENGLAND LONG DISTANCE TRAILS

- THE DALES WAY
- THE ISLE OF MAN COASTAL PATH
- THE PENNINE WAY
- THE ALTERNATIVE COAST TO COAST
- NORTHERN COAST-TO-COAST
- THE RELATIVE HILLS OF BRITAIN
- MOUNTAINS ENGLAND & WALES
  VOL 1 WALES
  VOL 2 ENGLAND

CYCLING

- BORDER COUNTRY BIKE ROUTES
- THE CHESHIRE CYCLE WAY
- THE CUMBRIA CYCLE WAY
- THE DANUBE CYCLE WAY
- LANDS END TO JOHN O'GROATS CYCLE GUIDE
- ON THE RUFFSTUFF –
  84 BIKE RIDES IN NORTH ENGLAND
- RURAL RIDES NO.1 WEST SURREY
- RURAL RIDES NO.1 EAST SURREY
- SOUTH LAKELAND CYCLE RIDES
- THE WAY OF ST JAMES
  LE PUY TO SANTIAGO – CYCLIST'S
- CYCLE TOURING IN SPAIN
- THE LOIRE CYCLE ROUTE

LAKE DISTRICT AND MORECAMBE BAY

- CONISTON COPPER MINES
- CUMBRIA WAY & ALLERDALE RAMBLE
- THE CHRONICLES OF MILNTHORPE
- THE EDEN WAY
- FROM FELL AND FIELD
- KENDAL – A SOCIAL HISTORY
- A LAKE DISTRICT ANGLER'S GUIDE
- LAKELAND TOWNS
- LAKELAND VILLAGES
- LAKELAND PANORAMAS
- THE LOST RESORT?
- SCRAMBLES IN THE LAKE DISTRICT
- MORE SCRAMBLES IN THE LAKE DISTRICT
- SHORT WALKS IN LAKELAND
  BOOK 1: SOUTH
  BOOK 2: NORTH
  BOOK 3: WEST
- ROCKY RAMBLER'S WILD WALKS
- RAIN OR SHINE
- ROADS AND TRACKS OF THE LAKE DISTRICT
- THE TARNS OF LAKELAND
  VOL 1: WEST
- THE TARNS OF LAKELAND VOL 2: EAST
- WALKING ROUND THE LAKES
- WALKS SILVERDALE/ARNSIDE
- WINTER CLIMBS IN LAKE DISTRICT

NORTH-WEST ENGLAND

- WALKING IN CHESHIRE
- FAMILY WALKS IN FOREST OF BOWLAND
- WALKING IN THE FOREST OF BOWLAND
- LANCASTER CANAL WALKS
- WALKER'S GUIDE TO LANCASTER CANAL
- CANAL WALKS VOL 1: NORTH
- WALKS FROM THE LEEDS-LIVERPOOL CANAL
- THE RIBBLE WAY
- WALKS IN RIBBLE COUNTRY
- WALKING IN LANCASHIRE
- WALKS ON THE WEST PENNINE MOORS
- WALKS IN LANCASHIRE WITCH COUNTRY
- HADRIAN'S WALL
  VOL 1 : THE WALL WALK
  VOL 2 : WALL COUNTRY WALKS

NORTH-EAST ENGLAND

- NORTH YORKS MOORS
- THE REIVER'S WAY
- THE TEESDALE WAY
- WALKING IN COUNTY DURHAM
- WALKING IN THE NORTH PENNINES
- WALKING IN NORTHUMBERLAND
- WALKING IN THE WOLDS
- WALKS IN THE NORTH YORK MOORS
  BOOKS 1 AND 2
- WALKS IN THE YORKSHIRE DALES
  BOOKS 1,2 AND 3
- WALKS IN DALES COUNTRY
- WATERFALL WALKS – TEESDALE & HIGH PENNINES
- THE YORKSHIRE DALES
- YORKSHIRE DALES ANGLER'S GUIDE

THE PEAK DISTRICT

- STAR FAMILY WALKS PEAK DISTRICT/STH YORKS
- HIGH PEAK WALKS
- WEEKEND WALKS IN THE PEAK DISTRICT
- WHITE PEAK WALKS
  VOL.1 NORTHERN DALES
  VOL.2 SOUTHERN DALES
- WHITE PEAK WAY
- WALKING IN PEAKLAND
- WALKING IN SHERWOOD FOREST
- WALKING IN STAFFORDSHIRE
- THE VIKING WAY

WALES AND WELSH BORDERS

- ANGLESEY COAST WALKS
- ASCENT OF SNOWDON
- THE BRECON BEACONS
- CLWYD ROCK
- HEREFORD & THE WYE VALLEY
- HILLWALKING IN SNOWDONIA
- HILLWALKING IN WALES VOL.1
- HILLWALKING IN WALES VOL.2
- LLEYN PENINSULA COASTAL PATH
- WALKING OFFA'S DYKE PATH
- THE PEMBROKESHIRE COASTAL PATH
- THE RIDGES OF SNOWDONIA
- SARN HELEN
- SCRAMBLES IN SNOWDONIA
- SEVERN WALKS
- THE SHROPSHIRE HILLS
- THE SHROPSHIRE WAY
- SPIRIT PATHS OF WALES
- WALKING DOWN THE WYE
- A WELSH COAST TO COAST WALK
- WELSH WINTER CLIMBS

THE MIDLANDS

- CANAL WALKS VOL 2: MIDLANDS
- THE COTSWOLD WAY
- COTSWOLD WALKS
  BOOK 1: NORTH
  BOOK 2: CENTRAL
  BOOK 3: SOUTH
- THE GRAND UNION CANAL WALK
- HEART OF ENGLAND WALKS
- WALKING IN OXFORDSHIRE
- WALKING IN WARWICKSHIRE
- WALKING IN WORCESTERSHIRE
- WEST MIDLANDS ROCK

SOUTH AND SOUTH-WEST ENGLAND

- WALKING IN BEDFORDSHIRE
- WALKING IN BUCKINGHAMSHIRE
- CHANNEL ISLAND WALKS
- CORNISH ROCK
- WALKING IN CORNWALL
- WALKING IN THE CHILTERNS
- WALKING ON DARTMOOR
- WALKING IN DEVON
- WALKING IN DORSET
- CANAL WALKS VOL 3: SOUTH
- EXMOOR & THE QUANTOCKS
- THE GREATER RIDGEWAY
- WALKING IN HAMPSHIRE
- THE ISLE OF WIGHT
- THE KENNET & AVON WALK
- THE LEA VALLEY WALK
- LONDON: THE DEFINITIVE WALKING GUIDE
- LONDON THEME WALKS
- THE NORTH DOWNS WAY
- THE SOUTH DOWNS WAY
- THE ISLES OF SCILLY
- THE SOUTHERN COAST TO COAST
- SOUTH WEST COAST PATH
- WALKING IN SOMERSET
- WALKING IN SUSSEX
- THE THAMES PATH
- TWO MOORS WAY
- WALKS IN KENT BOOK 1
- WALKS IN KENT BOOK 2
- THE WEALDWAY & VANGUARD WAY

SCOTLAND

- WALKING IN THE ISLE OF ARRAN
- THE BORDER COUNTRY –
  A WALKERS GUIDE
- BORDER COUNTRY CYCLE ROUTES
- BORDER PUBS & INNS –
  A WALKERS' GUIDE
- CAIRNGORMS, WINTER CLIMBS
  5TH EDITION
- CENTRAL HIGHLANDS
  6 LONG DISTANCE WALKS
- WALKING THE GALLOWAY HILLS
- WALKING IN THE HEBRIDES
- NORTH TO THE CAPE
- THE ISLAND OF RHUM

Since its foundation over 30 years ago, Cicerone has specialised in publishing guidebooks and has built a reputation for quality and reliability. It now publishes nearly 300 guides to the major destinations for outdoor enthusiasts, including Europe, UK and the rest of the world.

Written by leading and committed specialists, Cicerone guides are recognised as the most authoritative. They are full of information, maps and illustrations so that the user can plan and complete a successful and safe trip or expedition – be it a long face climb, a walk over Lakeland fells, an alpine traverse, a Himalayan trek or a ramble in the countryside.

With a thorough introduction to assist planning, clear diagrams, maps and colour photographs to illustrate the terrain and route, and accurate and detailed text, Cicerone guides are designed for ease of use and access to the information.

If the facts on the ground change, or there is any aspect of a guide that you think we can improve, we are always delighted to hear from you.

Cicerone Press

2 Police Square Milnthorpe Cumbria LA7 7PY

Tel:01539 562 069 Fax:01539 563 417

e-mail:info@cicerone.co.uk web:www.cicerone.co.uk

CICERONE